GENDER BASED VIOLENCE IN UNIVERSITY COMMUNITIES

Policy, prevention and educational initiatives

Edited by Sundari Anitha and Ruth Lewis

D1611172

P

First published in Great Britain in 2018 by

Policy Press
University of Bristol
1-9 Old Park Hill
Bristol
BS2 8BB
UK
t: +44 (0)117 954 5940
pp-info@bristol.ac.uk
www.policypress.co.uk

North America office:
Policy Press
c/o The University of Chicago Press
1427 East 60th Street
Chicago, IL 60637, USA
t: +1 773 702 7700
f: +1 773-702-9756
sales@press.uchicago.edu
www.press.uchicago.edu

© Policy Press 2018

British Library Cataloguing in Publication Data
A catalogue record for this book is available from the British Library

Library of Congress Cataloging-in-Publication Data
A catalog record for this book has been requested

ISBN 978-1-4473-3659-4 paperback
ISBN 978-1-4473-3657-0 hardcover
ISBN 978-1-4473-3660-0 ePub
ISBN 978-1-4473-3661-7 Mobi
ISBN 978-1-4473-3658-7 ePdf

The right of Sundari Anitha and Ruth Lewis to be identified as editors of this work has been asserted by them in accordance with the Copyright, Designs and Patents Act 1988.

Cover design by Hayes Design
Front cover image: istock
Printed and bound in Great Britain by CPI Group (UK) Ltd, Croydon, CR0 4YY
Policy Press uses environmentally responsible print partners

MIX
Paper from
responsible sources
FSC® C013604

Remembering Kate Cavanagh, from whom
I learned so much (Ruth Lewis)

For Jamaal, Nafisa and Charlie, with hope
for the changes to come (Sundari Anitha)

Contents

Notes on contributors

Sundari Anitha is a Reader in the School of Social and Political Sciences at the University of Lincoln. She has researched and published widely in her two areas of research interest – gender based violence, and gender and work. Her recent work has examined marriage migrants' experiences of domestic violence, forced marriage, transnational marriage abandonment, sex-selective abortion, dowry-related violence, gender based violence in university communities, and the position and struggles of South Asian women workers in the UK labour market. She has previously managed a Women's Aid refuge and is a trustee of Asha Projects, a specialist refuge for South Asian survivors of domestic violence and of ATLEU (Anti-Trafficking and Labour Exploitation Unit), which provides legal representation to victims of trafficking and labour exploitation.

Zowie Davy is a Senior Lecturer in LGBTQ Research at the Centre for LGBTQ Research, De Montfort University. Zowie's work centres on medicolegal constructions of gender and sexuality in healthcare. Her current research spans (trans)gender studies including critical approaches to gender dysphoria, a project on parents' experiences of school cultures while supporting their trans children, and LGBT sex work migration and health. Zowie has published a number of books and articles about transgender embodiment and her book *Recognizing Transsexuals* won the Philip Abrams Memorial Prize in 2012. Zowie is on the board of directors of the International Association for the Study of Sexuality Culture and Society, the Vice Chair of the European Sociological Association's Sexuality Research Network and a scientific advisor for the European Professional Association for Transgender Health.

Anni Donaldson is currently Knowledge Exchange Fellow/Project Lead for Equally Safe in Higher Education (ESHE) at the University of Strathclyde. ESHE is implementing a Gender Based Violence Strategy at the University. Anni was a Violence against Women (VAW) Lead Officer, VAW Partnership Coordinator and Service Manager in Scottish local government for 20 years. Anni is also a historian and is currently writing an oral history of domestic abuse in Scotland 1979–92, a VAW activist, writer and award winning journalist.

Andrea Durbach is Professor of Law at the University of New South Wales (UNSW) Sydney. She was Director of UNSW's Australian Human Rights Centre (AHRCentre) from 2004–17. She has held senior positions in the human rights field, including as Deputy Australian Sex Discrimination Commissioner and as a consultant to the Australian Defence Abuse Response Taskforce to develop a framework to address the needs of Defence Force victims of gender based violence. Andrea has published widely on a range of human rights issues, including gender justice, and is currently co-investigator on an Australian Research Council grant examining reparations for victims of sexual violence post-conflict. Between 2015 and 2017, Andrea led the AHRCentre's major research project, *Strengthening Australian University Responses to Sexual Assault and Harassment.*

Rachel Fenton is a Senior Lecturer in Law at the University of Exeter. She has published widely about gender and the law, in particular regarding sexual offences and the legal regulation of assisted reproduction and is co-editor of *Gender, Sexualities and Law* (Routledge, 2011). Recently, as the project lead for Public Health England, her work has focused on establishing the evidence base for bystander intervention for the prevention of sexual and domestic violence in university settings and the development and evaluation (with Helen Mott) of the first evidence-based bystander programme *The Intervention Initiative* for English universities.

Rosemary Grey is a Postdoctoral Fellow at Melbourne Law School, where she teaches the International Criminal Justice Clinic in partnership with Amnesty International. From 2015 to 2016, she was the inaugural research director on the *Strengthening Australian University Responses to Sexual Assault and Harassment* project. Since then, Rosemary has continued to research on gender issues in law, particularly on the prosecution of gender based crimes under international law. Her PhD, completed at the University of New South Wales in 2015, considered the prosecution of these crimes in the International Criminal Court. Her monograph on gender based crimes and the ICC will be published by Cambridge University Press in 2018.

Ellie Hutchinson is the Director of the Empower Project, a feminist, intersectional membership organisation working to challenge online and technology-based abuse against women and girls. Previously she was Prevention Policy Worker at Scottish Women's Aid, where she led

Get Savi over a period of four years. She holds an MSc in International Relations and European Politics from the University of Edinburgh and is passionate about children's rights, participation, feminism and change.

Jill Jameson is a Senior Lecturer in Criminology at the University of Lincoln and has interests in both Criminology and issues relating to the 'student experience'. She has undertaken research looking at student employability and engagement, teaching excellence, the 'student as producer' (with Katie Strudwick and Sue Bond Taylor, University of Lincoln), bystander schemes and gender based violence on the university campus (with Ana Jordan, Sundari Anitha and Zowie Davy). Jill's teaching interests include theories of crime, gender, feminisms, victimology and penology and she is particularly interested in encouraging undergraduate students to get involved in research and co-writing and presenting academic papers. She has facilitated students in presenting conference papers in a variety of settings and being published in academic publications such as *Enhancing Learning in the Social Sciences* (ELISS) and the *Student Engagement in Higher Education Journal*.

Ana Jordan is a Senior Lecturer in the School of Social and Political Sciences at the University of Lincoln. She has published on men's movements, including the construction of fatherhood(s) and masculinity/ies by fathers' rights movements, the gender politics of men's rights groups, and the relationship between backlash, postfeminism and men's movements. She has conducted research (along with co-investigators) into GBV in universities. The 'Stand Together' action research project at the University of Lincoln was one of the first bystander intervention programmes designed to challenge GBV in a UK university. This project investigated student attitudes to GBV and the potential of prevention education. Current research projects include a monograph on masculinities and men's movements in the UK and co-authored research on 'crisis', masculinity and suicide; future projects will be related to masculinities and violence.

A research psychologist by training, **Renate Klein** focuses on gender and violence with a variety of courses as well as research and scholarship. She has longstanding international research collaborations and is a recipient of major grants from large national institutions including the German Research Foundation, the UK National Lottery, and the US Department of Justice. Her framework is international, interdisciplinary and practice-oriented. She has conducted research for local community organisations such as the Penquis Law Project and the Maine Coalition to End Domestic Violence, and is the recipient of a Teal Award from Rape Response Services for outstanding community partner. She is the founder and long-time coordinator of the European Network on Gender and Violence, and a founding member of the UK-based network Universities against Gender Based Violence.

Ruth Lewis is Associate Professor in the Department of Social Sciences at Northumbria University. She has published widely on feminist activism and GBV, and has been involved in feminist activism of various kinds locally and nationally. Recent research examines: young women's engagements with feminism and the development of feminist communities (with Susan Marine); feminists' experiences of and resistance to online abuse (with Mike Rowe and Clare Wiper), and women–only space as a political strategy (with Elizabeth Sharp and Julie Scanlon). Earlier research with Rebecca Dobash, Russell Dobash and Kate Cavanagh includes the first UK evaluation of domestic violence perpetrators programmes and the first sociological UK examination of homicide.

Susan Marine, PhD is Associate Professor and Program Director in the Higher Education Master's Program at Merrimack College, Massachusetts, USA. With 24 years' experience leading initiatives in higher education for the advancement of women and trans★ students of all genders, Dr Marine has specific expertise in sexual violence prevention and response, and advocacy for the LGBTQ community. She was the founding director of the Harvard Office of Sexual Assault Prevention and Response and served in various advocacy roles on four different college campuses. Dr Marine's research focuses on building gender expansive campuses, including ending sexual violence against LGBTQ students and fostering full participation of trans★ students. Her work seeks to transform campus cultures and to continually advance social justice in higher education. She has contributed to numerous scholarly journals and books, and is the author of *Stonewall's Legacy: Bisexual, gay, lesbian and transgender students in higher education.*

Melanie McCarry is currently the Programme Director for the BA Social Policy, University of Strathclyde. She is also joint Principle Investigator, and Research Lead, on the Equally Safe in Higher Education project. Prior to joining Strathclyde University, Melanie was a Senior Research Fellow and founding member of the Connect Centre for International Research on Interpersonal Violence and

Harm, University of Central Lancashire. Previously, she spent over 13 years in the Centre for Gender and Violence Research, University of Bristol. Over the past 20 years Melanie has published widely in the area of men's violence against women and children, and GBV more broadly including abuse in young people's relationships, forced marriage, sexuality, gender constructions and research ethics. In addition to her academic work Melanie has been active in the feminist anti-male violence activist movements and other social justice campaigns.

Aimee McCullough is currently a Research Associate for the Equally Safe in Higher Education Project, based at the University of Strathclyde. She is responsible for generating qualitative data on attitudes to, and experiences of, GBV with both staff and students at the University. With a background in Human Geography and Social History, Aimee has experience across a diverse range of social, historical and policy research contexts. Her recently completed ESRC funded thesis at the University of Edinburgh explored fatherhood, masculinities and intimate family relationships in Scotland, and she has been involved in a number of contemporary social research projects at the Scottish Government and third sector organisation Citizens Advice Scotland. Aimee's main research interests are gender, families, parenthood and sexualities in 20th century Britain to present day.

Helen Mott is an independent researcher and academic. Her research examines cultures of sexism, discrimination and violence against women and girls (VAWG). She has been active in a variety of feminist campaigning and policy organisations in the UK over the past 20 years. Helen was a member of the UK Government and Universities UK taskforce on preventing sexual harassment and sexual violence in universities, which produced its 'Changing the Culture' report in November 2016. She was lead consultant for the British Council's report on the UK's performance against the UN Sustainable Development Goals for Gender Equality in 2016. With Rachel Fenton, Helen co-created and evaluated 'The Intervention Initiative'. She helped to develop The Bristol Ideal, a flagship programme to tackle abuse and promote healthy relationships and gender equality in schools. Helen is currently working as the specialist adviser on sexual harassment and sexual violence to the UK Parliament's working group tasked with improving Parliament's institutional response to sexual harassment.

Alison Phipps is Professor of Gender Studies at Sussex University. She co-authored *That's What She Said*, the first national study of 'lad culture' in university contexts, and has published extensively on sexual harassment and violence against students. She is co-founder of the Changing University Cultures project, developed from funded research at Imperial College, which combines sociology and organisational development techniques to help institutions promote equality and diversity and tackle bullying, harassment and violence.

Vanita Sundaram is currently Professor in Education at the University of York. Her research broadly covers gender and education, focusing more specifically on GBV and teenagers; tackling everyday sexism, harassment and abuse in education across the lifecourse; and lad cultures and sexual violence in higher education. She is the author of numerous publications on these issues, including *Global Debates and Key Perspectives on Sex and Relationships Education: Addressing Issues of Gender, Sexuality, Plurality and Power* (2016) and *Preventing Youth Violence: Rethinking the Role of Gender in Schools* (2014). She is an academic member of the NUS Strategy Team on Lad Culture, an advisory board member of the 1752 Group, and serves on the Gender and Education Association executive committee and the Gender and Education journal editorial board.

Louise Whitfield is a solicitor and partner at Deighton Pierce Glynn in London, where she specialises in challenging state bodies, particularly in relation to gender equality and disability discrimination. She has produced legal briefings for the End Violence Against Women coalition on sexual violence on campus and in schools. Her casework includes advising women's organisations, such as Southall Black Sisters and the Women's Resource Centre, on cuts to domestic violence support services. She has represented a wide range of feminist clients including those challenging the Bank of England's decision over historical characters on bank notes, and the heterosexual couple seeking a civil partnership. She is also a member of the Fawcett Society's panel reviewing sex discrimination law.

Acknowledgements

This book was originally conceived with Ruth Jones OBE of the University of Worcester; we gratefully acknowledge her contribution to the project and her work to address GBV in all its forms. We are grateful for the commitment each contributor has shown to this book as well as to their wider work to end GBV in universities; more power to you! We would like to thank Renate Klein for her additional role in providing characteristically insightful comments on our writing for this book, and anonymous reviewers at Policy Press. Thanks to Victoria Pittman who supported the project from its initial conception and guided it through to completion. Ruth Lewis would like to thank Anitha, Susan Marine and colleagues at Northumbria University Gender Research Hub who embody their feminism through sisterly support and by making work, even work about a grim topic like this, fun. Sundari Anitha would like to thank Ana Jordan, Jacqui Briggs, Sara Owen, Kathryn Brookfield and Ruth Pearson for their support and solidarity through the challenges of addressing this issue and to Ruth Lewis, my co-traveller on this intellectual and activist journey – onwards and upwards!

Introduction: some reflections in these promising and challenging times

Sundari Anitha and Ruth Lewis

This collection comes in the midst of some promising and challenging times for activists, students and academics in the UK and beyond who have been researching and campaigning on the issue of gender based violence (GBV) in university communities. In the context of emerging research evidence and in the face of increasing public awareness of and media attention on this problem, these are indeed the first steps towards acknowledging and addressing it in countries including the UK and Australia. This chapter explores the context and contours of some of the recent and emerging debates on GBV in university communities within which this collection is located.

We understand GBV as behaviour or attitudes underpinned by inequitable power relations that hurt, threaten or undermine people because of their (perceived) gender or sexuality. This definition recognises that GBV is influenced by and influences gender relations and problematises violence premised on hierarchical constructions of gender and sexuality. Women and girls constitute the vast majority of victims of GBV, and men the overwhelming majority of perpetrators (Watts and Zimmerman, 2002; Hester, 2009). GBV includes a continuum of behaviours and attitudes such as domestic violence, sexual violence, sexist harassment on the streets, trans/homophobic expressions and behaviours, and expressions on social media which normalise sexism and sexual objectification. These expressions and behaviours are connected through what Kelly (1988) described as a continuum of incidents and experiences. The continuum of incidents (Kelly, 1988, 1989) refers to the conceptual connections between acts that constitute the wallpaper of violations – the behaviours and expressions so commonplace that they often recede into the minutiae of everyday life – and the less common 'sledgehammer' events (Stanko, 1985) that are more widely recognised as harm, which are both underpinned by and reinforce gendered power hierarchies. The everyday expressions and behaviours scaffold a culture of gender inequalities that sustains and enables the rarer acts. The associated

1

concept of a continuum of experiences (Kelly, 1988) captures the subjective perceptions and the commonalities in how women and sexual minorities experience these expressions and behaviours as violations. Hence this conceptualisation suggests that we cannot address one end of the continuum – for example, rape and domestic homicide – without problematising the everyday manifestations of sexism and gendered hierarchies (Bates, 2014).

This concept of a continuum provides a useful framework for reflecting on the nature of the problem, with associated implications for how we perceive harm and craft responses to it. Feminist analysis of policymaking draws attention to the importance of explicating the framing of social problems, of 'making politics visible' (Bacchi, 2012). Such an approach enables analysis that goes beyond a focus on the impact or effectiveness of policies to one that can critically examine how a social issue has come to be defined as a problem and what are the exclusions and silences in this construction. For example, it has been argued that how GBV is conceptualised can enable or inhibit the naming of the problem and help-seeking (DeKeseredy and Schwartz, 2011). In the context of university communities, this approach can be applied to examine what the problem is represented to be – sexual assault with a narrow focus on individual victims and perpetrators (incidentalism), or a broader focus on GBV that recognises a continuum of harms, problematises the underpinning cultures that scaffold acts and attitudes, recognises disadvantage and inequalities on the basis of gender and sexuality, and tackles student-on-student, staff-on-student, and staff-on-staff GBV. A tendency to focus on particular acts, on particular countable manifestations of GBV and on particular individuals as the problem, can be critiqued for ignoring the connections between different manifestations of GBV. This elision reflects the broader gap in current theorising on GBV, whereby there is scant research that systematically examines both the empirical and theoretical links between different manifestations of GBV (for exceptions see Stockdale and Nadler, 2012). This failure to make the broader connections has implications – for example, the narrow focus on sexual violence in US campus policies may mean that institutions do not prioritise challenging the broader cultures which foster such acts (see Klein, Chapter Three in this volume).

In his reconceptualisation of domestic violence, Stark (2007) urges a shift from a focus on a corpus of incidents and a calculus of harm whereby the more frequent and severe the incidents, the more dangerous the violence is presumed to be. His concept of coercive control outlines the perpetrator's project of re-inscribing and enforcing gender inequality and limiting women's freedom and potential, primarily and effectively through isolation, degradation and control and occasionally through physical and other forms of violence. Stark (2007) ponders on the stalled revolution some four decades after the first refuges for 'battered wives' were established in the 1970s, a problem he identifies as stemming from a change in our project. He argues that by focusing on individual acts of physical, sexual, financial and emotional violence, we have taken our attention away from the cause of the problem – the structural inequalities that derive from and scaffold gendered power relations – to particular manifestations or symptoms of the problem. In the context of GBV in university communities, this collection is part of the wider project that seeks to consider how we might turn our attention to the causes while we also deal with the symptoms in the here and now.

The problem

Substantial evidence from the US indicates a high prevalence of GBV in student communities, which includes high levels of sexual violence on university campuses (Cantor et al, 2015; Fisher et al, 2000, 2010). A recent study of 27 institutions of higher education in the US, with responses from 150,000 students (Cantor et al, 2015), found that since enrolling at college, 23% of women students had experienced sexual contact involving physical harm or incapacitation, and 62% had experienced sexual harassment. Research from other countries in Europe and Australia (Feltes et al, 2012; Sloane and Fitzpatrick, 2011; Valls et al, 2016) indicates a similar problem in university communities that is only beginning to be acknowledged and documented.

Unlike the research and policy context in the US, the issue of domestic violence in young people's intimate relationships and GBV in student communities in the UK has been the focus of research only since the mid-2000s. Studies in the UK document the high prevalence of violence in young people's intimate relationships (Barter et al, 2009). Research by Girlguiding – a charity that works with young women and girls in the UK – found that 59% of girls and young women aged 13–21 years had faced some form of sexual harassment at school or college in the previous year (Girlguiding, 2014). The National Union of Students' (NUS) survey of 2,000 students studying in England, Wales, Scotland and Northern Ireland found that, while at university, one in seven female students had been victims of serious sexual assault or serious physical violence, while 12% had been stalked (NUS, 2010). Of those surveyed, 68% had been a victim of one or more kinds of sexual harassment on campus, with 16% having experienced unwanted kissing, touching or molesting. In the majority of cases in all incident categories surveyed, the perpetrator was known to the victim and was male. There is also evidence that 'lad cultures'[1] on campuses create 'conducive contexts' (Kelly, 2016) for a range of other manifestations of GBV (Phipps and Young, 2012).

GBV also affects other groups of students. Research that surveyed 4,205 LGBT students and support staff found that 31% LGB students had experienced homophobic/biphobic verbal abuse, while 7% received physical abuse (Valentine et al, 2009: 18), while 30% trans students had experienced verbal abuse and a greater percentage – 11.3% – had experienced physical abuse (Valentine et al, 2009: 24). An 'out in sport' report published by the NUS (2012) revealed that 14.3% of LGBT university and college students had experienced homophobia, biphobia or transphobia which put them off participating in sport. Almost a quarter of trans students have been bullied or discriminated against since starting university. Such accounts perhaps help explain why 20% (524) of LGB students and 28.5% (53) of trans students have taken time out of their course (Valentine et al, 2009: 25).

Together, this research indicates that such problematic cultures affect women and sexual minorities' experiences on university campuses, in social spaces such as night clubs surrounding universities (Brooks, 2011; Nicholls, 2015), in online communities and on social media (Lewis et al, 2017; Jane, 2017), and in the teaching and learning contexts within universities (Jackson and Sundaram, 2015; Jackson et al, 2015). There has also been recent attention to the issue of GBV in the broader university community, particularly in the context of the power differentials between staff and students and university practices which are slow to take responsibility for and investigate staff abuses of their power in relation to GBV against students (Ahmed, 2016a, 2016b; Weale and Batty, 2016). However, attention to broader institutional cultures should not take the focus away from the people with decision making power who uphold existing institutional cultures, who could be held accountable for their decisions and can indeed reshape these cultures.

The issue of staff-on-student sexual violence came into sharp focus when Professor Sara Ahmed recently resigned in protest against Goldsmith University's 'failure to address the problem of sexual harassment' (Ahmed, 2016a). Ahmed (2016b) outlined the reasons and context of her resignation in a widely circulated post on her blog called 'Resignation is a feminist issue'. Though aware of the existence of the problem of sexual harassment at universities, the process of pursuing particular student complaints made Ahmed come to an increasing realisation of the sexist ethos and culture in particular parts of her university. Ahmed argues that as she navigated (unsuccessfully) through the bureaucratic procedures, trying to address the issues raised by students, she 'began to realise how the system was working' and that indeed, '*I began to realise that the system was working*. ... I began to realise too my own complicity with that system' (emphasis in original). What Ahmed effectively articulated through her words and actions is the ways in which the neoliberal model of universities as businesses competing for rankings and student numbers has created a context whereby the gaps in addressing GBV effectively are not 'failings' of university policies and practice. In fact, what appears to be bureaucratic ineffectiveness or inefficiency/incompetence of particular staff members designated with redressing complaints can be better understood as the system working exactly as it is intended to do – to manage potential negative publicity, to dissuade potential complainants and thus minimise complaints-making, to deflect attention from the broader and pervasive cultural contexts within which particular acts and violations occur, and to shroud any successful redress by students through secrecy clauses designed to protect the reputations of academics and academic institutions.

Over the past decade, other institutions – in the UK and beyond – have found to their cost that the widespread prevalence of sexual violence and abuse and, more significantly, the subsequent culture of impunity and systematic cover-ups have inflicted irreparable damage to institutional reputations in the military (Alleyne, 2012), churches (BBC News, 2010; Ruhl and Ruhl, 2015; Sherwood, 2016), residential homes for children (HIA, 2017; Morris, 2013), media (Martinson and Grierson, 2016) and sports organisations (Rumsby, 2016). Where universities have been slow to even acknowledge the existence of GBV within their communities for fear of reputational damage, in the context of the increasing scrutiny of institutional cultures in relation to GBV, we may be witnessing a shift towards a normative frame whereby not (being seen to be) doing something about GBV will begin to seem more damaging than doing something about it. In these promising times, it seems apt to reflect on the challenges that lie ahead.

Understanding and responding to the problem: possibilities and challenges

Primary prevention programmes to tackle GBV have been advocated by the United Nations (CEDAW[2]) and the World Health Organization

(WHO and Butchart 2004). Government policy and practice on GBV in the UK have focused on criminal justice sanctions and to a lesser extent service provision, to the neglect of prevention (Walklate, 2008), a policy focus that has been mirrored in Australia (see Durbach and Grey, Chapter Four in this volume). While secondary prevention work with perpetrators has become established in UK government policy over the past decade, primary prevention remains the weakest part of the UK government response to GBV (Coy et al, 2009). GBV or, more narrowly, sexual violence have long been the subject of research, policy directives, and student activism in US universities (Fisher et al, 2010; Klein, Chapter Three in this volume). However, under the Trump administration, uncertainty remains about the extent of commitment to the policies and processes institutionalised by the federal government and courts over the past four decades. Recent wider policy developments in the UK (see Donaldson et al, Chapter Five in this volume) – such as the ratification of the Istanbul Convention with its prevention and monitoring requirements on the UK government and the amendments to the Children and Social Work Bill in March 2017 which will make it a requirement that all secondary schools in England teach relationships and sex education – present a shift in policy.

This policy shift towards a greater focus on prevention has come about following a period of increasing media attention and student activism against GBV in school and university communities. It was within this context that the first bystander intervention programmes in UK universities were piloted at the University of West of England, University of Lincoln, and by Scottish Women's Aid at Scottish universities and higher education institutions in 2014–16 (see Fenton and Mott (Chapter Eight), Jordan et al (Chapter Nine) and Hutchinson (Chapter Ten), in this volume). Around this same period, several initiatives were announced by some universities following negative publicity associated with an incident of GBV (Payne and Green, 2016; Weale and Batty, 2017). In 2015, Universities UK (UUK) – an advocacy organisation for UK universities comprising university vice-chancellors and principals – announced a taskforce to examine the issue of 'violence against women, harassment and hate crime affecting university students, with a focus on sexual violence and harassment' (Department for Business, Innovation and Skills, 2015). The taskforce's report (UUK, 2016a) makes a series of recommendations on addressing these issues through effective responses to complaints and prevention initiatives, which represents an overhaul of previous approaches to this issue (see Donaldson et al, Chapter Five in this volume). Although this report represents a significant first step, it fails to adopt a broad approach of

GBV which recognises a range of harms based on (perceived) gender and sexuality. For example, despite growing evidence about the high levels of domestic violence in young people's relationships, there is little explicit engagement with this issue in the report. The report also exclusively focuses on student-on-student incidents, which represents a missed opportunity to acknowledge and address staff-on-student and staff-on-staff GBV.

In the same period that UUK's taskforce was undertaking its work, Durham University instituted a Sexual Violence Task Force. In a context where few UK universities had stand-alone policies on GBV (Bows et al, 2015) and fewer still had dedicated staff that are trained to support students on this issue, Durham University's taskforce was a pioneering initiative (Durham University, 2015; Towl, 2016). While its recognition of a continuum of sexual violence beyond the limiting framework of sexual assault must be welcomed, the connections between sexual violence and other forms of GBV are elided from the frame. The Durham University initiative, however, has several positive elements such as the provision for anonymous reporting beyond that intended to trigger investigations in order to map the scale and nature of the problem and craft adequate responses to it. In a context where only a small minority of students report their victimisation (Fisher, 2009, NUS, 2012), this must be welcomed. As a result of the taskforce's work, Durham University has committed resources to establish a new dedicated full-time role, believed to be the first in the country, of Student Support & Training Officer (Sexual Violence and Misconduct), which indicates a welcome ongoing commitment to make a real difference at the institution.

At the time of going to press, a few other UK universities are undertaking a review of their policies on GBV, but the absence of a mandatory requirement for universities to address GBV through prevention and through recording of reported incidents means that any progress is likely to depend on individual institutions' commitment. This contrasts with the US, where mandatory requirements have been the basis of long-established initiatives on this issue. This collection comes at this unique moment and seeks to make the most of the rare opportunity to reflect on the US experience, draw upon the missteps and successes there and rethink how those new to the journey might start with somewhat different premises, and take somewhat different routes. In that vein, we discuss two themes that are important for work in this area: the significance of gender and the need to rethink a jigsaw of responses.

Gender in gender based violence: the elephant in the room?

Gender is a lens that is increasingly becoming obscured when considering the causes and consequences of a problem that is paradoxically gaining attention. This elision of gender is taking place in the context of the appeal of post-feminist equalisation discourses that deem gender equality as a *fait accompli* and any acts of violence as residual remnants from a previous era – idiosyncratic and individual rather than rooted in structural inequalities. This obscuring of gender and of the structural inequalities that intersect with gender can perhaps be better understood within prevailing narratives of individual emancipation and micro-politics that are in keeping with a well-documented shift towards neoliberal cultures of individualism where the onus for change is firmly located on the individual.

Within this discourse, concepts such as 'power-based violence' (Katz et al, 2011: 689) have become the means through which GBV is uncoupled from its structural roots while simultaneously becoming re-cast as something that 'could happen to anyone'. Resistance to GBV is framed in appealing terms such as 'equality and diversity' approaches of institutions on one hand, and through a common-sense appeal to the active pro-social bystander on the other. After all, no individual or institution casts oneself as aspiring to be unequal or anti-social. In ideological terms, such a degendering constructs the problem as that of particular (pathological) individuals who abuse their power, and the violence as ephemeral and power-based rather than rooted in historically persistent hierarchies of gender and sexuality. Hence the problem is not framed as arising from structural inequalities or institutional cultures, but as an individual aberration. Underlying this approach is the premise that at a simplistic level, some people are always going to abuse their power, some people hurt others; that the problem is 'bullying' rather than gendered violence that is supported by gendered norms, practices and structures. Particular bystander programmes in the US such as the Green Dot programme have come to adopt discourses of 'power-based violence' as they have evolved and been reshaped by students resistant to the idea that gendered structural inequalities form the basis of violence (Katz et al, 2011). Such framings may also hold appeal for programme designers and anti-violence educators keen to minimise resistance from students – particularly from men but also from women, who can be co-opted into 'lad cultures'.

However, a binary understanding of the problem as either systemic or individual prevents an understanding of the ways in which individual people act in relation to peer groups and how they form personal and institutional networks which both respond to and enact structural constraints. As Katz et al (2011: 689) argue, social justice-oriented approaches require that 'questions of gender, race, and sexual orientation, especially the role of complicit silence on the part of members of dominant groups' are at the forefront of any efforts to bring about change. As Lewis and Marine (Chapter Six in this volume) highlight, student feminist groups in the UK challenge that 'complicit silence' in an effort to bring about changes on campus. A feminist approach asserts that we must keep naming our activities and politics as feminist, in a bid to give the lie to the stereotypes, to better inform people about what feminism is and is not, and to prevent 'feminism' being co-opted (or 'taken account of' in McRobbie's (2009) terms) by the forces of neoliberalism and its narratives of individual responsibility and 'empowerment' (Lewis et al, 2016; Marine and Lewis, 2014).

Beyond orthodoxies: rethinking the jigsaw of punitive responses, service provision and prevention education

One of the key planks of the US policy directive to universities has centred on punitive responses to complaints of sexual assaults, a focus that was under critical spotlight in the much-acclaimed documentary, *The Hunting Ground*. The public screenings of this documentary on campuses in the UK and Australia were crucial to the shift in the perceptions of this issue and in enabling a conversation about GBV in university communities (see Durbach and Grey, Chapter Four in this volume). The complaints procedure is also a central plank of the UUK's recommendations (2016b).

Feminist scholars have long been critical of criminal justice solutions to the problem of violence against women and girls (VAWG) and have drawn attention to the many ways in which legal institutions, processes and conceptualisations of the legal subject are deeply gendered (for example, Anitha and Gill, 2009; LSE, 2017; Walklate, 2008). While acknowledging the need for robust criminal justice responses to VAWG, they have pointed out the gains and losses, the problems and possibilities incurred by this strategy (Gill and Anitha, 2009; Lewis, 2004; Walklate, 2008). In response to feminist campaigning and activism, we now have moved towards the criminalisation of behaviour that was not so long ago considered acceptable but women and sexual minorities continue to choose not to engage with these mechanisms and reporting rates of GBV remain low (Fisher et al, 2003). The wide chasm (Kelly et al, 2005) between the law in theory and practice raises questions relating to the appropriateness or, at the very least, the limits of devoting most of our energy to institutional and criminal justice investigatory and punitive mechanisms. However, the very existence of these mechanisms and the codifying of violations nonetheless contains within it the capacity to change social norms. It has been suggested in other contexts that the norms that underpin the perpetration of GBV may have not changed significantly over the past three decades, but women may have a greater sense of *entitlement* to safety and quality of life (Lewis, 2004), an expectation that was evident in account after account outlined by women and sexual minorities in *The Hunting Ground*. Increases in reporting of sexual and domestic violence in the UK over the last few years indicate that a similar expectation may be at work; however, if nothing else changes, then this risks even lower levels of satisfaction with the criminal justice system. In the university context, we risk a re-run of similar issues if our focus remains narrowly on reporting mechanisms and complaints policies and procedures. A crucial part of the jigsaw of responses also includes robust and gender-specific service responses and prevention education initiatives.

Post-violence community service provision has long been a key plank of responses to GBV in a range of countries in a context where the vast majority of survivors do not seek recourse to criminal justice or punitive responses, because of a combination of the costs of engaging with them (see Whitfield, Chapter Seven in this volume) including the risk of secondary victimisation (Laing, 2016). A range of community services such as women's refuges and support services for survivors of rape recognise the harm inflicted by the violence and work towards restoring survivors' sense of personal integrity and civil and political selves.

The impact of the ongoing dismantling of the welfare state across the UK and other industrialised democracies such as the US and Canada on women and children's equality and safety needs to be recognised and challenged (Sanders-McDonagh et al, 2016). These broader policy landscapes for service provision have an inevitable impact on potential responses to GBV in university communities, as they may well hinder collaborative efforts to bring together existing expertise in challenging GBV in a holistic manner that recognises universities' location within broader communities. But beyond these immediate and pressing problems, there has also been a longer term shift from a potentially more transformative focus that seeks to address both the violence and the root causes of such violence to a more individualistic project within a neoliberal context that seeks to provide support to the survivor to enable recovery from the violence and to restore them to the position they were in prior to the violence. This replaces the project of recognising the structural basis of the violence that might lead to a questioning of the contexts that sustain that violence for oneself and for others. A similar shift can be observed in feminist activism in other contexts from a collective project of empowerment to individualist service provision and rehousing; from the politics of refusal to 'request politics' (Alwis, 2009). In the context of GBV in university communities, when support is recognised as the crucial second plank of the responses to violence, we also need to reflect on the contours of this support. When structured around a punitive, individualistic response to GBV, such support risks becoming a means of managing expectations in the contexts of complaints made or anticipated, a means to student retention rather than a means of empowerment, resistance and indeed prevention of violence.

Prevention education has rightly drawn attention of anti-violence activists as a potential counterpoint to an individualistic focus on particular signal acts and individual perpetrators – the opportunity to reconceptualise a broader range of expressions and behaviours and the cultures underpinning them as harm, and of interrogating one's complicity in these cultures. Rather than pursuing such an inevitably challenging goal, the focus of bystander programmes may come to rest on tangible interventions in others' inflictions and expressions of violence. In this no doubt positive project of garnering bystanders as active citizens, the perpetrators seem to be missing, as do those who may be complicit and derive benefits from a culture that sustains such violence. How do we engage men in the project to call out and give up their gendered privilege? An approach which limits responsibility to individual men, rather than broader cultures of inequality that scaffold GBV and implicate rather more of us and the cultures we inhabit, may prove to be an effective strategy that seems to appeal to men and women, as well an institutions. But what do we lose in such a framing? What constitutes an intervention needs further interrogation, as does the possibility of defining/measuring 'success'. In addition, programmes must not become a tool used by institutions to hold students responsible for their own safety and must not shift scrutiny away from institutional cultures and institutional responsibility.

Organisation of this volume

The first section explores conceptualisations of violence and the role of gender norms in these. In the first of the two chapters in this section, Sundaram investigates young people's understandings of violence and the factors which influence their acceptance, and use, of violent behaviour. She argues that gender norms mediate young people's understandings of GBV and discourses around the perceived acceptability of such violence. Sundaram argues that young people's attitudes towards violence exist on a continuum, rather than in binary terms of the violence being perceived as 'right' and 'wrong'. This contribution points to the need to address broader gender norms as part of any prevention intervention.

Phipps' chapter on lad cultures continues this engagement with gender norms – as they intersect with social structures such as class – in order to examine forms of sexualised banter, 'everyday' sexism and sexual harassment in student communities, which has been termed 'lad cultures'. In exploring the links between 'lad cultures' and other forms of sexual violence, this chapter theorises 'lad cultures' in order to better understand them and develop effective interventions. It also offers a critical perspective that locates such aggressions and violence within the institutional cultures of neoliberal competitively-driven universities, and offers suggestions for interventions that can create cultural change and provide new tools for researchers wishing to theorise this issue.

The second section of this collection brings together an overview of policy and practice in various countries: the US, where responses to particular forms of GBV in university communities have been well established, as well as Australia and the UK, where these issues have only recently come under scrutiny. The contributions in this section locate recent debates in the UK within wider international debates and action on tackling GBV in student communities.

Klein's critical historical overview of US activity charts the early research which overlooked the gendered nature of the phenomenon it investigated and the initial efforts that sought to 'teach women how to stay safe' and were critiqued for implicit victim-blaming to more recent prevention approaches which focus on bystander intervention and the role of friends, peers and social networks in preventing violence. Three interrelated issues are examined in this chapter: the limitations of existing framing of campus sexual violence as sexual misconduct among individual students that takes little account of the interlocking structures of gender inequality and exploitation; the lack of institutional responses in terms of fundamental changes to university governance; and the limitations in university treatment of victims and perpetrators.

Durbach and Grey outline the limited attention to prevention within Australian policy responses to GBV in general and particularly within student communities. In the context of recent policy and media attention to these issues, they present the findings of the first nationwide survey directed at collating data on prevalence, student reporting experiences and preferred responses to sexual violence in university settings. This chapter provides a historical and political context for the survey, and considers how the survey results and analysis can inform the development of effective responses to sexual assault and sexual harassment in Australian universities and the shift of a culture that enables (and even encourages) harmful sexual behaviour.

Decades later than other countries, the UK is waking up to the fact that GBV blights the experiences of many students. Donaldson, McCarry and McCullough's chapter presents a critical analysis of the theoretical foundations of the dominant policy frameworks on GBV in the different nations in the UK and locates recent developments in universities' approaches to GBV within their national context. This chapter offers some observations on the opportunities and challenges facing the UK Higher Education sector as it develops its approach to GBV prevention.

The next section of this collection brings together some recent initiatives that seek to challenge GBV in UK universities, thereby documenting an emerging area of practice and research. In doing so, it addresses the complexities and challenges of developing, implementing and evaluating GBV prevention and educational initiatives.

Lewis and Marine's chapter draws on data from a qualitative study of young women feminists in UK and US universities to examine how they are creating communities of resistance to GBV. The university has a historical and contemporary role in providing important opportunities to create communities and networks, formal and informal, where activism against GBV can flourish, but structural and cultural changes in universities may threaten their scope to foster such developments. The chapter argues that feminist communities are vital in the struggle against GBV in universities.

Alongside activism and campaigning against GBV in universities, resistance to this troubling issue has also drawn on legal approaches. Whitfield's chapter explores the progressive potential of the existing legal frameworks such as the human rights and equality legislation to protect and provide justice for survivors of GBV and to hold institutions to account. Written by a leading public lawyer with unique expertise and experience of representing survivors of GBV at university communities, it demonstrates the limitations of existing university responses to sexual violence against students and reflects on the potential of existing legislation to bring universities to account, as well as the inherent challenges and tensions in such approaches.

Fenton and Mott's chapter outlines the history of the development of *The Intervention Initiative*, an evidence-based programme predicated on bystander and social norms theories and public health criteria for effective prevention programming, which incorporates skills-based training to enable participants to intervene safely and effectively when they witness problematic behaviours along the continuum of violence. It presents the evidence base and the theoretical rationale for the programme to demonstrate how it takes participants through each stage of change required for bystanders to intervene. The chapter ends with a discussion of the policy recommendations for further implementation of the programme in the context of current agendas for the university sector.

Jordan, Anitha, Jameson and Davy's chapter draws upon research conducted as part of a bystander intervention programme and reflects on some of the key challenges and potential of prevention education in a university context. It explores the possibilities and complexity of challenging gendered attitudes, behaviours and the broader cultural norms underpinning GBV in two sites where gender norms and everyday forms of GBV are re-inscribed, negotiated and resisted – social media and the night-time economy. Given the complexity of realising effective responses to GBV, it interrogates the possibilities for crafting activist responses to problematic campus cultures within neoliberal institutional contexts of UK universities.

Hutchinson's contribution is based on her experiences of developing the 'Get Savi' (students against violence initiative) prevention education programme while working for Scottish Women's Aid, the Scottish branch of a leading national charity that works to tackle domestic abuse. It outlines the role of a shifting policy context in Scotland in shaping particular responses to GBV more broadly, and to prevention education in particular. Hutchinson discusses the practical process of the development of 'Get Savi' and reflects on the conceptual basis of the programme in her engagement with themes relating to local policy contexts, institutional cultures, collaborative working and a gendered approach to GBV.

A final chapter consolidates some key themes of this volume, and considers the future directions of activism, policy, practice and research on the issue of GBV in university communities. We present some suggestions about the nature of activism and action that can address this problem as well as the role that academic research can play in this process.

Notes

[1] 'Lad culture' has been defined as 'a group mentality articulated through activities such as sport and heavy alcohol consumption, and characterised by sexist and

homophobic 'banter'" (Phipps and Young, 2012: 28). Broader terms such as 'sex object culture' (popularised by the campaign Object!) and 'rape culture' (developed by US feminists in the 1970s) have also been utilised to describe this phenomenon. The latter refers to a set of general cultural beliefs supporting men's violence against women.

[2] See www.un.org/womenwatch/daw/cedaw/

References

Ahmed, S. (2016a) 'Resignation', feministkilljoys, 30 May, https://feministkilljoys.com/2016/05/30/resignation/

Ahmed, S. (2016b) 'Resignation is a feminist issue', feministkilljoys, 27 August, https://feministkilljoys.com/2016/08/27/resignation-is-a-feminist-issue/

Alwis, M. (2009) 'Interrogating the 'political': feminist peace activism in Sri Lanka', Feminist Review, 91: 81–93.

Alleyne, R. (2012) 'Judge fears 'Deepcut' culture remains after 'cover up' of army recruit sexual abuse', Telegraph, 26 November, www.telegraph.co.uk/news/uknews/9703451/Judge-fears-Deepcut-culture-remains-after-cover-up-of-army-recruit-sexual-abuse.html

Anitha, S. and Gill, A. (2009) 'Coercion, consent and the forced marriage debate in the UK', Feminist Legal Studies, 17 (2): 165–84.

Bacchi, C. (2012) 'Why study problematizations? Making politics visible', Open Journal of Political Science, 2(1): 1–8.

Barter, C., McCarry, M., Berridge, D. and Evans, K. (2009) Partner Exploitation and Violence in Teenage Intimate Relationships, London: NSPCC, www.nspcc.org.uk/inform/research/findings/partner_exploitation_and_violence_report_wdf70129.pdf

Bates, L. (2014) Everyday Sexism, London: Simon & Schuster.

BBC News (2010) 'Catholic Church sex abuse scandals around the world', 14 September, www.bbc.co.uk/news/10407559

Bows, H., Burrell, S. and Westmarland, N. (2015) Rapid Evidence Assessment of Current Interventions, Approaches, and Policies on Sexual Violence on Campus, Durham: Durham University Sexual Violence Task Force, www.dur.ac.uk/resources/svtf/DUSVTFRAEfinalpdfversion.pdf

Brooks, O. (2011) '"Guys! Stop doing it!" Young women's adoption and rejection of safety advice when socializing in bars, pubs and clubs', British Journal of Criminology, 51: 635–51.

Cantor, D., Fisher, B., Chibnall S., Townsend, R., Lee, H., Bruce, C. and Thomas, G. (2015) *Report on the AAU Campus Climate Survey on Sexual Assault and Sexual Misconduct*, Maryland: Association of American Universities, www.aau.edu/sites/default/files/%40%20Files/Climate%20Survey/AAU_Campus_Climate_Survey_12_14_15.pdf

Coy, M., Kelly, L. and Foord, J. (2009) *Map of Gaps 2 – The Postcode Lottery of Violence against Women Support Services in Britain*, London: End Violence Against Women Coalition and Equality and Human Rights Commission.

DeKeseredy, W. and Schwartz, M.D. (2011) 'Theoretical and definitional issues in violence against women', in C. Renzetti, J.L. Edleson and R.K. Bergen (eds) *Sourcebook on Violence Against Women*, London: Sage, pp 3–20.

Department for Business, Innovation and Skills (2015) 'Business Secretary calls on universities to tackle violence against women on campus', Department for Business, Innovation and Skills, 6 September, www.gov.uk/government/news/business-secretary-calls-on-universities-to-tackle-violence-against-women-on-campus

Durham University (2015) *Durham University's Sexual Violence Task Force: A Higher Education Initiative to Address Sexual Violence and Misconduct on Campus – A guide for staff and student HE leaders in how the issue of sexual violence and misconduct may be addressed in a university environment*, Durham: Durham University, www.neevawg.org.uk/sites/default/files/SVTF%20brochure%20PROOF%20(1).pdf

Feltes, T., Balloni, A., Czapska, J., Bodelon, E. and Stenning, P. (2012) *Gender-Based Violence, Stalking and Fear of Crime*, Final report to European Commission, Directorate General Justice, Freedom and Security (Project JLS/2007/ISEC/415), https://vmits0151.vm.ruhr-uni-bochum.de/gendercrime.eu/pdf/gendercrime_final_report_smaller_version.pdf

Fisher, B.S. (2009) 'The effects of survey question wording on rape estimates: Evidence from a quasi-experimental design', *Violence Against Women*, 15 (2): 133–47.

Fisher, B.S, Cullen, F. and Turner, M. (2000) *The Sexual Victimization of College Women*, Washington, DC: National Institute of Justice and Bureau of Justice Statistics.

Fisher, B.S., Daigle, L.E. and Cullen, F.T. (2010) *Unsafe in the Ivory Tower: The Sexual Victimisation of College Women*, Thousand Oaks, CA: Sage.

Fisher, B.S., Daigle, L.E., Cullen, F.T. and Turner, M.G. (2003) 'Reporting sexual victimization to the police and others: Results from a national-level study of college women', *Criminal Justice and Behavior*, 30 (1): 6–38.

Gill, A. and Anitha, S. (2009) 'The illusion of protection? A policy analysis of forced marriage legislation in the UK', *Journal of Social Welfare and Family Law*, 31 (3): 257–69.

Girlguiding (2014) *Girls' Attitudes Survey*, London: Girlguiding, www.girlguiding.org.uk/globalassets/docs-and-resources/research-and-campaigns/girls-attitudes-survey-2014.pdf

Hester, M. (2009) *Who Does What to Whom? Gender and Domestic Violence Perpetrators*, Bristol: University of Bristol.

HIA (2017)' Historical Institutional Abuse Inquiry. The Inquiry into Historical Institutional Abuse 1922 to 1995 and The Executive Office', www.hiainquiry.org/historical-institutional-abuse-inquiry-report-chapters

Jackson, C. and Sundaram, V. (2015) *Is 'Lad Culture' a Problem in Higher Education? Exploring the Perspectives of Staff Working in UK Universities*, Society for Research into Higher Education, Lancaster University, University of York, www.srhe.ac.uk/downloads/JacksonSundaramLadCulture.pdf

Jackson, C., Dempster, S. and Pollard, L. (2015) 'They just don't seem to really care, they just think it's cool to sit there and talk': laddism in university teaching-learning contexts', *Educational Review*, 67 (3): 300–14.

Jane, E.A. (2017) *Misogyny Online: A Short (and Brutish) History*, London: Sage.

Katz, J., Heisterkamp, H.A. and Fleming, W.M. (2011) 'The social justice roots of the mentors in violence prevention model and its application in a high school setting', *Violence Against Women*, 17 (6): 684–702.

Kelly, L. (1988) *Surviving Sexual Violence*, Minneapolis: University of Minnesota Press.

Kelly, L. (1989) 'The continuum of sexual violence', in M. Maynard, and J. Hanmer (eds) *Women, Violence and Social Control*, London: Macmillan, pp 46–60.

Kelly, L. (2016) 'The conducive context of violence against women and girls', *Discover Society*, 30, 1 March, https://discoversociety.org/2016/03/01/theorising-violence-against-women-and-girls/

Kelly, L., Lovett, J. and Regan, L. (2005) *Gap or Chasm: Attrition in Reported Rape Cases*, Home Office Research study 293, London: HMSO.

Laing, L. (2016) 'Secondary victimization: Domestic violence survivors navigating the family law system', *Violence Against Women*, published online 23 August.

Lewis, R. (2004) 'Making Justice Work: Effective Interventions for Domestic Violence', *British Journal of Criminology*, 44: 204–24.

Lewis, R., Marine, S and Keeney, K (2016) '"I get together with my friends and I change it": Young feminist students resist 'laddism', 'rape culture' and 'everyday sexism"', *Journal of Gender Studies*, 27 (1): 56–72, http://dx.doi.org/10.1080/09589236.2016.1175925

Lewis, R., Rowe, M. and Wiper, C. (2017) 'Online abuse of feminists as an emerging form of violence against women and girls', *British Journal of Criminology*, 57 (6): 1462–81.

LSE (2017) *Confronting Gender Inequality: Findings from the LSE Commission on Gender, Inequality and Power*, London: London School of Economics and Political Sciences, http://eprints.lse.ac.uk/66802/1/Confronting-Inequality.pdf

Marine, S. and Lewis, R. (2014) '"I'm in this for real": Revisiting young women's feminist becoming', *International Women's Studies Forum*, 47: 11–22.

Martinson, J. and Grierson, J. (2016) '"Serious failings' at BBC let Jimmy Savile and Stuart Hall go unchecked', *Guardian*, 25 February, www.theguardian.com/media/2016/feb/25/serious-failings-bbc-jimmy-savile-abuse-72-woman-children-report

McRobbie, A. (2009) *The Aftermath of Feminism: Gender, Culture, and Social Change*, London: Sage.

Morris, S. (2013) 'Jillings report confirms 'extensive' abuse at North Wales children's homes', *Guardian*, 8 July, www.theguardian.com/uk-news/2013/jul/08/jillings-report-north-wales-child-abuse

National Union of Students (NUS) (2010) *Hidden Marks: A Study of Women Students' Experiences of Harassment, Stalking, Violence and Sexual Assault*, London: NUS.

Nicholls, E.M.L. (2015) 'Running the Tightrope: Negotiating femininities in the night time economy in Newcastle', PhD Thesis, Newcastle University, UK.

NUS (2012) *Out in Sport: LGBT Students' Experiences of Sports*, London: NUS, www.nus.org.uk/global/final%20out%20in%20sport_new_web.pdf

Payne, F.M. and Green, D. (2016) 'Alison Smith speaks out on domestic abuse scandal', *The Badger*, 12 October, http://thebadgeronline.com/2016/10/alison-smith-speaks-out-on-domestic-abuse-scandal-students-will-feel-safe/

Phipps, A. and Young, I. (2012) *'That's What She Said': Women Students' Experience of 'Lad Culture' in Higher Education*, London: NUS.

Phipps, A., Ringrose, J., Renold, E. and Jackson, C. (2017) 'Rape culture, lad culture and everyday sexism: researching, conceptualizing and politicizing new mediations of gender and sexual violence', *Journal of Gender Studies*, 27 (1): 1–8.

Ruhl, J. and Ruhl, D. (2015) 'NCR research: Costs of sex abuse crisis to US church underestimated', *National Catholic Reporter*, 2 November, www.ncronline.org/news/accountability/ncr-research-costs-sex-abuse-crisis-us-church-underestimated

Rumsby, B. (2016) 'English football's child sexual abuse scandal set to spread to other sports', *Telegraph*, 26 November, www.telegraph. co.uk/football/2016/11/26/english-footballs-child-sexual-abuse-scandal-set-spread-sports/

Sanders-McDonagh, E., Neville, L. and Nolas, S. (2016) 'From pillar to post: Understanding the victimisation of women and children who experience domestic violence in an age of austerity', *Feminist Review*, 112: 60–76.

Sherwood, H. (2016) 'Damning report reveals Church of England's failure to act on abuse', *Guardian*, 15 March.

Sloane, C. and Fitzpatrick, K. (2011) *Talk About It Survey*, National Union of Students, Australia, https://d3n8a8pro7vhmx.cloudfront. net/nus/pages/33/attachments/original/1435818157/talk-about-it-survey-results-and-recommendations.pdf?1435818157

Stanko, B. (1985) *Intimate Intrusions: Women's Experience of Male Violence*, London: Unwin Hyman

Stark, E. (2007) *Coercive Control: How Men Entrap Women in Personal Life*, Oxford: Oxford University Press.

Stockdale, M.S. and Nadler, J.T. (2012) 'Situating sexual harassment in the broader context of interpersonal violence: Research, theory and policy implications', *Social Issues and Policy Review*, 6 (1): 148–76.

Towl, G. (2016) 'Tackling sexual violence at UK universities: a case study', *Contemporary Social Science*, 11 (4): 432–7.

UUK (2016a) *Changing the Culture: Report of the Universities UK Taskforce Examining Violence Against Women, Harassment and Hate Crime Affecting University Students*, Universities UK, www.universitiesuk. ac.uk/policy-and-analysis/reports/Documents/2016/changing-the-culture.pdf

UUK (2016b) *Guidance for Higher Education Institutions: How to Handle Alleged Student Misconduct Which May Also Constitute a Criminal Offence*, Universities UK, www.universitiesuk.ac.uk/policy-and-analysis/reports/Documents/2016/guidance-for-higher-education-institutions.pdf

Valls, R., Puigvert, L., Melgar, P. and Garcia-Yeste, C. (2016) 'Findings from the first study of violence against women on campuses in Spain', *Violence Against Women*, 22 (13): 1519–39.

Valentine, G., Wood, N. and Plummer, P. (2009) *The Experience of Lesbian, Gay, Bisexual and Trans Staff and Students in Higher Education*, Equality Challenge Unit, www.ecu.ac.uk/wp-content/uploads/2015/04/Experiences-of-LGBT-staff-and-students-in-he.pdf

Walklate, S. (2008) 'What is to be done about violence against women?', *British Journal of Criminology*, 48 (1): 39–54.

Watts, C. and Zimmerman, C. (2002) 'Violence against women: global scope and magnitude', *The Lancet*, 359 (9313): 1232–7.

Weale, S. and Batty, D. (2016) 'Sexual harassment of students by university staff hidden by non-disclosure agreements', *Guardian*, 26 August, www.theguardian.com/education/2016/aug/26/sexual-harassment-of-students-by-university-staff-hidden-by-non-disclosure-agreements

Weale, S. and Batty, D. (2017) 'New sexual harassment claims at Goldsmiths spark calls for inquiry', *Guardian*, 6 March, www.theguardian.com/education/2017/mar/06/new-sexual-harassment-claims-goldsmiths-university-of-london-calls-inquiry

WHO and Butchart, A. (2004) *Preventing Violence: A Guide to Implementing the Recommendations of the World Report on Violence and Health*, Geneva: World Health Organisation.

Section I
The problem

1

A continuum of acceptability: understanding young people's views on gender based violence

Vanita Sundaram

Introduction

There is an increasing focus on sexual violence in higher education in the UK. A growing body of research suggests that experiences of sexual harassment and violence are widespread in university communities (Phipps and Young, 2013). Recent research also suggests that institutional knowledge and action to tackle sexual harassment and violence (often described as 'lad culture') is sparse, with most university-led initiatives adopting a reactive and, often, punitive approach (Jackson and Sundaram, 2015). Violence *prevention* initiatives in higher education are not yet well-developed. However, increasing attention is being given to how to 'tackle' or 'challenge' sexual harassment and violence in universities.

In 2016, the UK Women's and Equalities Committee launched an enquiry into sexual harassment in schools. The final enquiry report noted the prevalence of various forms of sexual violence in schools, including unwanted sexual touching, sexual name-calling and sexual violence in teenage partner relationships (WEC, 2016). A major recommendation of the report, which was based on quantitative and qualitative research from a range of expert organisations and individuals, was that in order to tackle 'lad culture' in universities more work must be done to understand and prevent gender based violence (GBV) earlier in the educational life course.

This chapter therefore discusses research on secondary school pupils' views and experiences of gender based harassment and violence, in order to improve our understanding of how such practices arise and become entrenched. In particular, the research focuses on the ways in which young people talk about the acceptability of violence in different situations. A number of studies have noted that young people have high levels of tolerance in relation to various forms of GBV (Burton et al, 1998; Prospero, 2006; Barter et al, 2009, 2015; McCarry, 2010) but few have analysed why these views are held.I will argue that, in terms of developing violence prevention in schools and in universities, it is crucial to understand the nuances, contradictions and complexities in young people's views on violence. My work on this (Sundaram, 2013, 2014a, 2014b) suggests that young people's views exist on a *continuum of acceptability* and that binary positions on violence are rarely adopted. The positions young people take up along this continuum are fundamentally shaped by their understandings of normal and appropriate gender behaviour. The discourse used about violence as 'acceptable' or not is shaped by context and setting, perceived relationship dynamics, and gender – such that similar forms of violence may be justified in one instance but viewed as unacceptable in another. Teaching about GBV in particular, then, is unlikely to be effective if simplistic messages about violence being 'wrong' are dominant, especially if these are not accompanied by critical consciousness-raising about the gender norms and expectations underlying perspectives on violence. Recent violence prevention initiatives in higher education (for example, *The Intervention Initiative*, discussed in Chapter Eight in this volume) have similarly focused on culture and norm change, rather than on behavioural improvement.

Compulsory heterosexuality, young people and violence

In the following section, I review the recent UK research on young people and GBV. The focus will primarily be on young people's views and attitudes towards violence in order to situate this chapter in relation to questions about why GBV might exist in university communities and what actions might be necessary to engendering cultural change at higher education institutions. It is key to understand how values and attitudes around GBV manifest among younger people and the key factors influencing these views.

A growing body of research in the UK and elsewhere suggests that GBV, including sexual harassment, coercion and assault, are prevalent experiences for young people. Findings from a recent EU study showed that 48% of young women aged 14–17 years report having experienced sexual violence from an intimate partner (Barter et al, 2015) and a recent UK parliamentary enquiry into sexual harassment in schools found that sexual violence (in a range of forms) is a common experience for young school-aged girls in particular. Over 5,000 separate cases of sexual harassment or assault were recorded in UK schools between

2012 and 2015 and a Girlguiding poll in 2015 found that 75% of girls experience anxiety related to sexual harassment. The parliamentary enquiry found that sexual harassment covered a range of experiences, including unwanted sexual touching, groping, sexual jokes, name-calling that focuses on appearance, homophobic bullying, spreading of sexual rumours on- and offline, sharing of nude photos, coercion to participate in sexual activity, and sexual assault by intimate partners.

While the negative emotional, physical, social and psychological impacts of sexual harassment and violence have been well-documented, there appears to be a high degree of toleration of these practices too. Research with young women, in particular, suggests that their enjoyment of school is negatively impacted in a range of ways by coercive sexualised practices (for example, Ringrose and Renold, 2011; Keddie, 2009). Existing literature notes that practices such as phone-checking, monitoring friendships and contact with peers, and restrictions on dress are commonly perpetrated forms of harassment and abuse. Yet, young women normalise and accept these behaviours, narrating them as caring, loving or to be expected (even if not desirable). The normalisation of sexual violence by young people is key to their reproduction. Sexual violence becomes recast as 'relationship practices' that signify seriousness, possession, love and are accepted, even if not uniformly seen as 'good'. Young men adopt these practices as signifiers of 'proper' masculine behaviour (for example McCarry, 2010), demonstrating control, dominance and manliness to their peers and partners in doing so.

The pervasive normalisation and acceptance of GBV by young people is well-documented in UK and US research literature. Studies by the Zero Tolerance Trust (Burton et al, 1998), Prospero (2006), Barter et al (2009, 2015), McCarry (2010) and Coy et al (2016) have shown that young people justify and rationalise violence against women and girls in a range of situations. Violence against women is viewed as sometimes justified and women are varyingly viewed as having provoked violence towards them. Coy et al (2016) found that consent is a poorly understood concept among teenagers and numerous instances of sexual harassment or coercion were seen either as a 'normal' part of relationships or as something that the woman in the scenario had brought upon herself. The perpetration of relationship violence/s by young men is narrated as 'normal', if not desirable, and is therefore widely tolerated by young men and women. This produces a 'truth' about gendered interactions in which violence does not need to be automatically challenged or rejected. Following Foucault, it is imperative that we acknowledge the ways in which social arrangements produce discourses about gender and other hierarchies, such that particular knowledges become common-sensical and alternative interpretations are marginalised, denigrated or silenced (Waitt, 2010). This has significance for our understanding of how and why young people – and adults – come to normalise toxic heteronormative practices and to rationalise them through essentialist understandings of gender.

A wide-ranging body of research suggests that sexual harassment and violence are common experiences in educational settings (see, for example, Sundaram and Sauntson, 2015). There is also increasing evidence to suggest that young people tolerate, justify and even normalise a range of forms of violence, and that women themselves are sometimes blamed for having provoked violence towards them (see, for example, Barter et al, 2009). Less theorisation has been done around the reasons why young people (and adults) might perpetrate, accept and excuse violence in a range of contexts.

Heteronormativity as a framework for justifying violence

Gendered social norms are a key influence on young people viewing violence as 'violence' and understanding it as 'wrong' or as acceptable. Young people's expectations of appropriate and expected gender behaviour within the context of relationships are a fundamental influence on their definition of specific practices as violence and on their acceptance of violent practices. The centrality of heteronormative gender expectations to young people's justifications of violence is such that I would argue that heterosexual hegemony (Butler et al, 1994) can, itself, be understood as violent, in its policing of young people's views and practices to 'misrecognise' violence (in Bourdieu's sense of the term). Violence is not always recognised for what it is (Bourdieu, 2000) because of the salience of heteronormative gender expectations in shaping young people's understandings of 'normal' gender behaviour.

It is clear that young people hold strong expectations about 'appropriately feminine' behaviour. This has been shown in work with primary aged children (Davies, 1989; Reay, 2001; Renold, 2005), as well as older children and young adults. These discursive constructions of 'normal' gender behaviour also play out in the ways young people view violence, what constitutes violence and the acceptability of violence (Sundaram, 2013, 2014a).

The findings from my own research (Sundaram, 2014a) suggest that young people employ varying and contradictory discourses around the acceptability of violence, alternately labelling it as 'wrong' and 'unacceptable' to use violence against women, or calling it 'understandable' or even 'deserved'. The narratives young people draw on in relation to the acceptability of violence are heavily influenced by the context of the violence, the relationship dynamic between the social actors involved, and their imposition of gender expectations onto these two aspects of a given scenario. Expectations of women were a particular hinge-point around which narratives of violence as acceptable or not were centred. The expectations were not explicitly used to justify violence *a priori* but emerged through discussions about violence, in which young people revealed that their position towards violence was influenced by their understandings of how women should behave in different situations. They thus positioned themselves on a continuum of acceptability, where their understandings of violence were shown to be complex, nuanced and not-binary. Crucially, their positions on the continuum were influenced by their gendered expectations of behaviour within a given situation.

Young people appear to be well acquainted with formal school and governmental discourses about violence against women. A number of young people I interviewed were familiar with the governmental *This is Abuse* campaign which was launched in 2010 as a public information campaign about relationship violence among young people. The campaign had a dedicated website with sources of support, examples and stories illustrating the range of violences in relationships, and a discussion board for young people. It also included short films that depicted different scenarios of violence between young people and that presented viewers with a moral choice about whether to challenge and reject violence or whether to be a perpetrator. The campaign was discussed as a positive form of awareness-raising by many participants, although views challenging the gender-relatedness of violence was strong in almost all of the focus groups. There was a fairly widely-held view that girls can be, and are, violent within intimate relationships and within same-sex friendships too. Challenges were also presented to the notion that all violence was necessarily undeserved and there were some views expressed that were disparaging of people feeling like 'victims' over relatively 'mild' forms of violence, such as pushing, a slap or putting sexual pressure on someone.

The value of asking young people about 'real world' scenarios, rather than solely presenting them with abstract moral dilemmas to discuss, became apparent in the use of mixed methods for this study (see Sundaram, 2014a). When relatively generalised discussions about 'violence' were initiated, the vast majority of participants were quick to reject violence against women and to label perpetrators negatively.

Some of the judgements expressed about perpetrators were heavily classed and close links were made between substance use, certain forms of attire or socialising, and the use of violence. No young person in this study expressed a positive view on 'violence' per se. Violence against women was described as 'wrong', 'unacceptable' and as something that young people know, almost intuitively, not to do.

Yasin: 'It's a thing we know, but we can't put into words.'

The use of 'real world' vignettes generated a different, more nuanced response from young people in relation to violence. Details about the (presumed) context, relationship dynamics and setting were invoked to sustain a narrative of violence as unacceptable or, in many cases, of violence as understandable, excusable or even as deserved. Acts of violence were re-classified, as 'self-defence', 'caring too much' (being too emotionally invested in a situation), or as 'natural [male] reaction'. So, young people's views on what violence actually is began to shift as they imagined and imposed more details onto the different scenarios being discussed. Participants hypothesised about the sequence of events leading up to a particular scenario of violence, collectively generating stories about, and in defence of, harassment, coercion and acts of physical violence (Sundaram, 2014a).

Mark: 'If he cheated, like if he cheated on his wife or something, then you would probably expect it [one man to hit another]'. (in response to being shown a photograph of one man hitting another)

Laura: 'If she wasn't used to it, she'd probably fight back, but she's probably in the past hit him back and then it's got worse so she probably thinks 'oh just sit there and do nothing'.' (in response to being shown a photograph of a man acting in a threatening manner towards a woman)

Across different school settings, young people expressed consistent views on what they thought might be 'normal' emotions, practices and reactions for men. These included jealousy, pride, needing to show dominance or control, not being seen as weak, feeling anger or embarrassment if they are turned down, and doing what other men or boys would expect you to do. The naturalisation of these emotions as gendered, as specifically expected of 'men', was used as a means to rationalise or explain men's use of violence. An essentialist discourse about (heterosexual) 'men' was used to normalise their use of violence and, in some ways, to undermine its significance or noteworthiness.

> Josh: 'I think do you know like how the Romans before they used to have gladiators and everything and they just, they had like a lust for violence, it's the same with all of us. Like, say if Elliott and John, they had been arguing a lot and then we think they might have a fight, everyone is going to try and make them have a fight. Because like, school days, to be honest they are pretty boring and there's not much to do.'

In some cases, expectations of 'male' behaviour were used to defend their use of violence, indirectly and explicitly. Assumptions around the 'nature' of men in relation to sexual appetite and pride were invoked to rationalise violence, in a range of forms, including harassment and coercion. For example, violence was seen as excusable or justifiable if a man had been sexually rejected or if their dominance within the relationship or family dynamic had been challenged (by a female partner or relative or by another man). This reification of socially constructed expectations for male behaviour as 'natural' was thus used to excuse the use of violence by men.

> Tallyia: 'Some guy whistled at my sister and my [male] cousin realised and he gave him a black eye.'

> Isobel: 'It depends on how she goes about it because if she turns him away and [...] he feels rejected and embarrassed, then it could turn into a violent situation.'

Expectations of appropriate behaviour for girls or women were also clearly articulated and provided the complement to narratives about 'normal' male behaviours. While on the one hand, men's use of violence was narrated as justifiable depending on the scenario being discussed, girls' or women's perceived transgressive behaviour (especially within the context of intimate partner relationships) was used to excuse harassment, coercion or violence. Young people's expectations of appropriate behaviour for women and girls became apparent through their narratives about when violence might be used. Their justifications for violence were illustrative of these normative expectations of women. Normative 'feminine' behaviour included sexual compliance and acquiescence, honesty, listening and doing what you are asked to do. The scenarios that young people discussed and constructed together revealed that infidelity, sexual rejection and 'not listening' were situations in which violence might be justified to varying extents.

> Marta: 'If she slept with someone else, then there could be a little bit of violence but he shouldn't take it to the extreme.'

> Farah: '[...] Some guys do not mind you talking to [another] guy, it's just that they are like, if you cheat on them the guy is obviously going to get 'messy'.'

Gender norms are powerful in shaping their views on what constitutes violent behaviour and where the boundaries of acceptability lie (the use of euphemisms for violence – as above – also signals the parameters for naming a practice as 'violent'). Young people's views are fluid and often contradictory, shifting between imagined scenarios. Gender norms may be varyingly invoked to label violence as unacceptable (Richard: "a man should know better than that"), or as understandable (Emma: "she shouldn't have lied to him like that"). As discussed earlier, assumptions about the temporal and spatial contexts and relationship dynamics are imposed onto scenarios of violence to render them acceptable or not. The fluidity and tensions inherent in the varying accounts young people have of violence are important to acknowledge and to draw upon in thinking about how best to educate them about violence and gender. In the following section, I argue that a continuum of violence emerges in relation to the acceptability of violence in young people's narratives.

Re-theorising young people's views on violence: towards a 'continuum of acceptability'

Liz Kelly's (1988) work has been fundamental to our understanding of violence – and of sexual violence in particular – as comprising multiple and overlapping forms. Existing work shows the range of forms of violence young people perpetrate and experience, including sexist name-calling, groping and sexual touching, coercion and physical assault. Kelly (1988) argued that sexual violence should be conceptualised as a continuum of aggressions that might be visual, verbal, physical or sexual (and all of these might co-occur) and that are experienced as degrading or invasive by the victim and take away their ability to control intimate contact (Kelly, 1988: 41). This conceptualisation of violence has been pivotal to a survivor-led understanding of the experience and impact of violence. In the current political and cultural climate in which women's experiences of sexual harassment and assault are routinely trivialised, mocked and dismissed (as exemplified by US President Donald Trump, for example) (WEC, 2016; Bates, 2015), a theorisation of sexual violence which positions the survivor's experience at the centre is necessary.

Building on this concept of a continuum of violence, I propose that in terms of understanding why young people accept and excuse violence, it is helpful to think of their views as existing on a *continuum of acceptability*. Young people do not straightforwardly conceptualise violence in binary terms of 'right' and 'wrong'; rather they sometimes label violence as 'wrong' and at other times construct narratives to excuse or justify violence. Sometimes, violence is narrated as a negative practice but its use in a particular situation is still accepted. Their positions on this continuum are heavily influenced by their views on what is appropriate or 'normal' gender behaviour. So, violence against women may generally be viewed as a bad thing, but if a woman has transgressed expectations for appropriate 'feminine' behaviour within a given situation, expressions of understanding or empathy for the perpetrator were made. Similarly, if a 'male' reaction to a situation was understood as 'natural' then violence, which had previously been rejected, might be justified.

Conceptualising young people's views on violence as existing on a continuum is significant to thinking about prevention work aimed at this group. Previous national action on violence against women and girls prevention has tended to take as its starting point and primary focus the need to teach young people that violence against women is 'wrong'. While it is clearly imperative that young people are taught, unequivocally, that violence against women and girls is wrong, existing research suggests that this might not be an effective way to challenge social and cultural norms that inform young people's thinking about violence. My own, and other, research (for example, Prospero, 2006; Sundaram, 2014b; Barter et al, 2015) shows that young people 'know' that violence is wrong, morally and legally speaking. They are aware of school, social, cultural and legal 'rules' that reject violence – and violence against women in particular. They repeat these formal, learned discourses fluently and express this knowledge with conviction in its value. This tension between formal knowledge and more implicit values and attitudes towards violence needs to be acknowledged in our development of educational programmes aimed at young people.

Using a feminist research base (as additional to a feminist political approach) to inform school- and university-based prevention programmes would be a novel approach in the UK context. Over the past decade, feminist research has shown that young people are, by and large, accepting of violence against women and that cultural norms and expectations for gender are key to their acceptance and justification of violence. A fundamental aspect of prevention work therefore must be to challenge these entrenched gender expectations. Given that gender norms are embedded more widely in culture, including in local cultures (for example, school or university cultures), one element of violence prevention work should be to influence and change these local cultures. Connell (2006) has described public sector organisations, including universities, as 'gender regimes' that uphold – and even protect – the gendered distribution of power, labour and emotion, thereby producing conducive contexts for gender inequality, including abuses of gendered power. Making changes to institutional cultures therefore necessitates an approach to violence prevention which goes beyond identifying problematic individuals or having effective policies in place for responding to individual acts of harassment or violence. It necessitates an understanding of violence in its range of manifestations (so as to avoid an unhelpful focus on one-off, 'severe' incidents), an understanding of values and practices within the educational setting as closely linked to those reflected in wider society (and therefore a need to engage with critical consciousness-raising about these wider cultural norms), and an understanding that teachers, parents and pupils are all responsible for creating cultural norms and expectations within the school. Interventions that seek to alter prevailing social norms are therefore key to bringing about change. However, in increasingly marketised higher education contexts, where the generation of revenue and the protection of institutional reputations is paramount, challenging gendered, racialised and classed power relations may be difficult.

Critical consciousness-raising, which is rarely done in work to empower young people (Allen and Carmody, 2012), implies, in this case, that gender norms and the socially and culturally constructed nature of these, should be made explicit and visible to young people. The impact on the lived experiences of young women and men should be made visible and pedagogical strategies to help young people reflect on the positive and negative ways in which gender norms impact on their lives should be used. As Donaldson, McCarry and McCullough also argue in this collection, there is a need to move away from the gender-neutral focus on 'healthy relationships' that is currently employed. Some young people do find a criminal justice or legalistic approach to violence prevention attractive. The ability to categorically identify certain practices as 'criminal' and to have clear consequences for engaging with these behaviours is appealing (Sundaram, 2014b). It is straightforward to see the appeal of boundaried, consistent messages that link action to consequence and in these teenagers' narratives, the threat of punishment was cast as a primary incentive to avoid using violence.

> Connor: 'If there are police about to issue, like, proper verbal warnings and then a few times afterwards, they could like, get fined or something, something to really make them stop.'

> Farah: 'Information could be given about how, like, say if you don't realise how violent you've been, then how far it could go [in terms of severity of punishment].'

One limitation of this approach is in its lack of challenge to contexts in which it is seen as acceptable to use violence. Young people do not consistently see all acts of violence as negative or, indeed, as 'violent', and their views on violence are fluid across different situations. So, taking an exclusively legalistic approach that might assume a consistent understanding of violence, straightforward categorisations of violent practices, and linearity between action and consequence would overlook the challenges in young people's conceptualisations of violence. Second, and related, an approach focused heavily on individual acts of violence and legal recourse overlooks the cultural norms that produce violence, and young people's values around violence. Phipps (2016) has noted the ways in which punitive approaches are adopted in university contexts too, serving to reinforce cultural myths about 'a few naughty boys' being responsible for violent behaviour. The punitive approach also stands at odds with what survivors of violence say they would like prevention programmes to include. In research by Coy et al (2016), survivors said that young people should be taught to respect each other, to practice consent in a range of ways, and not to be controlling or dominating within a relationship. Sex and relationships education provides an obvious educational space in which to challenge gendered social norms with young people, exploring ways in which they restrict and confine their practices and identities.

I therefore argue in favour of making explicit the ways in which heteronormativity shapes and limits young people's lives and experiences in violence prevention work, and giving young people the skills to begin to recognise and differentiate gender norms from biological realities and then to challenge sexist expectations and practices. Such an approach also gives young people the knowledge and tools to recognise gender normative expectations and practices around them, for example, in the media, in the behaviour of celebrities or role models they look up to, and to be critical of these in a wider sense, as well as in relation to violence. Bystander intervention is an approach to responding to violence, which has been used widely in the US higher education context (Katz, 2001). The bystander approach has been relatively widely seen as an effective approach to tackle attitudes around GBV in the US context (for example, the Mentors in Violence Prevention programme) and is now being introduced in the UK context (for example, *The Intervention Initiative*, University of the West of England), as discussed by Fenton and Mott (in Chapter Eight of this volume). The bystander approach is based on the premise that social actors can be given a positive and active role in challenging violence towards women (Fenton et al, 2015) and, thereby, in changing social norms and institutional cultures. Bystander interventions comprise knowledge development as well as skills acquisition; so, for example, knowledge about causes and forms of GBV, and skills to challenge harassing or violent behaviour.

One potential limitation of bystander approaches may be that while they strive to 'reinforce shared social identit(ies)' (Fenton et al, 2015: 2) that can outweigh perceived differences between social actors (for example ethnicity, disability, and so on), one's ability to understand a given situation as potentially harassing or violent, and one's ability to feel empowered and safe to act to challenge this, are intimately linked to characteristics such as ethnicity, gender, disability and class. However, used in the context of a 'closed community' such as a school and reinforced by institutional commitment to challenging sexual harassment and violence, giving young people the knowledge and skills to recognise sexual violence and to intervene (when safe to do so) might be an effective way to tackle sexual harassment.

Making links to 'lad culture', sexual harassment and sexual violence in universities

In 2016, the UK government's Women's and Equalities Committee made the recommendation that in order to tackle 'lad culture' in further and higher education, we need to look at origins of aspects of 'lad culture', such as sexual harassment and abuse, earlier on in school.

'Lad culture' has not been precisely defined by the few existing studies that have been conducted on sexual harassment in higher education (for example NUS, 2010, 2014; Phipps and Young, 2013; Jackson and Sundaram, 2015). It has been characterised as a set of values and practices that frequently revolve around heavy alcohol consumption, competitive games or activities, and the public abuse of gendered and cultural 'others'. Phipps and Young (2013) noted that 'lad culture' often involved a discourse of sexist stereotyping, the sexual objectification of women, and the trivialisation of violence against women and rape. The National Union of Students found that 'lad culture' included sexual harassment, unwanted touching, sexual name–calling and rape jokes (NUS, 2010, 2014). Jackson and Sundaram (2015) found that 'lad culture' was associated with the humiliation and degradation of women students and staff in social contexts, as well as teaching and learning spaces. Examples of 'lad culture' in classroom spaces included homophobic graffiti, sexist contributions in seminars, systematic refusal to engage with teaching and attempts to undermine women lecturers.

Many of the values and practices that are associated with 'lad culture' closely resemble behaviours that are reported as occurring in schools. The inscription of gendered norms for appropriate sexual behaviour and identity onto women's bodies, in particular, is also clear in work we have done on 'lad culture' in university settings (Jackson and Sundaram, 2015). Women participants in our study on institutional perspectives on 'lad culture' narrated personal experiences of being sexually shamed in online and offline spaces, as a means to undermine their authority and credibility by discursively positioning them as 'whore' or 'slut' – as not appropriately 'feminine'. In one instance, a senior officer at the university students' union disclosed that she had been targeted and bullied online over a matter of months, with sexualised texts and images of her being posted in public social media accounts. Public posts were made about her sexual life, as well as that of her female family members, accompanied by nude photographs of women that were doctored to look like this particular participant. The catalyst for the harassment and visual violence (Kelly, 1988) was that our participant had challenged the behaviour of a men's sports team at her university (which included misogynistic chanting in public spaces and verbal harassment of the equivalent women's team), eventually preventing them from participating in future events for a period of time.

Other participants (men and women) in our study narrated instances of gendered sexual shaming and harassment that they had witnessed in university settings. These included the harassment of university staff in teaching interactions, in professional evaluations and in teaching spaces more generally.

'For Sports programmes in particular, this can be problematic for staff. Male students can be disruptive in lectures and male staff don't help because they tolerate those behaviours or don't challenge these behaviours.' (HEI 3, interview 3, female provost/dean of school)

'We've seen instances of sexualised feedback regarding lecturers, for example, MILF.' (HEI 1, interview 2, female dean of school)

A few women staff in our study suggested that this 'laddism' or reinforcement of male privilege prevailed in senior levels of the academy, making it difficult to challenge or to report. Some women said that they had attempted to raise instances of sexualised harassment or sexist behaviour and had not felt supported by senior management at their institutions. Other staff (men and women) trivialised sexual jokes, name-calling and harassment as 'banter', suggesting that sexism was not the underlying driver for such practices. Practices that could be described as forms of sexual harassment, such as sexualised chanting or cat-calling, were narrated as young men taking a bit of fun 'too far' and alcohol was seen as the major contributing factor to such abusive behaviour.

Thus, the normalisation of sexual harassment was evident among some university staff as well. It was narrated as inevitable, natural and even desirable for big groups of young men to behave in this way. Essentialist and pseudo-evolutionary perspectives were used to excuse boys having "*a bit of fun*". (HEI1, interview 4, female head of subject). Narratives about this being 'the' way young men behave when they get together in groups carried an implication that this is the *normal* way for young men to behave, nothing to be overly alarmed or concerned about. There was a degree of defensiveness about the naturalised discourse being used; indeed, when pushed to explore why young men might behave in these ways, a number of participants countered this with assertions about the high numbers of young women who behaved in similar ways (although this tended to be narrated as more 'concerning' behaviour among young women).

There are overlaps and recurring similarities in terms of the forms in which sexual harassment occurs and the spaces in which young people feel targeted. We can enhance our understanding of the links between these behaviours across the educational stages and settings by drawing on existing research about young people's views on and acceptance of sexual harassment and violence. The knowledge we have can improve our understanding of the development of these behaviours over the educational life course, as well as the normalisation of these practices by young people. It can also inform prevention at the university level, offering us important insights into the myths, assumptions and values that need to be challenged among university students and staff engaging in similar practices.

Finally, existing research on young people's acceptance of sexual harassment, coercion and violence potentially offers us an understanding of why some women engage in, or normalise and accept, 'lad culture'. Expectations for appropriate gender behaviour are deeply embedded in the cultural fabric and are reinforced by wider societal and cultural discourses, representations and structural factors. However, I argue that a simplistic argument around internalised misogyny is not sufficient; it does not acknowledge the racialised and classed elements of 'lad culture' and sexual harassment and violence more generally. This is clearly a gap in existing work, including that discussed here, and one that future work should seek to address. In 'Brexit' UK and Trump-era North America, it is imperative to think about the ways in which gender identities intersect with race, religion, disability and class and how these hierarchies are maintained and reinforced through the deployment of sexual and physical harassment and abuse.

References

Allen, L. and Carmody, M. (2012) "Pleasure has no passport': revisiting the potential of pleasure in sexuality education', *Sex Education: Sexuality, Society and Learning*, 12 (4): 445–68.

Barter, C., McCarry, M., Berridge, D. and Evans, K. (2009) *Partner Exploitation and Violence in Teenage Intimate Relationships*, London: National Society for the Prevention of Cruelty to Children.

Barter, C., Stanley, N., Wood, M., Aghtaie, N., Larkins, C., and Øverlien, C. (2015) *Safeguarding Teenage Intimate Relationships (STIR): Connecting Online and Offline Contexts and Risks*, http://stiritup.eu/wp-content/uploads/2015/06/STIR-Exec-Summary-English.pdf.

Bates, L. (2015) *Everyday Sexism*, London: Simon and Schuster.

Bourdieu, P. (2000) *Pascalian Meditations* (trans. R. Nice), Stanford, CA: Stanford University Press.

Burton, S. Kelly, L., Kitzinger, J. and Regan, L. (1998). *Young People's Attitudes Towards Violence, Sex and Relationships: A Survey and Focus Group Study*, Research Report 002, Glasgow: Tolerance Charitable Trust.

Butler, J., Osborne, P. and Segal, L. (1994) 'Gender as Performance', in P. Osborne (ed) (1996) *A Critical Sense: Interviews with Intellectuals*, London: Routledge.

Coy, M., Kelly, L., Vera-Gray, F., Garner, M. and Kanyeredzi, A. (2016) 'From 'no means no' to 'an enthusiastic yes'. Changing the discourse on sexual consent through Sex and Relationships Education', in V. Sundaram and H. Sauntson (eds) *Global Perspectives and Key Debates in Sex and Relationships Education: Addressing Issues of Gender, Sexuality, Plurality and Power*, Basingstoke: Palgrave Pivot.

Connell, R. (2006) 'Glass Ceilings or Gendered Institutions? Mapping the Gender Regimes of Public Sector Worksites', *Public Administration Review*, 66 (6), 837–49.

Davies, B. (1989) *Frogs, Snails and Feminist Tales. Preschool Children and Gender*, Sydney: Allen and Unwin.

Fenton, R.A., Mott, H.L. and Rumney, P. (2015) *The Intervention Initiative: Theoretical Rationale*, Documentation, University of the West of England, http://eprints.uwe.ac.uk/27671Girlguiding (2015) *Girls' Attitudes Survey 2015*, London: Girlguiding.

Jackson, C. and Sundaram, V. (2015) *Is 'Lad Culture' a Problem in Higher Education? Exploring the Perspectives of Staff Working in UK Universities*, Funder report, Society for Research into Higher Education.

Katz, J. (2001) *Mentors in Violence Prevention 2000–2001 Evaluation Report*, Mentors in Violence Prevention, www.mvpnational.org/wp-content/uploads/2011/12/MVP-HS-Eval-Report-2000-2001.pdf

Keddie, A.(2009) "Some of those girls can be real drama queens'. Issues of sexual harassment, gender and schooling', *Sex Education: Sexuality, Society and Learning*, 9 (1): 1–16.

Kelly, L. (1988) *Surviving Sexual Violence*, London: Polity Press.

McCarry, M. (2010) 'Becoming a 'proper man': young people's attitudes about interpersonal violence and perceptions of gender', *Gender and Education*, 22 (1): 17–30.

National Union of Students (NUS) (2010) *Hidden Marks: A Study of Women Students' Experiences of Harassment, Stalking, Violence and Sexual Assault*, London: NUS.

NUS (2014) *Lad Culture and Sexism Survey*, August–September 2014. London: NUS.

Phipps, A. (2016) 'The university campus as 'hunting ground", gender, bodies, politics, 24 February, https://genderate.wordpress.com/2016/02/24/hunting-ground/

Phipps, A. and Young, I. (2013). *That's What She Said: Women Students' Experiences of 'Lad Culture' in Higher Education*, Project report. London: NUS.

Prospero, M. (2006) 'The Role of Perceptions in Dating Violence Among Young Adolescents', *Journal of Interpersonal Violence*, 21 (4): 470–84.

Reay, D. (2001) "Spice girls', 'nice girls', 'girlies'and 'tomboys': Gender discourses, girls' cultures and femininities in the primary classroom', *Gender and Education*, 13 (2): 153–66.

Renold, E. (2005) *Girls, Boys and Junior Sexualities: Exploring Children's Gender and Sexual Relations in the Primary School*, Oxford: Routledge.

Ringrose, J. and Renold, E. (2011)' 'Slut-shaming', girl power and sexualisation: thinking through the politics of the international SlutWalks with teenage girls', *Gender and Education*, 24 (3), 333–43.

Sundaram, V. (2013) 'Violence as understandable, deserved or unacceptable? Listening for gender in teenagers'talk about violence', *Gender and Education*, 25 (7), 889–906.

Sundaram, V. (2014a) *Preventing Youth Violence: Rethinking the Role of Gender and Schools*, Basingstoke: Palgrave Pivot.

Sundaram, V. (2014b) "You can try but you won't stop it. It will always be there'. Youth Perspectives on Violence and Prevention in Schools', *Journal of Interpersonal Violence*, 31(4): 652–76.

Sundaram, V. and Sauntson, H. (eds) (2015) *Global Perspectives and Key Debates in Sex and Relationships Education: Addressing Issues in Gender, Sexuality, Plurality and Power*, Basingstoke: Palgrave Pivot.

Waitt, G. (2010) 'Doing Foucauldian discourse analysis: revealing social realities', in I. Hay (ed) *Qualitative Research Methods in Human Geography*, Don Mills, Ontario: Oxford University Press, pp 217–40.

Women's and Equalities Committee (WEC) (2016) *Sexual Harassment and Sexual Violence in Schools. Third Report of Session 2016–17*, House of Commons.

2

'Lad culture' and sexual violence against students[1]

Alison Phipps

Introduction

This chapter addresses the issue of sexual violence against students and the concept of 'lad culture' which has been used to frame this phenomenon in the UK and has connections to similar debates around masculinities in other countries. This issue is much-researched and debated but under-theorised and, due to a lack of intersectionality, radical feminist frameworks around violence against women are useful but incomplete. The chapter sketches a more nuanced approach to the understanding of campus sexual violence and the masculine cultures that frame it, which also engages with the intersecting structures of patriarchy and neoliberalism. It argues that framing these issues structurally and institutionally is necessary in order to avoid individualistic and punitive approaches to tackling them which may seem feminist but are embedded in neoliberal rationalities.

Background

From concerns about 'eve teasing' or gendered and sexual harassment on South Asian campuses, to debates about 'lad culture' and freedom of speech in the UK, to Lady Gaga's performance at the 2016 Oscars when dozens of US survivors joined her silently on stage, the issue of sexual violence against students has recently been high on the international agenda. Starting in the 1980s, the sexual victimisation of women students has been studied in many countries including Japan, China (Nguyen et al, 2013), South Korea (Jennings et al, 2011), Haiti, South Africa, Tanzania (Gage, 2015), Jordan (Takash et al, 2013), Chile (Lehrer et al, 2013), Canada (Osborne, 1995), Germany, Italy, Poland, Spain (Feltes et al, 2012), Bangladesh, India, Sri Lanka (Chudasama et al, 2013; Nahar et al, 2013), the US and the UK (Phipps and Smith, 2012). Beginning in the US, initial studies were often psychological and individualistic, focused on motivations of male perpetrators, acceptance of 'rape myths' and experiences of post-traumatic stress. This orientation, as well as a largely positivist slant, continues in much academic and policy work, as the 'problem' is established and explorations begin in new international contexts. However, there has also been a strong thread of feminist analysis grounded in the concept of patriarchy, and the continuum between more 'everyday' forms of sexual harassment and more 'serious' manifestations of sexual violence. More recently, there have been attempts to contextualise campus violence within theories of masculinity, shaping discussions of 'lad culture' in the UK, 'bro culture' in the US and a new/renewed interest in 'rape culture' internationally.

Our study

In the UK, the first major study of women students' experiences of harassment and violence was released by the National Union of Students (NUS) in 2010. This found that one in seven women students had experienced a serious physical or sexual assault during their studies, and 68% had been sexually harassed (NUS, 2010). Following this, Isabel Young and I were commissioned by NUS to explore the links between sexual violence and 'laddish' masculinities characterised by competitive displays of sexism and misogyny. Our research (NUS, 2013) was a qualitative interview study with 40 female students at British universities, exploring their experiences of and feelings about 'lad culture' in their communities. We defined 'lad culture' as a group mentality residing in behaviours such as sport, heavy alcohol consumption, casual sex and sexist/discriminatory 'banter', and found that many of the behaviours collected under this banner actually constituted sexual harassment. We also found that much of this was normalised within student communities, with 'casual' non-consensual groping being commonplace at parties and in social venues, and expectations around sexual activity which required young women to be constantly available yet almost entirely passive. This, we suggested, created the conditions in which potentially serious boundary violations, including sexual assault, could occur. The release of our report was met by a wave of grassroots activism and policy conversation, and a deluge of media stories which incorporated both genuine concern and moral panic (Phipps and Young, 2015a, b).

These debates in the UK echoed similar ones around 'bro cultures' (Chrisler et al, 2012), 'hookup cultures' (Sweeney, 2014) and 'rape culture' (Heldman and Brown, 2014) in the US and internationally. In many countries there has tended to be a sensationalisation of the issue amidst calls for retaliatory and punitive responses, exemplified in the 2015 film *The Hunting Ground*, for which Lady Gaga's song provided the soundtrack. However, as yet there is little useful theorisation of why and how particular types of masculinities might shape and produce sexual violence among students, which means that the evidence base for prevention is thin. Radical feminist work on violence against women, in which anti-violence policy in Western countries tends to be grounded (Phillips, 2006; Jones and Cook, 2008; Bumiller, 2009), has established sexual violence as a gendered phenomenon primarily perpetrated by men against women and framed by the power relations between the sexes which also construct typically masculine and feminine sexual roles and expectations. However, this theory lacks nuance and does not give insight into why particular types of men perpetrate sexual violence in specific contexts for different reasons. Similarly, the term 'lad culture' is not helpful analytically, as it tends to collapse a variety of behaviours and motivations together (Phipps, 2016). There is a need, then, to (re)theorise 'laddish' masculinities and revisit theoretical frameworks around violence against women. To do this properly, we need to take an intersectional approach.

Theorising sexual violence

Radical feminists were not the first to politicise rape. As McGuire (2011) documents, the US Civil Rights movement was rooted in a powerful (and now largely obscured) strand of anti-rape resistance, which prefigured many of the insights of second-wave feminism. Generations of activists such as Ida B. Wells (McGuire, 2011: xviii) and Rosa Parks, who was an anti-rape campaigner 'long before she became the patron saint of the bus boycott' (McGuire, 2011: xvii), situated both the sexual abuse of black women and allegations of rape against black men within a broader analysis of the dynamics of racist oppression (see also Davis, [1981] 2011). 'Decades later', McGuire (2011: 46) writes, 'when radical feminists finally made rape and sexual assault political issues, they walked in the footsteps of [these] black women'. Radical feminists appeared blissfully unaware of this, instead believing that anti-rape organising was a Women's Liberation Movement invention (see for example Brownmiller, 1975: 397). The fact that the huge historical contribution of black women was erased (and the work of feminists of colour continues to be so) speaks to dynamics of racism and privilege within the feminist movement. These have also shaped the production of rather one-dimensional theory.

'I have never been free of the fear of rape', wrote Susan Griffin in 1971 (p 26). Today it is often taken for granted within feminist circles that rape is everyday rather than uncommon and more often committed by someone the victim knows than a stranger. However, this idea has a relatively short life in the political and cultural mainstream. In the 1970s and 1980s, radical feminist theorising and empirical research (see for example Russell, 1983; Hall, 1985) helped give the lie to the widely-held idea that rape was both rare and necessarily graphically violent (Jones and Cook, 2008: 5). Like those of the black activists preceding them (McGuire, 2011), radical feminist definitions of rape were expansive, reflecting women's experiences and refusing to let spouses and family members off the hook. This centring of lived realities defined rape as a violation of women's bodies, not men's property rights; both the testimonial politics of black women within Civil Rights movements (dating back to slavery) and subsequent radical feminist activism based on the slogan 'the personal is political' (Hanisch, 1971) focused on women helping women through sharing, healing and politicising trauma (Jones and Cook, 2008; McGuire, 2011).

Brownmiller (1975) and others focused on the 'violence' in sexual violence, conceptualising it as a tool of gender oppression which functioned to preserve male dominance rather than express uncontrolled sexuality (which was the popular belief). The threat of the 'stranger rapist' was seen as key to maintaining structural relations of patriarchal power; this created generalised fear and also caused women to look to specific men for protection, which often put them at greater risk of abuse (Brownmiller, 1975; MacKinnon, 1989). This structural interpretation echoed (without credit) the black feminist politics of the Civil Rights movement in its conceptualisation of sexual violence as a strategy of oppression and terror, albeit focusing only on the dimension of gender rather than the interconnections between gender and race.[2] Kelly's (1988) continuum of violence defined a collection of behaviours, from sexual harassment to sexualised murder, all with the social and political function of keeping women in their place. Radical feminists argued that a range of acts (some of which had been normalised or defined as 'minor') could be harmful, and that this was not adequately reflected in legal codes.

Important legislative gains were made from this conceptualisation of rape as violence rather than sex, including prohibitions on the use of sexual history evidence in court, although in practice this continued to happen (Kelly et al, 2006). In contrast, other radical feminists centred the 'sexual' in sexual violence, examining in particular the institution and practice of heterosexuality. For Dworkin (1976) and MacKinnon

(1989) heterosexuality constituted the gendered eroticisation of dominance and submission, with the latter regarded as consent. This meant that coercion and violence were a constitutive part of 'normal' sexual relations, and defined rape as committed by men who exemplified rather than deviated from extant social norms. The conceptualisation of femininity as a socialised state of embodied submission has since been rightly criticised for both playing into misogynist tropes and for being a specific representation of the identities and experiences of middle class, white women (hooks, 1981; Skeggs, 1997; Serano, 2009; Phipps, 2009). However, it provided a useful critical analysis of the construction of consent in conditions of inequality, and allowed for an appreciation of the conditioned reality in which many women did not fight back against assaults, challenging prevailing myths which defined 'real rape' as being one in which there was evidence of a struggle (Lees, 1996).

Radical feminist ideas were important in understanding the co-constitution of gender, sexuality and violence and were responsible for a number of legislative and political achievements (Cahill, 2001). However, from the 1980s onwards they came under increasing critique from black feminists and others for their lack of appreciation of differences between women which shaped experiences of gender, sexuality and violence in divergent and often directly contradictory ways (Davis, [1981] 2011; Carby, 1982; Crenshaw, 1991; Skeggs, 1997). Furthermore, the meanings of structures such as the family and the state, taken for granted within radical feminist theorising, were exposed as largely specific to the white middle classes, erasing the often completely different experiences of other women (Carby, 1982; Crenshaw, 1991). Although it had established strong links between masculinity and violence, radical feminist work had largely failed to explore how sexual violence was central to relations of power other than gender, for instance colonial and racist systems (see for example Mohanty, 1988; Ahmed, 1992). The space for thinking through issues connected to class, race or colonialism was limited within radical feminist frameworks in which, as MacKinnon (1989: 12) maintained, the 'woman question' was *the* question.

The concept of intersectionality, codified within black feminist thought from the 1980s onwards partly in response to these debates (Crenshaw, 1991; Hill Collins, 1998), is invaluable in its exhortation to move away from one-dimensional notions towards ideas of a co-constitution of social categories, positions and encounters which produces important differences in subjectivity, experience and practice. In relation to sexual violence, an intersectional perspective allows for an understanding of why particular types of men may be violent in specific situations, and how violence is experienced by victims and survivors in different social locations. It also encourages us to examine how both acts *and allegations* of sexual violence are part of gendered and other oppressive systems, including the oppressive power of the state wielded against some groups of citizens more than (or for the protection of) others. When applied to discussions of 'lad culture' and sexual violence in universities, an intersectional framework raises important questions around how performances of classed and racialised, as well as gendered and heterosexualised, superiority are at play, as well as the influence of broader intersecting structures such as patriarchy and neoliberalism. It also raises issues around the carceral solutions currently being proposed and implemented, in terms of which men they may construct and target as 'violent', and how these men may be dealt with.

Theorising laddish masculinities

Laddism in the UK has long been associated with the white working classes, at least since Paul Willis' iconic study *Learning to Labour* (1977), which focused on rebellions against academia and authority performed by young men who had been constructed as 'failures' in a hostile education system and job market. This type of laddish rebellion is still at work in many school and university classrooms, in higher education particularly within institutions with a more diverse social class intake (see for example Barnes, 2012; Jackson et al, 2015; Jackson and Sundaram, 2015).[3] Interpretations of laddism in schools have largely followed the Willis framework, and 'laddish' behaviours in university classrooms can similarly be positioned as an expression of alienation from neoliberal, middle class (and allegedly feminised) higher education. When laddism has been reported in the classrooms of more elite universities, this has tended to be a more domineering behaviour which has been defined as intimidating rather than disruptive, and which also appears more likely to be overtly sexist (NUS, 2013), although of course sexism and violence against women are issues that cross class boundaries.

In contrast to the mainly lower-middle and working class framing of classroom disruption, the sexist 'lad culture' which has been identified recently in the social and sexual spheres of university life appears to be largely (although not exclusively) the preserve of privileged men. This is reflected in our research findings and in recent media reports (NUS, 2013; Phipps and Young, 2015a, b), although more research is needed especially on the differences between 'new' and 'old' universities and those in campus and more urban settings. Recent discussion of university laddism brings to mind the 'new lad' of the 1990s, a more middle class version incorporating binge-drinking, drug-taking, casual sex and extreme sports (Phipps and Young, 2015a). There are also associations with masculinities which would not historically have been granted the epithet 'laddish', due to its working class connotations. The rugby players, drinking and debating society members from elite universities who exemplify contemporary UK laddism (Phipps and Young, 2015b) bring to mind the men and masculinities typified by the Bullingdon Club, a centuries-old all-male exclusive dining club at Oxford University which boasts high-profile former members including former British Prime Minister David Cameron.

This class profile is mirrored in the debate around 'rape culture' in the US, where elite white fraternities have been singled out (Valenti, 2014). In one high-profile story, Delta Kappa Epsilon at Yale was suspended en masse for an incident in which pledges chanted 'No means yes! Yes means anal!' around campus (Burgoyne, 2011). Elite men have been the focus of concerns around sexism and sexual harassment and violence in other Anglo-Western countries; in 2013, students at the prestigious church-run Wesley College at Sydney University won the annual 'Ernie' award for sexism for distributing beer holders branded 'It's not rape if it's my birthday' (AFP, 2013). Within an intersectional analysis, behaviours such as these cannot and should not be interpreted using the same ideas of alienation and resistance which are pertinent to discussions of working class laddism. The aggressive sexism of more privileged men can be seen as an attempt to preserve or reclaim territory, contextualised in relation to the patriarchal backlash against feminism, and attempts to diversify the UK student population along gender, race and class lines.

Intersections of power and privilege

Laddism cannot be theorised by a framework that only names gender and the patriarchal construction of men's violence against women; although gendered violence is perpetrated by men of all social classes, it is also necessary to appreciate the motivations and contexts informing different performances of masculinity. There is a distinction between *being* dominated as a working class young man navigating a middle class education system, and *feeling* dominated as a middle or upper class young man dealing with a loss of privilege (Phipps, 2016). Both can be seen in relation to the construction of white middle class young women as ideal neoliberal educational subjects, but there are also classed relations between these masculinities which warrant investigation. This means that an analysis of laddism as a reassertion of traditional gender binaries, which accords well with the radical feminist conception of sexual harassment and violence as tools to keep women in their place (Kelly, 1988), is resonant but ultimately incomplete.

There are strong currents of classism and racism in contemporary middle class 'lad culture', perhaps linked to the growth of widening participation agendas focused on increasing the numbers of working class and black, Asian and minority ethnic (BAME) students. In the classroom, it could be argued that the domineering behaviour of more privileged men (Jackson and Dempster, 2009; NUS, 2013) is both an attempt to intimidate women and a way to position middle class 'lads' as the intellectually superior counterparts of their 'disruptive' working class peers. Similarly the jokiness and self-conscious irony of this laddism could be viewed as a counterpoise to the construction of black masculinity as dangerously sexual (Williams et al, 2008), both invisibilising white men as perpetrators and preserving the idea of black men as inherently more threatening (Phipps, 2016). Its postfeminist 'raunchiness' could also be examined as it relates to perceptions of Asian men as fragile and sexually inadequate (Wong et al, 2014). In racialised terms then white middle class laddism may be an assertion of superior virility that nevertheless positions itself as less threatening than (and therefore also superior to) the black hyper-masculine Other (Phipps, 2016).

Homophobia is also a central component of laddish cultures and behaviours (NUS, 2013; Muir and Seitz, 2004), which can be seen in relation to ideas about 'inclusive masculinity' or 'hybrid masculinity' as a new middle class norm (Anderson and McGuire, 2010; Bridges, 2014). Retro-sexist performances may reply to this softening of masculinity, as well as the potential blurring of gender lines which has accompanied the greater visibility of trans, genderqueer, non-binary people and others, especially within student communities (Dugan et al, 2012; Rankin and Beemyn, 2012). Inclusive masculinities may be more style than substance, and thus obscure continued gender oppressions (Sweeney, 2014). Celebrations of these masculinities should also be related to geopolitical discourses constructing Western men as evolved and Other cultures as inherently misogynistic and homophobic (Bhattacharyya, 2008). Nevertheless, the representation, if not the reality, of these masculinities may be significant in understanding contemporary laddism in social and sexual spaces.

All these intersecting issues complicate interpretations of contemporary middle class white laddism as solely an anti-feminist backlash. Of course, this is also at work; white middle class girls and young women now frequently outperform boys and young men and embody the confident adaptability that is a contemporary employment requirement (Skelton, 2002; Williams et al, 2008). The idea that women are winning the 'battle of the sexes', popular in many Western countries, is a key framing factor in relation to 'lad culture' (Phipps and Young, 2015b) as well as retro-sexism more generally. Within this narrative the successful white middle class woman becomes universal, disregarding evidence that many gendered inequalities remain and that women from minoritised groups continue to struggle (Karamessini and Rubery, 2013). Furthermore, there is no acknowledgement of the fact that the masculinised values and power structures of education persist (Skelton, 2002; Leathwood and Read, 2009). Such sensationalist notions of a 'crisis of masculinity' thought to have been prompted by gains in women's rights have had a significant purchase on policy and popular debate (Skelton, 2002; Francis and Archer, 2005; Phipps, 2016), and in the context of these ideas, there is evidence that white middle class boys are being hothoused by parents who see them as frail and imperilled (Williams et al, 2008).

Viewed more sympathetically, performances of laddism could be seen as a pressure release for white, middle class young men who may be struggling to occupy neoliberal educational subjectivities, or a reaction against being cosseted by over-protective parents. This potential element of rebellion provides continuity with working class forms; however, a *sense* of victimisation on the part of the privileged does not mean victimisation has occurred. Furthermore, this oppression narrative has recently been used to great political advantage by the dominating classes, in debates about 'free speech' on campuses in both the US and the UK which have featured defences of 'lad culture' as a form of sexual self-expression in a repressive and repressed society (see for example Hayes, 2013; O'Neill, 2014; Palmer, 2015). It should be acknowledged that radical feminist initiatives around sexual violence have been co-opted in the past by moralistic and carceral agendas; this will be discussed later in the chapter (Bumiller, 2009; Phipps, 2014). However, to note, this is not to position laddism as progressive when it is in fact a reactionary phenomenon.

Intersections of patriarchy, neoliberalism and carceral feminism

Also challenging the generalised 'crisis of masculinity' narrative is the fact that white middle class and elite masculinities are often seen as harmonious with the contemporary context of corporate neoliberalism

(Connell, 2005; McGuire et al, 2014). In our work on laddism, and drawing on research exploring how norms of individualism, competition and consumerism are shaping and reshaping sexualities (Gill and Donaghue, 2013), Isabel Young and I have argued that it embodies neoliberal rationalities through its characteristic modes of sexualised audit (Phipps and Young, 2015b). Many of the elements of student 'lad cultures' are not new; however, conventional patriarchal modes of misogyny and one-upmanship (Jackson, 2010) have been reshaped by neoliberal values in the university environment. We argue that the market-political rationality of neoliberalism (Brown, 2006), which has come to predominate in the academy (Lynch, 2006; Ball, 2012), can be observed in laddish performative regimes.

Within contemporary middle class laddism, older practices such as the legendary 'fuck a fresher' race exist alongside more neoliberalised systems of monitoring and measurement such as charting sexual conquests and giving women grades for their sex appeal. Our research highlighted a variety of sexual scoring matrices and practices by which men appraise women. These were widely exposed in May 2013 when a number of Facebook pages entitled 'Rate Your Shag' appeared, linked to various universities, which were 'liked' by over 20,000 users of the social network in 72 hours before being deleted by administrators (Datoo, 2013). Similarly, more traditional modes of male entitlement have been reframed within these youth cultures, with ideas about 'having' women augmented by the notion of maximising sexual capital. This, in turn, reflects the idea of maximum outcomes for minimal effort which now underpins educational consumption (Molesworth et al, 2009). It can be suggested that the domineering 'effortless achievement' which characterises middle class laddism in educational contexts (Jackson, 2003; Jackson and Dempster, 2009) also animates the quest for an 'easy' lay.

As well as framing contemporary student laddism, neoliberal and patriarchal universities are complicit in overlooking the harassment and violence that can result from it. In the US, where higher education markets are well established and despite a legislative framework mandating the publication of campus crime statistics (Phipps and Smith, 2012), institutions have been criticised for covering these up, or encouraging students to drop complaints in order to preserve reputation in a competitive field (Sack, 2012). There have also been reports of this in the UK (Younis, 2014), and it is likely that the privatisation of essential services such as campus security and student support and counselling (Williams, 2011) will threaten student safety and the quality of pastoral care. The developing 'pressure-cooker culture' among academics (Grove, 2012) and fears about casualisation (Lynch, 2006) are also creating an individualism which may mean that academics turn a blind eye while trying to keep our jobs (at best) and advance our careers (at worst).

When universities do take action, it is usually in an individualistic and punitive fashion that both fails to address the roots of problems and has tremendous potential to exacerbate other inequalities. Calls for such measures in the US, exemplified in the 2015 film *The Hunting Ground*, are based on the research of Lisak (2008) who argues that campus offences are committed by a handful of violent sociopaths who 'groom' their targets and coerce and terrify them into submission. These claims however have been challenged; Lisak and Miller's initial paper (2002) was based on four different student dissertations, none on campus sexual assault specifically. It also did not distinguish between assaults committed on different victims and multiple assaults on the same person (LeFauve, 2015). In contrast to this picture of the violent serial rapist, the theorisation in this chapter suggests that many acts of sexual violence at university stem from a variety of more spontaneous boundary-crossings shaped by intersectional cultures of masculinity and scaffolded by the patriarchal and neoliberal rationalities of the institution. A retribution-restitution approach which is embedded in these frameworks may be entirely inappropriate in this context.

Furthermore, there are important intersectional questions about appealing to carceral systems, either within or outside institutions, which may be riddled with racism, classism and other injustices. It is here that radical feminist and neoliberal models meet, and from the 1980s onwards radical feminist theorisations of sexual violence were critiqued by black feminists for mounting uncritical appeals to state apparatuses which were deeply implicated in racist oppression (see for example Carby, 1982; Davis, [1981] 2011; Crenshaw, 1991). Radical feminist-inspired service provision has also been challenged on its co-optation by, or in some cases active collaboration with, neoliberal agendas around crime control, which have been focused on criminalising particular groups of men (usually black and working class) in the service of protecting particular types of women (usually white and middle class) (Bumiller, 2009).

Elizabeth Bernstein (2010) has coined the phrase 'carceral feminism' to describe these relationships between a rather one-dimensional gender theory and neoliberal projects which, in protecting white middle class women, exacerbate the domination of others. Such an intersectional analysis also needs to be applied to policy frameworks and interventions in higher education; questions need to be asked about who may be defined as violent within these and targeted for surveillance and punishment, and who will be considered worthy of protection. Just as black and working class boys and young men are more likely to be labelled 'disruptive' in the classroom (Monroe, 2005; McDowell, 2007),[4] the construction of these men as inherently more aggressively sexual than their white, middle class counterparts (see for example Phipps, 2009; Roberts, 2013; McGuire et al, 2014) may be reflected in the application of disciplinary codes. These punitive approaches also lack pedagogy, reflecting the callousness of the neoliberal institution which is not conducive to student welfare or the creation of healthy and positive communities. Intersectionality, then, needs to be embedded in our theorisations of laddism *and* in attempts to tackle it.

Conclusion

Contemporary student laddism can be seen as an enactment of power and privilege over multiple intersecting lines. This means that radical feminist frameworks are useful but incomplete; we must acknowledge the universality of men's violence against women but we also need to explore the differences that produce particular masculine cultures and forms and experiences of violence in specific contexts. Student 'lad culture' also reflects the intersections between patriarchy and neoliberalism, and attempts to address it need to take account of how it is institutionally and structurally framed rather than resorting to individualistic approaches which are embedded in neoliberal rationalities and are punitive rather than pedagogic. Indeed the carceral solutions favoured by both neoliberal institutions and radical feminists detract from addressing the intersecting hegemonies in higher education which shape, produce and conceal a variety of forms of bullying and violence.

Notes
[1] This chapter was originally published as Chapter 13 in N. Lombard (ed) (2018) *The Routledge Handbook of Gender and Violence*, Routledge: Oxford, pp 171–182.
[2] As Davis (1981 [2011]: 180) pointed out, the prevailing construction of the 'police-blotter rapist' as black and the function of this within structures of racist oppression was generally ignored.
[3] Research conducted by Jackson and Sundaram (2015) found that classroom laddism was more common in universities with lower entry grades, which tend to be those with a more diverse class intake (Sutton Trust, 2011).
[4] This also applies to young black women (see Morris, 2007). Furthermore, due to prevailing stereotypes of black women as aggressive and overly sexual, they are less

likely to be the 'ideal victim' in criminal justice terms (Phipps, 2009), an inequality that may be replicated in the university context.

References

AFP (2013) 'Beer Holder Slogan Wins 'Ernies' Sexism Prize', *The Australian*, www.theaustralian.com.au/news/nation/beer-holder-slogan-wins-ernies-sexism-prize/story-e6frg6nf-1226736840058

Ahmed, L. (1992) *Women and Gender in Islam: Historical Roots of a Modern Debate*, New Haven, CT: Yale University Press.

Anderson, E. and McGuire, R. (2010) 'Inclusive Masculinity Theory and the Gendered Politics of Men's Rugby', *Journal of Gender Studies*, 19 (3): 249–61.

Ball, S. (2012) 'Performativity, commodification and commitment: An I-spy guide to the neoliberal university', *British Journal of Educational Studies*, 60 (1): 17–28.

Barnes, C. (2012) 'It's No Laughing Matter... Boys' Humour and the Performance of Defensive Masculinities in the Classroom', *Journal of Gender Studies*, 21 (3): 239–51.

Bernstein, E. (2010) 'Militarized Humanitarianism Meets Carceral Feminism: The Politics of Sex, Rights, and Freedom in Contemporary Antitrafficking Campaigns', *Signs*, 36 (1): 45–72.

Bhattacharyya, G. (2008) *Dangerous Brown Men: Exploiting Sex, Violence and Feminism in the War on Terror*, London: Zed Books.

Bridges, T. (2014) 'A Very 'Gay' Straight? Hybrid Masculinities, Sexual Aesthetics, and the Changing Relationship between Masculinity and Homophobia', *Gender & Society*, 28 (1): 58–82.

Brown, W. (2006) 'American nightmare: Neoliberalism, neoconservatism, and de-democratization', *Political Theory*, 34 (6): 690–714.

Brownmiller, S. (1975) *Against Our Will: Men, Women and Rape*, London: Penguin.

Bumiller, K. (2009) *In an Abusive State: How Neoliberalism Appropriated the Feminist Movement against Sexual Violence*, Durham, NC: Duke University Press.

Burgoyne, M. (2011) 'Yale Bans "No Means Yes" Fraternity for Five Years', *Ms Magazine* blog, 18 May, http://msmagazine.com/blog/2011/05/18/yale-bans-no-means-yes-fraternity-for-five-years/

Cahill, A.J. (2001) *Rethinking Rape*, Ithaca, NY: Cornell University Press.

Carby, Hazel (1982) 'White Woman Listen! Black Feminism and the Boundaries of Sisterhood'. In *Centre for Contemporary Cultural Studies, Empire Strikes Back: race and racism in 70s Britain*, London: Hutchinson.

Chrisler, J.C., Bacher, J.E., Bangali, A.M., Campagna, A.J. and McKeigue. A.C. (2012) 'A Quick and Dirty Tour of Misogynistic Bro Culture', *Sex Roles*, 66 (11–12): 810–11.

Chudasama R.K., Kadri, A.M., Zalavadiya, D., Joshi, N., Bhola, C., and Verma, M. (2013) 'Attitude and Myths Towards Rape among Medical Students in Rajkot, India', *Online Journal of Health and Allied Sciences* 12(3): 1-6.

Collins, P.H. (1998) 'It's All in the Family: Intersections of Gender, Race, and Nation', *Hypatia*, 13 (3): 62–82.

Connell, R.W. (2005) *Masculinities*, second edition, Berkeley: University of California Press.

Crenshaw, K. (1991) 'Mapping the Margins: Intersectionality, Identity Politics, and Violence against Women of Color', *Stanford Law Review*, 43 (6): 1241–99. doi:10.2307/1229039

Datoo, S. (2013) 'Facebook just Deleted Every University's "Rate Your Shag" Page', Buzzfeed, 28 May, www.buzzfeed.com/sirajdatoo/facebook-just-deleted-all-of-the-rate-your-shag-pa-9o1f

Davis, A.Y. ([1981] 2011) *Women, Race, & Class*, New York: Knopf Doubleday Publishing Group.

Dugan, J.P., Kusel, M.L. and Simounet, D.M. (2012) 'Transgender College Students: An Exploratory Study of Perceptions, Engagement, and Educational Outcomes', *Journal of College Student Development*, 53 (5): 719–36.

Dworkin, A. (1976) *Our Blood: Prophecies and Discourses on Sexual Politics*, New York: Perigee.

Feltes, T., List, K., Schneider, R., Hofker, S., Balloni, A., Bisi, R., Sette, R., Czapska, J., Klosa, M., Lesińska, E., Bodelon, E., Igareda, N., Casas, G., Stenning, P., Mitra-Kahn, T., and Gunby, C. (2012) *Gender-Based Violence, Stalking, and Fear of Crime*, Bochum: Ruhr-Universitat Bochum.

Francis, B. and Archer, L. (2005) 'Negotiating the Dichotomy of Boffin and Triad: British-Chinese Pupils' Constructions of "laddism"', *The Sociological Review*, 53 (3): 495–521.

Gage, A.J. (2015) 'Exposure to Spousal Violence in the Family, Attitudes and Dating Violence Perpetration Among High School Students in Port-Au-Prince', *Journal of Interpersonal Violence*, 13 (14): 2445–74, https://doi.org/10.1177%2F0886260515576971

Gill, R. and Donaghue, N. (2013) 'As if postfeminism had come true', in S. Madhok, A. Phillips and K. Wilson (eds) *Gender, Agency and Coercion*, Basingstoke: Palgrave Macmillan, pp 240–58.

Griffin, S. (1971) 'Rape: The All-American Crime', *Ramparts*, 10: 26–35.

Grove, J. (2012) 'Stressed academics are ready to blow in pressure-cooker culture', *Times Higher Education*, 4 October.

Hall, R. (1985) *Ask Any Woman: A London Inquiry into Rape and Sexual Assault*, Report of the Women's Safety Survey conducted by Women Against Rape, Bristol: Falling Wall Press.

Hanisch, C. (1971) 'The Personal Is Political'. Archive text available at: http://www.carolhanisch.org/CHwritings/PIP.html

Hayes, P. (2013) 'The NUS's prissy war on "lad culture"', *Spiked*, 10 April, www.spiked-online.com/newsite/article/nus/13517Heldman, C. and Brown, B. (2014) 'Why Colleges Won't (really) Address Rape Culture', *Ms Magazine* blog, 8 October, http://msmagazine.com/blog/2014/10/08/why-colleges-wont-really-address-rape-culture

hooks, b. (1981) *Ain't I a Woman: Black Women and Feminism*, Boston: South End Press.

Jackson, C. (2003) 'Motives for "laddishness" at school: Fear of failure and fear of the "feminine"', *British Educational Research Journal*, 29(4): 583–98.

Jackson, C. (2010) '"I've sort of been laddish with them – one of the gang": Teachers' perceptions of 'laddish' boys and how to deal with them', *Gender and Education*, 22 (5): 505–19.

Jackson, C. and Dempster, S. (2009) '"I sat back on my computer ... with a bottle of whisky next to me": Constructing "cool" masculinity through "effortless" achievement in secondary and higher education', *Journal of Gender Studies*, 18 (4): 341–56.

Jackson, C. and Sundaram, V. (2015) *Is 'Lad Culture' a Problem in Higher Education? Exploring the Perspectives of Staff Working in UK Universities*, London: Society for Research into Higher Education.

Jackson, C., Dempster, S., and Pollard, L. (2015) '"They just don't seem to really care, they just think it's cool to sit there and talk": Laddism in university teaching-learning contexts', *Educational Review*, 67 (3): 300–14.

Jennings, W.G., Park, M., Tomsich, E.A., Gover, A.R. and Akers, R.L. (2011) 'Assessing the Overlap in Dating Violence Perpetration and Victimization among South Korean College Students: The Influence of Social Learning and Self-Control', *American Journal of Criminal Justice*, 36 (2): 188–206.

Jones, H. and Cook, K. (2008) *Rape Crisis: Responding to Sexual Violence*, Lyme Regis: Russell House Publishing.

Karamessini, M. and Rubery, J. (2013) *Women and Austerity: The Economic Crisis and the Future for Gender Equality*, Oxford: Routledge.

Kelly, L. (1988) *Surviving Sexual Violence*, Chichester: John Wiley & Sons.

Kelly, L., Temkin, J. and Griffiths, S. (2006) 'Section 41: An Evaluation of New Legislation Limiting Sexual History Evidence in Rape Trials (Home Office Online Report 20/06)', London: HMSO, http://citeseerx.ist.psu.edu/viewdoc/download?doi=10.1.1.628.3925&rep=rep1&type=pdf

Leathwood, C., Read, B. and Society for Research into Higher Education (2009) *Gender and the Changing Face of Higher Education: A Feminized Future?* Maidenhead, Berkshire: Society for Research into Higher Education/Open University Press.

Lees, S. (1996) *Carnal Knowledge: Rape on Trial*, London: Hamish Hamilton.

LeFauve, L.M. (2015) 'Campus rape expert can't answer basic questions about his sources', *Reason*, 28 July.

Lehrer, J.A., Lehrer, E.L., and Koss, M.P. (2013) 'Sexual and Dating Violence among Adolescents and Young Adults in Chile: A Review of Findings from a Survey of University Students', *Culture, Health & Sexuality*, 15 (1): 1–14.

Lisak, D. (2008) 'Understanding the predatory nature of sexual violence', unpublished paper, www.middlebury.edu/media/view/240951/original

Lisak, D. and Miller, P.M. (2002) 'Repeat rape and multiple offending among undetected rapists', *Violence and Victims*, 17 (1): 73–84.

Lynch, K. (2006) 'Neo-liberalism and marketisation: The implications for higher education', *European Educational Research Journal,* 5(1): 1–17.

MacKinnon, C.A. (1989) *Toward a Feminist Theory of the State*, Cambridge, MA: Harvard University Press.

McDowell, L. (2007) 'Respect, Deference, Respectability and Place: What Is the Problem With/for Working Class Boys?' *Geoforum*, 38 (2): 276–86. doi:10.1016/j.geoforum.2006.09.006.

McGuire, D.L. (2011) *At the Dark End of the Street: Black Women, Rape, and Resistance-a New History of the Civil Rights Movement from Rosa Parks to the Rise of Black Power*, London: Vintage Books.

McGuire, K.M., Berhanu, J., Davis, C.H.F. and Harper, S.R.(2014) 'In Search of Progressive Black Masculinities Critical Self-Reflections on Gender Identity Development among Black Undergraduate Men', *Men and Masculinities*, 17 (3): 253–77, doi:10.1177/1097184X13514055

Mohanty, C.T. (1988) 'Under Western Eyes: Feminist Scholarship and Colonial Discourses', *Feminist Review*, 30: 61–88, doi:10.2307/1395054

Molesworth, M., Nixon, E. and Scullion, R. (2009) 'Having, being, and higher education: The marketisation of the university and the transformation of student into consumer', *Teaching in Higher Education*, 14 (3): 277–87.

Monroe, C.R. (2005) 'Why Are "Bad Boys" Always Black? Causes of Disproportionality in School Discipline and Recommendations for Change', *The Clearing House*, 79 (1): 45–50.

Morris, E.W. (2007) '"Ladies' or 'Loudies?" Perceptions and Experiences of Black Girls in Classrooms', *Youth & Society*, 38 (4): 490–515.

Muir, K.B. and Seitz, T. (2004) 'Machismo, Misogyny, and Homophobia in a Male Athletic Subculture: A Participant-Observation Study of Deviant Rituals in Collegiate Rugby', *Deviant Behavior*, 25 (4): 303–27.

Nahar, P., van Reeuwijk, M. and Reis, R. (2013) 'Contextualising Sexual Harassment of Adolescent Girls in Bangladesh', *Reproductive Health Matters*, 21 (41): 78–86.

National Union of Students (NUS) (2010) *Hidden Marks: A Study of Women Students' Experiences of Harassment, Stalking, Violence and Sexual Assault*, London: NUS.

NUS (2013) *That's What She Said: Women Students' Experiences of "Lad Culture" at Universities*, London: NUS.

Nguyen, T.T., Morinaga, Y., Frieze, I.H., Cheng, J., Li, M., Doi, A., Hirai, T., Joo, E. and Li, C. (2013) 'College Students' Perceptions of Intimate Partner Violence: A Comparative Study of Japan, China, and the United States', *International Journal of Conflict and Violence*, 7 (2): 261–73.

O'Neill, B. (2014) 'The Moral McCarthyism of the War on Lads', *Spiked*, 8 October, www.spiked-online.com/freespeechnow/fsn_article/the-moral-mccarthyism-of-the-war-on-lads

Osborne, R.L. (1995) 'The Continuum of Violence against Women in Canadian Universities: Toward a New Understanding of the Chilly Campus Climate', *Women's Studies International Forum*, 18 (5–6): 637–46.

Palmer, J. (2015) 'The real victim of "rape culture"? Free speech', *Spiked*, 23 April, www.spiked-online.com/newsite/article/the-real-victim-of-rape-culture-free-speech/16901

Phillips, R. (2006) 'Undoing an Activist Response: Feminism and the Australian Government's Domestic Violence Policy', *Critical Social Policy*, 26 (1): 192–219, doi:10.1177/0261018306059771

Phipps, A. (2009) 'Rape and Respectability: Ideas about Sexual Violence and Social Class', *Sociology*, 43 (4): 667–83, doi:10.1177/0038038509105414

Phipps, A. (2014) *The Politics of the Body: Gender in a Neoliberal and Neoconservative Age*, Cambridge: Polity Press.

Phipps, A. (2016) '(Re)theorising laddish masculinities in higher education', *Gender and Education*, 29 (7): 815–30, doi:10.1080/095 40253.2016.1171298

Phipps, A. and Smith, G. (2012) 'Violence against Women Students in the UK: Time to Take Action', *Gender and Education*, 24 (4): 357–73, doi:10.1080/09540253.2011.628928

Phipps, A. and Young, I. (2015a) 'Neoliberalisation and "Lad Cultures" in Higher Education', *Sociology*, 49 (2): 305–22.

Phipps, A. and Young, I. (2015b) 'Lad Culture' in Higher Education: Agency in the Sexualization Debates', *Sexualities*, 18 (4): 459–79.

Rankin, S. and Beemyn, G. (2012) 'Beyond a Binary: The Lives of Gender-Nonconforming Youth', *About Campus*, 17 (4): 2–10.

Roberts, S. (2013) 'Boys Will Be Boys … Won't They? Change and Continuities in Contemporary Young Working-Class Masculinities', *Sociology*, 47 (4): 671–86, doi:10.1177/0038038512453791

Russell, D.E. (1983) 'The Prevalence and Incidence of Forcible Rape of Females', *Victimology*, 7: 81–93.

Sack, K. (2012) 'Reform campus rape policy to prevent complaints becoming a "second assault"', *Observer*, 18 November.

Serano, J. (2009) *Whipping Girl: A Transsexual Woman on Sexism and the Scapegoating of Femininity*, Emeryville, CA: Seal Press.

Skeggs, B. (1997) *Formations of Class & Gender: Becoming Respectable*, London: SAGE.

Skelton, C. (2002) 'The "Feminisation of Schooling" or "Re-Masculinising" Primary education?' *International Studies in Sociology of Education*, 12 (1): 77–96.

Sutton Trust (2011) *Degrees of Success: University Chances by Individual School*, London: Sutton Trust.

Sweeney, B. (2014) 'To Sexually Perform or Protect: Masculine Identity Construction and Perceptions of Women's Sexuality on a University Campus in the Midwestern USA', *Gender, Place & Culture*, 21 (9): 1108–24.

Takash, H., Ghaith, S. and Hammouri, H. (2013) 'Irrational Beliefs About Family Violence: A Pilot Study Within Jordanian University Students', *Journal of Family Violence*, 28 (6): 595–601.

Valenti, J. (2014) 'Frat Brothers Rape 300% More. One in 5 Women Is Sexually Assaulted on Campus. Should We Ban Frats?' *Guardian*, 24 September.

Williams, K., Jamieson, F. and Hollingworth, S. (2008) '"He was a bit of a delicate thing": white middle-class boys, gender, school choice and parental anxiety', *Gender and Education*, 20 (4): 399–408.

Williams, R. (2011) 'Supporting students in a time of change', in *Higher Education and Society in Changing Times: Looking Back and Looking Forward* (CHERI Project Report), Buckingham: Open University, pp 46–53.

Willis, P.E. (1977) *Learning to Labor: How Working Class Kids Get Working Class Jobs*, New York: Columbia University Press.

Wong, Y.J., Tsai, P.C., Liu, T., Zhu, Q. and Wei, M. (2014) 'Male Asian International Students' Perceived Racial Discrimination, Masculine Identity, and Subjective Masculinity Stress: A Moderated Mediation Model', *Journal of Counseling Psychology*, 61 (4): 560–69.

Younis, J. (2014) 'Rape culture at university needs urgent action', *Guardian*, 27 January, www.theguardian.com/education/mortarboard/2014/jan/27/rape-culture-campus

Section II
Histories and politics of educational interventions against gender based violence in international contexts

3

Sexual violence on US college campuses: history and challenges

Renate Klein

In the United States, research about sexual violence on campus goes back into the 1950s (Kanin, 1957; Kirkpatrick and Kanin, 1957). Many more studies have followed (Fisher, Daigle and Cullen, 2010), and successive waves of rape prevention programmes have been rolled out on campuses across the country. The US Congress has weighed in with federal legislation, the White House took on the issue in 2014,[1] and media reporting of campus sexual assault scandals has soared. Yet, the problem continues. Why this is is difficult to answer. This chapter makes three points:

1. It is necessary to take a historical perspective to see where things have changed and where they have not.
2. While we know much about victimisation, the interplay between perpetration dynamics, campus culture, and institutional governance are not well understood.
3. The current policy emphasis on reporting is troubling because it ignores most of what we know about crime reporting and challenges neither perpetration nor university governance.

Use of terms

In this chapter the terms higher education institution (HEI), college and university are used interchangeably to refer primarily to four-year institutions in the US granting advanced degrees (typically, a Bachelor's degree is based on a four-year programme; a Master's degree may require an additional two years in graduate school). The expression 'on campus' is used to refer to sexualised violations in the context of higher education whether incidents occur on or off university premises. Regardless of place, the involvement of students or staff raises questions about a university's responsibility and its capacity to intervene, support and protect. When discussing specific findings, the terminology of the authors is used. Otherwise, the term 'sexualised violations' is used to refer to a broad range of actions from sexualised text messages to rape. Referencing such a range with one broad term has advantages and disadvantages. Broad terms allow an overarching analysis that examines diverse patterns of behaviour and links campus debates to broader issues of sexual violence in contemporary societies. However, for practical interventions, broad terms may be less useful. Specific violations need tailored interventions which require specific naming. Speaking of, and advocating against, sexualised violations or sexual violence in general also means that all forms of transgressions need to be taken seriously, from the seemingly trivial to the blatantly brutal. This does not mean that these actions have the same impact on victims. Actual impact is highly personal and depends on individual, social and cultural context. What is important, though, is to recognise that even seemingly minor incidents of sexual harassment are serious in that they constitute discriminatory contexts that undermine academic learning, personal development and social equality. The current US President is on record making disturbing misogynist remarks about men's sexual aggression against women. His electoral success shows that significant numbers of voters, women included, either condone or trivialise sexualised violations. Against such attitudes it is important to emphasise the seriousness of the entire range of sexual aggression, from online insults to bodily assaults. The term 'sexual misconduct', common in campus debates, is unsatisfying because it puts rape within the framework of student conduct codes and thus in the vicinity of transgressions such as drinking beer in public or cheating on coursework.

Next, very early research is described in detail because it serves to set the stage for an examination of the progress and stagnation that followed. A discussion of victimisation and perpetration follows, which leads into questions of policy framing, and the current focus on crime reporting.

Beginnings

In 1957, Clifford Kirkpatrick and Eugene Kanin published two studies with which they pioneered research on campus sexual violence. The studies show that in some ways little has changed over the past 50 years; male cultures of sexual aggression against women continue, underreporting by victims remains a problem, the social networks of victims and perpetrators play a role, and perhaps prevalence has remained similar, although because of methodological differences that is difficult to determine. The authors were outspoken about the existence of a male culture of sexual aggression against women. Indeed, they seemed to take it for granted. With bitter academic irony both studies illustrate how sexist assumptions can blind researchers to their own findings, stare misogynist practices in the face, and yet ignored them in the advancement of 'knowledge'.

The first paper, 'Male sex aggression on a university campus', appeared in a top academic journal, *American Sociological Review*, and thus was a piece of cutting-edge research done to the highest academic standards of the time (Kirkpatrick and Kanin, 1957). From today's vantage point, the language is sexist and the theoretical framework lacks a gender analysis even though gendered inequities scream off the page. In the 1950s, the civil rights movement was gaining strength, second wave feminism was in its infancy; gender was not yet an analytical category; there where were no intersectional frameworks. Yet, there were sociological concepts of social stigma and exploitation in unequitable relationships. The study was prompted by 'some case material reporting instances of violent male aggression with reluctance on the part of the offended girls to invoke protection and punishment' (Kirkpatrick and Kanin, 1957: 52–3). Here already are two observations still relevant today; university authorities were aware that sexual violence occurred on campus and victims were reluctant to report assaults to them.

The study was a survey of female students on one university campus. Two key findings, as well as the overall tenor of the conclusions, ring strikingly familiar even today. First, instances of sexual violence (from unwanted fondling 'above the waist' and 'below the waist' to attempted rape) were common. Of 291 female students, 162 (55.7%) 'reported themselves offended [by male students] at least once during the [1954–55] academic year at some level of erotic intimacy' (Kirkpatrick and Kanin, 1957: 53). Second, the majority of assaults (over 90%) were not reported to the authorities and none of the attempted rapes were. Of the recommendations, the first focuses on the victim; 'college girls should be trained in *informed* self-reliance' (p 58, emphasis in original). Measures addressing victims still rank high on today's agendas. However, the authors also emphasis that 'parents, peer groups and formal agencies should operation so as to avoid stigmatization [of the victim]' (p 58). No recommendations concern the perpetrators (who, as fellow students, are also part of the peer groups that ought to avoid stigmatising the victim). Today, victims are still concerned about stigma and shame, policies against alcohol consumption can deter reporting, peer groups are not effectively restraining perpetrators, and the campus officials responsible for advice are often the same officials responsible for punishment.

The violations were serious; 27% of them were what we would now call attempted rape. The women experienced a range of emotions, including a lot of anger and fear as well as guilt and disgust. The authors ignore the findings about anger, fear and disgust and focus only on guilt. Yet, despite their explicit theoretical premise that stigma may make victims more vulnerable to exploitation, they do not relate women's guilt over pre-marital sexual activity to 1950s societal norms expecting young women to be chaste before marriage. Instead, the authors speculate that guilt may be associated with emotional involvement in the relationships and 'possibly provocation' (p 57). Nowhere in the paper is there any empirical evidence of provocation or misunderstanding. There is evidence that a high proportion of offenders were fraternity men but in conclusion the authors emphasise misunderstanding instead of fraternity culture. The text shows how deep-seated assumptions about male sexual aggression against women remain unquestioned despite contradictory evidence. Facts alone are unlikely to unseat such assumptions.

In a follow-up study Kanin (1957) interviewed first year female students about their experiences in the last year of high school and the summer before attending university. This study was to 'test hypotheses suggested by the earlier investigation', namely 'the protective influence of the family, the provocation of the aggressive episodes, and situation factors, such as the influence of alcohol and the site of occurrence' (Kanin, 1957: 197). Note that 'provocation' is now a hypothesis even though Kirkpatrick and Kanin (1957) did not find any evidence of provocation. Alcohol also features, although Kirkpatrick and Kanin (1957) did not even mention alcohol. Of 262 young women in Kanin (1957), 62% reported 'offensive episodes at some level of erotic intimacy', including 30% who reported attempted rape and violent attempted rape. Overall, only 16% of attacks were reported to parents or other authorities (10% of the attempted rapes).

Kanin (1957) makes frequent mention of 'male sex exploitation' and 'the male culture' that threaten women with 'erotic aggression and the tactics of exploitation' (p 199). He writes that to 'some extent, both the male and the female subcultures contain the notion that sex aggression is somehow the "fault" of the female' (p 201) but what the young women actually report is that they had done nothing to provoke the men but rather were attacked out of the blue. What is remarkable is how a sexist male culture of sexual aggression and exploitation is explicitly mentioned but never acknowledged as the central problem in men's sexual violence against women.

Victimisation

Since this early research much has changed. Inspired by the civil rights movement, second wave feminists refused to take sex discrimination for granted and revealed rape and other forms of violence against women as unacceptable social problems. Civil rights activists and feminists lobbied to end sex discrimination in employment and education. As a result, federal legislation from the early 1970s (Title IX of the Higher Education Amendments) banned sex discriminatory practices in the entire education system, from kindergarten to university. In studies that pioneered measurement and nationally representative sampling, academic researchers developed methodologies to assess 'the true scope' of rape (Koss et al, 1987: 162; Koss and Oros, 1982). The work by Koss and colleagues initially did not focus on campuses per se but saw students as representative of the population age group at high risk of perpetration and victimisation. Over the years, evidence has accumulated from different types of studies including national surveys of college students (Fisher et al, 2000; Koss et al, 1987), studies restricted to one campus or a small number of campuses (Krebs et al, 2007), and the National Crime Victimization Survey (NCVS) that surveys the general population but can distinguish between students and non-students (Sinozich and Langton, 2014). Because the NCVS is built as a crime survey it uses narrower definitions of rape and sexual assault and narrower screening questions than studies that focus on public health, use broader definitions and more specific questions (Fisher et al, 2000; Krebs et al, 2007). In addition, different studies have assessed prevalence over different time periods such as since age 14, during the year prior to the survey, or while in college. Estimates vary accordingly. Based on an analysis of NCVS data from 1995 to 2013, Sinozich and Langton (2014) estimated a prevalence rate of rape and sexual assault of 6.1 per 1,000 students and 7.6 per 1,000 non-students in the 18 to 24 year age bracket (over the previous 12 months). Using a longer time period from age 14, Koss et al (1987) reported that among 3,187 women 44% had experienced unwanted sexual contact; 2% had been raped. Ten years later Fisher et al (2000) found that, of 4,446 college women, 2.8% had experienced an attempted or completed rape over the past seven months. Because some women were victimised more than once, the rate of incidents was higher (35.3 per 1,000 female students) than the rate of victimised individuals (27.7 per 1,000 female students).

Sexualised violations can have serious health and mental health consequences (Centers for Disease Control and Prevention, 2016). Of particular concern to universities should be impacts on students' academic performance and employment prospects due to a range of long-term problems including depression, eating disorders, alcohol or drug use, suicidal thoughts, loss of confidence, fear of leaving the house, and difficulty trusting other people (Feltes et al, 2012; Horsman, 2006). Victimised students may come to the attention of university staff not because they disclose abuse but because they fall behind academically (Freeman and Klein, 2012, 2013). Victims may miss classes to avoid the perpetrator, and some students drop out of higher education altogether (Feltes et al, 2012; Freeman and Klein, 2013). Sexual assault impacts students' grades with more severe violence associated with worse academic performance (Jordan et al, 2014).

Perpetration

Research on perpetration has taken two different approaches, one focusing on perpetrator behaviour and attitudes, the other on social contexts that may encourage rape (Buchwald, et al, 2005). Of 341 unmarried male undergraduates who Kanin interviewed in 1969, 87 (25.5%) reported aggressive attempts at sexual intercourse in which the perpetrator saw 'the female responding with offended reactions, e.g., fighting, screaming, crying, etc.' (p 13). A decade later, Rapaport and Burkhart (1984) found that ,among 190 male undergraduates, 28% self-disclosed acts of sexual coercion of a woman; 15% disclosed raping a woman. Koss, et al (1985) reported that, of 1,846 male students, 4.6% self-disclosed having raped. In Koss et al (1987) 19% of college men self-disclosed having coerced a woman to have sexual contact; 1% of men admitted oral or anal penetration by force.

According to Lisak and Miller (2002), of 1,882 male undergraduates, 120 (6.4%) self-disclosed rape or sexual assault or attempted rape/sexual assault, a small fraction of the entire sample. The 120 self-disclosed rapists admitted a total of 483 rapes. Of these, 44 rapes (9%) were admitted by men who said they raped only once. This leaves 439 (91%) rapes committed by 76 repeat rapists. Thus, it is conceivable that a small but critical minority of college men commit the vast majority of rapes. However, Swartout et al (2015) argue that too much emphasis on serial rapists is misguided. Based on an analysis of the trajectory of rapist behaviour over a period of about ten years the authors found that of 1,642 male college students 10.8% (178) disclosed that they had perpetrated at least one rape from when they were 14 years old through to the end of college. Over this time period, 93% of self-acknowledged rapists raped only once or stopped after a short while; 2% raped more over time. However, during the time in college only 52% of rapists had a brief trajectory of raping, and 15% increased their raping. Even though such trajectories are not yet well understood (Lussier and Cale, 2016), they raise the disturbing possibility that campuses provide contexts that offer opportunities to rapists, which they would otherwise not have. In the college context debates are wrapped up with concern over excessive drinking and the role of fraternities (Marine, 2016; Sanday, 2007) and athletics departments (Crosset, 2016). The interplay of drug use, peer pressure, popularity rankings and misogynist practices at parties and around sports events create rape-prone contexts in that they may encourage men to be sexually aggressive, to be disrespectful to women, and to boast of sexual conquest to other males. Fraternities and athletics departments may also be able to shield perpetrators from scrutiny, and victims who were drunk or high on other drugs make easy targets for victim-blaming, regardless of whether they consumed drugs willingly or were manipulated, and even though drug consumption and sexual violence are separate issues. Thus, misogynist rituals and subcultures (Godenzi et al, 2001; NUS, 2012) could model, encourage or demand that college men who want to participate enact the very misogynist, hostile and aggressive attitudes and behaviours that have been observed in convicted rapists (Lisak and Miller, 2002). Such contexts may also attract men with a propensity of violence against women by promoting shared norms in which violence against women is acceptable and giving perpetrators 'cover' under which they can proceed with impunity (DeKeseredy and Schwartz, 2013; Raghavan et al, 2009; Silverman and Williamson, 1997). Still, how rape-prone contexts, or attitudes for that matter, translate into actual raping is not well understood and probably involves the confluence of multiple factors (Hagemann-White et al, 2010).

Sexist dating cultures have continued for decades, supported by rape myths and victim-blaming (Burt, 1980). Kanin (1969) simply assumed 'female-provoked sex aggression' which, even though he had no empirical evidence, he thought 'reasonable to suspect' (p 17). He took 'for granted ... that there are sufficient numbers in the male population who will aggressively respond to provocative females' but rather than investigating male sexual aggression he chose to 'concentrate on the conduct of the female and the perceptions made of her conduct by the male' (p 18). Rape myths and victim-blaming include troubling ideas of 'communication' that continue to this day. Instead of examining male sexual aggression, women are blamed for not understanding 'the male subculture'; 'Some females, deficient in socialization in the male subculture, unwittingly engage in provocative behavior' (Kanin, 1969; p 19). Women are blamed for not deferring to men's expectations. While young women today may be more outspoken about sex than they were decades ago, they still describe dating cultures imbued with victim-blaming and male aggression (Mogilevsky, 2016).

Our understanding of perpetration is hampered further by the fact that what is perpetrated includes a broad array of problematic behaviours and actions that range from 'minor' sexual harassment to forceful rape. Terminology, methodology and policy have yet to settle on a better way to take the entire range of sexualised violations seriously, without dismissing any as trivial but also without treating all violations as the same. In addition, the policy response to sexual violence, which will be addressed next, has focused more on the risk of victimisation, and how to manage that risk, than on the risk of perpetration; in university policies perpetrators are nearly invisible (Iverson, 2016).

Problem framings in law and policy

Notwithstanding the significance of research, in the US two pieces of federal legislation – Title IX and the Clery Act – have had a profound impact on the university response to sexual violence on campus. Both will be discussed below along with their impacts and limitations. As influential as this legislation has been, it also has led to a relatively narrow focus on student-to-student violence and formal crime reporting. A more comprehensive approach would be desirable that also considers sexual harassment of employees and thus the entire cluster of problematic practices indicative of structural inequality and exploitative hierarchies in HEIs and society at large (Armstrong et al, 2006; Marine, 2016; Weale and Batty, 2016). Worryingly, underreporting of sexual violence remains a complex social problem that is unlikely to be resolved by legislation.

From the 1960s, when many HEIs were still closed to women, pressure from the civil rights and women's movements forced Congress to address sex and racial discrimination in successive pieces of legislation; Title VII of the Civil Rights Act 1964 prohibiting employment discrimination on the basis of sex, race, religion, and national origin; the Equal Credit Opportunity Act 1974 allowing women to own credit cards; the Pregnancy Discrimination Act 1978 prohibiting the firing of female employees who became pregnant. Since 1972, Title IX of the Education Amendments has prohibited sex discrimination in all federally funded education programmes and activities (from kindergarten to college, and including private institutions that benefit from federal financial aid programmes). Title IX focuses on equal access to educational opportunities for male and female students and is best known for its impact on college athletics where it led to increased spending on women's sports. 'The principal objective of Title IX is to avoid the use of federal money to support sex discrimination in education programmes and to provide individual citizens effective protection against those practices'.[2] For decades, debates about sexual violence on campus have focused almost exclusively on students and the implementation of Title IX, rendering this issue separate from sex discrimination against employees and the institutional structures implicated in all forms of discrimination.

Under Title IX students can sue HEIs for damages, which raises the question at which point and according to what standard of liability campuses can be held responsible for failing to provide equal access to education opportunities. Since a 1998 court ruling, the legal standard for liability has been *deliberate indifference* to known instances of sexual harassment (*Gebser v. Lago Vista Independent School District*, 524 U.S. 274, 290 (1998)). MacKinnon (2016) argues that this standard is inconsistent with Title IX's mandate and should be replaced with the 'due diligence' standard of human rights law. According to MacKinnon, to focus only on deliberate indifference to known harassment does not meet the law because many other practices contribute to unequal access such as inequality, hierarchical relations and climates of abuse.

The Office for Civil Rights (OCR) in the US Department of Education is responsible for enforcing Title IX. This is done by issuing guidance to HEIs and threatening to withdraw federal funds should campuses be found in violation of the law. In 1997, the OCR interpreted sexual harassment as a form of sex discrimination; in 2001 it emphasised that 'preventing and remedying sexual harassment in schools is essential to ensuring a safe environment in which students can learn'; and in 2011 it specifically addressed sexual violence as a form of sexual harassment and sex discrimination (OCR, 2011). HEIs need to investigate allegations of sexual violence even though their own investigation may conflict with investigations by police. HEIs come to know of harassment through 'responsible employees', defined by the OCR as employees who have

> the authority to take action to redress the harassment, who [have] the duty to report to appropriate school officials sexual harassment or any other misconduct by students or

employees, or an individual who a student could reasonably believe has this authority or responsibility.[3]

Who exactly is a responsible employee has been controversial. One response by HEIs has been to include teaching staff among responsible employees, expecting them to report disclosures of sexualised violations even if the disclosing student does not want the matter to be shared with campus officials. For instance, the University of Maine has been requiring its teaching staff to put language into their syllabi that warns students that the lecturer needs to report disclosures. Despite the guidance, critical matters remain unresolved such as balancing the institutional need to know with students' need to remain confidential. In addition, loopholes exist. For instance, at the point of this writing the University of Maine System's 'Policy Manual – Sexual Harassment'[4] states that the university does not consider itself to know of sex discrimination if disclosures were made in the context of research projects or at public speak-outs. As a result, a 'cottage industry' (Napolitano, 2014: 400) has sprung up in consulting firms trying to help universities to interpret and implement legal mandates. Lastly, although several hundred HEIs have been investigated by the OCR (Kingkade, 2016), and withdrawal of federal funds has been threatened, it seems that as of August 2016 in no case had funding actually been withdrawn.

While Title IX focused specifically on eliminating discrimination, the Clery Act of 1990 concerns crime reporting. It is based on the premise that crimes may be averted if students, parents and staff were aware of campus crime statistics. Under Clery, HEIs are required to compile and publish crime statistics (not limited to but including sex crimes) and crime prevention and safety policies. So-called 'campus security authorities' must report crimes in and around campus. They include police, security staff, officials with significant responsibility for student and campus activities, and persons designated campus security authorities. As with Title IX, enforcement of the Clery Act lies with the US Department of Education. It can fine HEIs up to $35,000 for a violation of the law such as noncompliance with regard to sexual assault policies and procedures. The Campus Sexual Violence Elimination Act 2013 amends Clery by requiring HEIs to address dating violence, domestic violence and stalking as well as sexual violence. The need to pass legislation that includes additional forms of violence reflects the fragmented framings of these issues in policy (and practice; while I was project director of VAWA (Violence Against Women Act) campus grant from 2002–06 grantees had to focus strictly on sexual assault, dating and domestic violence, and stalking against students and were barred from addressing sexual harassment of employees).

As of 2013, the three most common violations of the Clery Act included '(1) failure to disclose crimes based on Clery Act geography; (2) improper classification and disclosure of crimes; (3) lack of or inadequate policy statements' (Kiss and Feeney White, 2016). Campuses continue to struggle with the requirements of Title IX and Clery; the gap between officially reported and informally disclosed violations remains wide; it is unclear to what extent campuses have the capacity and training to adequately investigate allegations; it is unclear and perhaps doubtful if investigations, when they do happen, contribute to improved gender equality on campus (MacKinnon, 2016).

> The still evolving Department of Education … regulatory apparatus that surrounds campus sexual violence and sexual assault drives [HEIs] to devote significant resources to prescriptive compliance regimes, often at the expense of improving prevention, response, and support programmes. Both by federal rule and by agency 'guidance,' universities and colleges are required to act as investigators and adjudicators of sexual violence and sexual assault cases, even where victims choose not to pursue criminal prosecution and do not want law enforcement involvement. At the same time, university student conduct processes may be inadequate if they end up supplanting the criminal justice system. (Napolitano, 2014: 388)

Campus-based victim advocates (specialist service providers) fear that the current legislative environment has created a narrow focus among universities on technical and procedural compliance to avoid institutional liability, while fundamental changes towards gender equality and violence prevention have yet to happen (Moylan, 2016). While many campus officials believe that the Clery Act has improved law enforcement and students' ability to protect themselves, there is no clear evidence that students are safer and campuses are more gender equal (Kiss and Feeney White, 2016; Sloan et al, 1997). The current emphasis on formal reporting illuminates the challenges that have plagued campus violence prevention for decades and that still lie ahead.

Formal reporting, campus culture and university governance

Spurred by the activist movement – Know your IX – more students who were sexually assaulted have filed Title IX complaints against their university. Even so, formal reporting significantly underestimates the extent of the problem. Fisher et al (2000) estimated that in a single academic year there may be 35 rapes per 1,000 female students on US college campuses. This figure is much higher than the number of rapes that appear in official campus crime reports. Fisher et al (2003) found that only 2% of female students who experience sexual violence reported the incident to police, and only 4% reported to campus authorities. Similar low reporting rates have been found in other countries (NUS, 2010; Sloane and Fitzpatrick, 2011) and in comparison with other offences (Hart, 2003) with students less likely than non-students to report (Sinozich and Langton, 2014).

However, lack of formal reporting does not mean lack of informal disclosure (Klein, 2012). Fisher et al (2003) found that although fewer than 5% of victims reported sexual victimisation to police or a campus administrator, 70% told somebody in their social networks (mostly friends). This discrepancy is not unique to student populations nor to the US (Smith et al, 2011; Stenning et al, 2012).

The difference between what is formally reported and what is informally disclosed is so large that reporting and disclosure can be considered separate social and interpersonal processes. They may intersect at some point, such as when a victim, after consultation with and support from specialist services or informal contacts, decides to file a formal report. However, disclosure is based on trust (and opportunity), and can be a long process (Ullman, 2010). It seems unlikely that this could be forced by legislation or that this would be desirable. Informal third parties know more about sexualised violations because they are trusted confidants or happened to witness an attack (Ahrens et al, 2007). Authorities know less because they often are not trusted and are not part of victims' lives. Furthermore, only a small number of victims ever access specialist services such as rape crisis centres or domestic violence projects although when they do, they tend to be highly satisfied with the support received, (Klein, 2012). Thus, the formal systems responsible, respectively, for apprehending perpetrators and supporting victims are also the ones who know the least about what actually happened. Formal reporting is a poor way to get a sense of how many sex crimes and sexualised violations actually occur on campuses. The emphasis on reporting and compliance with procedural detail has led HEIs to frame the problem as a need to know (about incidents) rather than a need to act to change campus culture and university governance (Klein, 2013).

In recognition of the limits of formal reporting the White House has been pushing HEIs to undertake regular climate surveys (Krebs et al, 2016). And while university members such as deans of students, equal opportunity officers, and legal counsel may be focusing on procedural compliance, students and faculty, for decades, have been organising awareness events and prevention education. Since 1999, with funding from the Campus Grant Program under the Violence Against Women Act, many HEIs have overhauled their policies, increased staff training, and experimented with outreach to students (Karjane et al, 2006). Early rape prevention workshops were often limited to short-term improvement in self-reported attitudes with little evidence of long-term behaviour change (Anderson and Whiston, 2005). Such programmes may have other beneficial impact such as helping victims to connect with services. The recent bystander intervention programmes promise to be effective in educating students how to intervene in the build-up of a sexual assault and support victims (Foubert et al, 2007; Moynihan et al, 2011). On balance, these approaches to violence prevention have aimed at students (not employees, or the institution), in particular female students and students as bystanders. Programmes to teach women how to stay safe have been criticised for implicit victim-blaming but such programmes continue, and self-defence courses seem to offer women benefits (Senn et al, 2015). From today's perspective, much of the history of campus policies and prevention programmes reveals a white, heterosexist bias is evident (Wooten, 2016). Yet, although we now have a better understanding of intersecting oppressions, the current focus on 'student sexual misconduct' is in danger of losing sight of the structural inequalities in higher education that continue to this day (Marine, 2016). They concern the reproduction of inequality and sexism in elements of student life and institutional practices. Although different on the surface (binge drinking at parties versus sober meetings of the president's cabinet), these practices have in common the role of high status males in enacting and reinforcing particular forms of sexist masculinity, to which those who want to belong need to adapt (Armstrong et al, 2006; Hsu and Reid, 2012; Sanday, 2007). '[S]exualized peer cultures organized around status' (Armstrong et al, 2006: 484) may seem a far cry from the mundane work of authoring campus policy. Yet, in the process of implementing policy, institutional practices occur that are shaped by a legacy of high status (often white) men in leadership positions with little or no understanding of sexual violence.

Even a thoughtful and thorough process of creating a campus sexual assault policy is only a small step towards changing campus culture and university governance. The process of creating a sexual assault policy usually involves the formation of a committee charged to produce the text, followed by a period of drafting, discussing and editing versions of the text. The policy document then moves through the institutional chain of command across the desks of deans, vice presidents, legal counsel, presidents and perhaps boards of trustees. Once approved, a policy may be implemented by publicising the text among students and staff members, perhaps even training staff on how to implement the policy. The institutional actions taken after a policy text has been officially adopted involve informal practices that go beyond what is stated on the written page: university authorities discuss cases among their peers and with their supervisors; case details that ought to be confidential are nonetheless shared with colleagues or parents; deans may decide whether to feed allegations of sexual violence through the official hearing process or decide the matter for themselves; athletics departments often have their own rules; donors (often former members of fraternities) and 'boosters' of athletic programmes may weigh in, perhaps threatening legal consequences if the university goes too hard on a star athlete; university lawyers may counsel caution in pursuing alleged offenders. Some staff members can speak their mind, while others are afraid to jeopardise their job if they do. If anything seeps out, it is in the form of rumour. Unlike policy documents, much of this activity is not accessible to the public. It occurs behind closed doors and is shielded from scrutiny.

In an ironic twist, HEIs are capable of, on one hand, producing progressive, feminist research on sexual violence, while on the other ignoring the import of that research for governance. Noting decades of useless change work at Harvard, Marine (2016) deplored that while this university 'has produced ... and employed ... a small army of noted feminists who have written copiously on the topic of men's violence against women, these analyses were mistrusted and muted from the analysis of the issues at Harvard' (Marine, 2016: 67). In particular, confronting violent masculinity, male white privilege and sexual subordination of women at Harvard 'was untenable' (Marine, 2006: 67).

Final thoughts

In 2016, the state of media reporting about sexual violence at US universities is dominated by a seemingly endless stream of scandals in which institutions failed to investigate, did not support victims and treated perpetrators with impunity. While institutions are blamed for not responding well or at all, they have, in fact, tried to respond, writing and revising policies, investigating allegations and teaching prevention programmes. They have been doing this for decades. Occasionally, high-ranking officials do step down, victims win lawsuits, and perpetrators are held to account. The question is whether this adds up to true change or whether it is a new normal in which abusive practices are more visible yet continue as before. Since the 1950s the volume of research about sexual violence on campus has increased considerably, measurement has been refined, and significant strictures have been placed on universities through legislation and policy. But none of these changes has fundamentally changed the nexus between gender inequality and sexual violence. Indeed, the presence of gender equality policies in areas of equal employment opportunity or family policy does not necessarily translate into less sexual violence against women (Michalski, 2004). It is debatable whether campus sexual assault policies have produced radical change in sexual violence on campus. It seems that campuses still struggle to truly overcome victim-blaming and rape myths (Stoll, Lilley and Pinter, 2017). In some ways, much progress has been made: sexual violence is talked about more openly, and truly inspiring efforts have been made to educate campus communities. Yet, it sometimes seems as though underneath these positive changes sexual violence continues unabated. University leaders may need to take a closer look at university governance. In contrast to the remit of a rape crisis organisation, sexual violence prevention is not the primary mission of a university. But nor are fire safety, food safety and building safety. Yet, these are fully incorporated into campuses' core operating procedures. It is time to do the same with sexual violence prevention.

Notes

[1] www.changingourcampus.org

[2] US Department of Justice, 'Overview Of Title IX Of The Education Amendments Of 1972, 20 U.S.C. A§ 1681 Et. Seq.', www.justice.gov/crt/overview-title-ix-education-amendments-1972-20-usc-1681-et-seq

[3] Revised Sexual Harassment Guidance, www2.ed.gov/about/offices/list/ocr/docs/shguide.html

[4] www.maine.edu/about-the-system/board-of-trustees/policy-manual/section402/

References

Ahrens, C.E., Campbell, R.M., Ternier-Thames, N.K., Wasco, S.M. and Sefl, T. (2007) 'Deciding whom to tell: Expectations and outcomes or rape survivors' first disclosures', *Psychology of Women Quarterly*, 31: 38–49.

Anderson, L.A. and Whiston, S.C. (2005) 'Sexual assault education programs: A meta-analytic examination of their effectiveness', *Psychology of Women Quarterly*, 29: 374–88.

Armstrong, E.A., Hamilton, L. and Sweeney, B. (2006), 'Sexual assault on campus: A multilevel, integrative approach to party rape', *Social Problems*, 53 (4): 483–99.

Buchwald, E., Fletcher, P. and Roth, M. (2005) *Transforming a Rape Culture*, Minneapolis, MN: Milkweed Editions.

Burt, M.A. (1980) 'Cultural myths and support for rape', *Journal of Personality and Social Psychology*, 38 (2): 217–30.

Centers for Disease Control and Prevention (2016) 'Sexual violence: Consequences', www.cdc.gov/violenceprevention/sexualviolence/consequences.html

Crosset, T.W. (2016) 'Athletes, sexual assault, and universities' failure to address rape-prone subcultures on campus', in S.C. Wooten and R.W. Mitchell (eds) *The Crisis of Campus Sexual Violence,* New York: Routledge, pp 74–91.

DeKeseredy, W.S. and Schwartz, M.D. (2013) *Male Peer Support and Violence Against Women,* Boston: Northeastern University Press.

Feltes, T., Balloni, A., Czapska, J., Bodelon, E. and Stenning, P. (2012) *Gender-Based Violence, Stalking and Fear of Crime,* Final report to European Commission, Directorate General Justice, Freedom and Security, Project JLS/2007/ISEC/415.

Fisher, B.S., Cullen, F.T. and Turner, M.G. (2000) *The Sexual Victimization of College Women,* Research report, US Department of Justice, National Institute of Justice, Bureau of Justice Statistics.

Fisher, B.S., Daigle, L.E. and Cullen, F.T. (2010) *Unsafe in the Ivory Tower: The Sexual Victimization of College Women,* Thousand Oaks, CA: Sage.

Fisher, B.S., Daigle, L.E., Cullen, F.T. and Turner, M.G. (2003) 'Reporting sexual victimization to the police and others: Results from a national-level study of college women', *Criminal Justice and Behavior,* 30: 6–38.

Foubert, J.D., Newberry, J.T. and Tatum, J. (2007) 'Behavior differences seven months later: Effects of a rape prevention program', *NASPA Journal,* 44 (4): 728–49.

Freeman, M. and Klein, R.C.A. (2012) 'University responses to forced marriage and violence against women in the UK: Report on a pilot study', *International Family Law*, September: 285–99.

Freeman, M., and Klein, R. (2013) *College and University Responses to Forced Marriage*, Report to the Forced Marriage Unit.

Godenzi, A., Schwartz, M.D. and DeKeseredy, W.S. (2001) 'Toward an integrated gendered social bond/male peer support theory of university woman abuse', *Critical Criminology*, 10 (1): 1–16.

Hagemann-White, C., Kavemann, B., Kindler, H., Meysen, T. and Puchert, R. (2010) *Review of Research on Factors at Play in Perpetration*, Report prepared for the European Commission.

Hart, T.C. (2003) *Violence Victimization of College Students, 1995–2000*, Washington, DC: Bureau of Justice Statistics (NCJ 196143).

Horsman, J. (2006) 'Moving beyond "stupid": Taking account of the impact of violence on women's learning', *International Journal of Educational Development*, 26(2): 177–88.

Hsu, C.L. and Reid, L.D. (2012) 'Social status, binge drinking, and social satisfaction among college students', paper presented at the 2012 Annual Meeting of the American Sociological Association.

Iverson, S.V. (2016) 'A policy discourse analysis of sexual assault policies in higher education', in S.C. Wooten and R.W. Mitchell (eds) *The Crisis of Campus Sexual Violence*, New York: Routledge, pp 15–32.

Jordan, C.E., Combs, J.L. and Smith, G.T. (2014) 'An exploration of sexual victimization and academic performance among college women', *Trauma, Violence, and Abuse*, 15 (3): 191–200.

Kanin, E.J. (1957) 'Male aggression in dating-courtship relations', *American Journal of Sociology*, 63 (2): 197–204.

Kanin, E.J. (1969) 'Selected dyadic aspects of male sex aggression', *The Journal of Sex Research*, 5 (1): 12–28.

Karjane, H.M., Fisher, B.S. and Cullen, F.T. (2006) *Sexual Assault on Campus: What Colleges and Universities Are Doing About It*, Office of Justice Programs, US Department of Justice.

Kingkade, T. (2016) 'There are far more Title IX investigations of colleges than most people know', Huffington Post, 16 June, www.huffingtonpost.com/entry/title-ix-investigations-sexual-harassment_us_575f4b0ee4b053d433061b3d

Kirkpatrick, C. and Kanin, E. (1957) 'Male sex aggression on a university campus', *American Sociological Review*, 22 (1): 52–8.

Kiss, A. and Feeney White, K.N. (2016) 'Looking beyond the numbers: Understanding the Jeanne Clery Act and sexual violence', in S.C. Wooten and R.W. Mitchell (eds) *The Crisis of Campus Sexual Violence*, New York: Routledge, pp 95–112.

Klein, R. (2012) *Responding to Intimate Violence Against Women: The role of Informal Networks*, New York: Cambridge University Press.

Klein, R. (2013) 'Language for institutional change: Notes from US higher education', in R. Klein (ed) *Framing Sexual and Domestic Violence Through Language*, New York: Palgrave Macmillan, pp 163–178.

Koss, M.P. and Oros, C.J. (1982) 'Sexual experiences survey: A research instrument investigating sexual aggression and victimization', *Journal of Consulting and Clinical Psychology*, 50 (3): 455–7.

Koss, M.P., Gidycz, C.A. and Wisniewski, N. (1987) 'The scope of rape: Incidence and prevalence of sexual aggression and victimization in a national sample of higher education students', *Journal of Consulting and Clinical Psychology*, 55: 162–70.

Koss, M.P., Leonard, K.E., Beezley, D.A. and Oros, C.J. (1985) 'Nonstranger sexual aggression: A discriminant analysis of the psychological characteristics of undetected offenders', *Sex Roles*, 12 (9–10): 981–92.

Krebs, C., Lindquist, C., Berzofsky, M., Shook-Sa, B. and Peterson, K. (2016) *Campus Climate Survey Validation Study: Final Technical Report*, Bureau of Justice Statistics.

Krebs, C.P., Lindquist, C.H., Warner, T.D., Fisher, B.S. and Martin, S.L. (2007) *The Campus Sexual Assault (CSA) Study*, National Institute of Justice.

Lisak, D. and Miller, P.M. (2002) 'Repeat rape and multiple offending among undetected rapists', *Violence and Victims*, 17 (1): 73–84.

Lussier, P. and Cale, J. (2016) 'Understanding the origins and the development of rape and sexual aggression against women: Four generations of research and theorizing', *Aggression and Violent Behavior*, 31 (Nov-Dec): 66–81.

MacKinnon, C. (2016) 'In their hands: Restoring institutional liability for sexual harassment in education', *The Yale Law Journal*, 125 (7): 2038–105.

Marine, S. (2016) 'Combating sexual violence in the Ivy League', in S.C. Wooten and R.W. Mitchell (eds) *The Crisis of Campus Sexual Violence*, New York: Routledge, pp 55–73.

Michalski, J.H. (2004) 'Making sociological sense out of trends in intimate partner violence: The social structure of violence against women', *Violence Against Women*, 10 (6): 652–75.

Mogilevsky, M. (2016) '5 Problems with Hookup Culture – And How to Take It Back from Sexism', Everyday Feminism, 16 February', http://everydayfeminism.com/2016/02/hook-up-culture-is-sexist/

Moylan, C.A. (2016) '"I fear I'm a checkbox": College and university victim advocates' perspectives of campus rape reforms', *Violence Against Women*, 6 July (online).

Moynihan, M.M., Banyard, V.L., Arnold, J.S., Eckstein, R.P. and Stapleton, J.G. (2011) 'Sisterhood may be powerful for reducing sexual and intimate partner violence: An evaluation of the Bringing in the Bystander in-person program with sorority members', *Violence Against Women*, 17 (6): 703–19.

Napolitano, J. (2014) 'Only yes means yes: An essay on university policies regarding sexual violence and sexual assault', *Yale Law and Policy Review*, 33 (2): 387–402.

National Union of Students (NUS) (2010) *Hidden Marks: A Study of Women Students' Experiences of Harassment, Stalking, Violence and Sexual Assault*, London: NUS.

NUS (2012) *That's What She Said: Women Students' Experiences of 'Lad Culture' in Higher Education*, London: National Union of Students.

Office for Civil Rights (OCR) (2011) 'Dear Colleague Letter', 4 April, www2.ed.gov/about/offices/list/ocr/letters/colleague-201104.html

Raghavan, C., Rajah, V., Gentile, K., Collado, L. and Kavanagh, A.M. (2009) 'Community violence, social support networks, ethnic groups differences, and male perpetration of intimate partner violence', *Journal of Interpersonal Violence*, 24 (10): 1615–32.

Rapaport, K. and Burkhart, B.R. (1984) 'Personality and attitudinal characteristics of sexually coercive college males', *Journal of Abnormal Psychology*, 93 (2): 216–21.

Sanday, P.R. (2007) *Fraternity Gang Rape: Sex, Brotherhood, and Privilege on Campus*, New York: New York University Press.

Senn, C.Y., Eliasziw, M., Barata, P.C., Thurston, W.E., Newby Clark, I.R., Radtke, H.L. and Hobden, K.L. (2015) 'Efficacy of a sexual assault resistance program for university women', *The New England Journal Of Medicine*, 372 (24): 2326–35.

Silverman, J.G. and Williamson, G.M. (1997) 'Social ecology and entitlements involved in battering by heterosexual college males: Contributions of family and peers', *Violence and Victims*, 12 (2): 147–65.

Sinozich, S. and Langton, L. (2014) *Rape and Sexual Assault Victimization Among College-Age Females, 1995–2013*, Bureau of Justice Statistics, US Department of Justice.

Sloan, J.J., Fisher, B.S. and Cullen, F.T. (1997) 'Assessing the Student-Right-to-Know and Campus Security Act of 1990: An analysis of the victim reporting practices of college and university students', *Crime and Delinquency*, 43 (2): 148–68.

Sloane, C. and Fitzpatrick, K. (2011) *Talk About It Survey*, National Union of Students (Australia).

Smith, K., Coleman, K., Eder S. and Hall, P. (2011) *Homicides, Firearm Offences, and Intimate Violence 2009/10-Supplementary Volume 2 to Crime in England and Wales*, Home Office Statistical Bulletin, 01/2011.

Stenning, P., Mitra-Kahn, T. and Dunby, C. (2012) *Gender-Based Violence, Stalking and Fear of Crime. Country Report United Kingdom*, European Commission, EU–Project 2009–2011 JLS/2007/ISEC/415.

Stoll, L.C., Lilley, T.G. and Pinter, K. (2017) 'Gender-blind sexism and rape myth acceptance', *Violence Against Women*, 23 (1): 28–45.

Swartout, K.M., Koss, M.P., White, J.W., Thompson, M.P., Abbey, A. and Bellis, A.L. (2015) 'Trajectory analysis of the campus serial rapist assumption', *JAMA Pediatrics*, 169 (12): 1148–54.

Ullman, S.E. (2010) *Talking About Sexual Assault: Society's Response to Survivors*, Washington, DC: American Psychological Association.

Weale, S. and Batty, D. (2016) 'Sexual harassment of students by university staff hidden by non–disclosure agreements', *Guardian*, 26 August.

Wooten, S.C. (2016) 'How feminist theory shaped campus sexual violence policy', in S.C. Wooten and R.W. Mitchell (eds) *The Crisis of Campus Sexual Violence*, New York: Routledge, pp 33–51.

4

Grounds for concern: an Australian perspective on responses to sexual assault and harassment in university settings

Andrea Durbach and Rosemary Grey

Introduction

> ... it is much easier to focus on the successes of an institution, rather than its failures. However, it is honourable to be able to acknowledge that we have failed; but that we refuse to continue to fail on this issue. (Sophie Johnston, President, Student Representative Council, University of New South Wales, 2016)

In August 2017, the Australian Human Rights Commission (the Commission) released a report on its findings and analysis of the first national student survey on sexual assault and harassment in Australian universities. The report, *Change the Course: National Report on Sexual Assault and Sexual Harassment at Australian Universities (Change the Course)*, provided a significant indication of the nature and extent of university sexual violence. More importantly, it revealed widespread student dissatisfaction with university responses to reports of sexual violence, the adequacy of support services, and the utility of prevention measures.

In relation to prevalence, the report found that 51% of student respondents were sexually harassed in 2016, with 26% reporting sexual harassment in a university setting. A further 6.9% reported sexual assault in 2015 or 2016, with 1.6% of respondents reporting sexual assault in a university setting (Australian Human Rights Commission, 2017: 3–4). Importantly, the report also found that the vast majority of student respondents who reported sexual harassment or sexual assault did not make a formal complaint to their university.

The release of the Commission's report was a milestone in the struggle to address and prevent sexual harassment and sexual assault in Australian universities. However, the 2017 report was released decades after student activism first brought these issues to the attention of universities (Australian Human Rights Centre, 2017a: 15). Moreover, the report was published six years after the Commission's review into the treatment of women in the Australian Defence Force Academy (ADFA), an academic facility operated jointly with the Department of Defence which warned that sexual harassment and assault was 'a problem across Australian universities' and that ADFA was 'not alone in facing these challenges.' (Australian Human Rights Commission, 2011: 33, xxv).

Despite these efforts to compel university action, it was not until the Australian release of *The Hunting Ground* documentary in 2015, and a series of interventions discussed in this chapter, that Australian universities collectively undertook to address campus sexual violence. Although the documentary highlights the problem of sexual assault and harassment in American universities, it has also functioned as a visual reminder of a struggle waged by Australian student and gender activists and as a critical 'disrupter' of university complacency, resurrecting the issue of sexual violence as a priority for Australian university leaders and representative bodies such as Universities Australia. Importantly, the documentary triggered a national conversation about the issue and reframed its focus from individual student misconduct to institutional failure.

This chapter provides an Australian perspective on developments in universities to sexual assault and harassment based on our experience in developing and implementing the *Strengthening Australian University Responses to Sexual Assault and Harassment* project. The chapter does not focus on the scale of sexual assault and sexual harassment in Australian universities (despite its disquieting presence). Rather, it seeks to explore the progression of institutional responses from disavowal or bureaucratic opacity to more proactive and pre-emptive measures. It examines the shift in university and government responses to an issue that has long been overlooked in Australian legal and policy responses to gender based violence. We argue that in a comparatively short period, Australian universities have taken steps to enable a national student survey and submission process, enhance reporting procedures and support services, publicly denounce campus sexual violence, and commit to certain prevention strategies.

However, despite these initiatives, the capacity of universities to effectively respond to student needs continues to be constrained by structural barriers and the protection of institutional interests. The chapter ends by highlighting challenges that Australian universities must address if the critical gains secured from the implementation of the national student survey and the release of three major reports and their recommendations are to effectively reshape Australian university responses to campus sexual violence.

Recognising the problem of sexual violence in Australian universities: a long and winding road

Universities are complex environments. About three in five Australian university students are under 24, many are away from home for the first time, and there's a vibrant social life on campus. We know too that 18- to 24-year-olds are the group most likely to drink harmful levels of alcohol on a single occasion. All these factors compound the issue of sexual harassment and sexual assault, but none excuse it.

In her 2016 book *My Life on the Road*, Gloria Steinem writes about the evolution over decades of American university administration responses to 'sexualised violence on campus'. She recalls that many universities 'obscured the rates of sexual assault, in order to protect a campus reputation and encourage parents to send their daughters' to certain universities (Steinem, 2016: 98–9). Steinem describes how students, who were previously arrested on charges of vandalism for 'painting a big read X on sidewalks wherever a woman had been sexually assaulted,' now have access to Title IX legislation to 'threaten campuses with the loss of federal funding if sexual assault creates an environment hostile to women's education' (p 99).

In Australia, allegations of universities obscuring rates of sexual assault have been similarly surfaced in recent years (End Rape on Campus, 2017). These allegations follow decades of advocacy by women students and NGOs to expose, address and prevent campus sexual violence. While this activism began with calls for improved infrastructure such as 'adequate lighting, more security personnell (sic) [and] immediate, confidential counselling' (Figure 4.1), more recent action has seen the National Union of Students (NUS) conduct two student surveys on sexual violence and reporting experiences in university settings in 2011 and 2015. These survey results have led the NUS to make recommendations for institutional responses including campaigns to challenge gender stereotypes, respectful relationship training for students and campus residents, adequate training and resources for sexual violence counsellors, clear and accessible reporting procedures, stand-alone sexual violence policies, and accessible information on external services such as rape crisis centres, legal aid, and police (NUS, 2011, 2016).

Figure 4.1: Poster produced by the NUS Women's Department, 1994 (courtesy of Heidi La Paglia, NUS Women's Officer, 2016)

Although Australian student activism led to minimal and uneven changes in university responses over the years, unlike developments in the US, these efforts have yet to translate into substantive legislative or policy reforms to specifically address university sexual violence (Australian Human Rights Centre, 2017a: 43–6). In the policy realm, the 12-year *National Plan to Reduce Violence against Women and their Children 2010–2022* commits to 'sharpen[ing] our focus on sexual violence' (Commonwealth of Australia, Department of Social Services, 2016: 24). However, universities and campus sexual violence have not been the subject of specific consideration under the Plan to date (see Australian Human Rights Centre, 2017a: 47). At the state level, and clearly in response to recent initiatives, the New South Wales Minister for the Prevention of Domestic Violence and Sexual Assault conducted a university students sexual assault consultation in mid-2017 as part of the development of a Sexual Assault Strategy (NSW Family & Community Services, 2017).

As noted above, the issue of sexual violence in university settings was also highlighted by the Commission's 2011 ADFA review. The review, based on the results of an internal 'unacceptable behaviour survey', identified institutional features that discourage the reporting of sexual misconduct in ADFA, including fear of stigmatisation, retaliation or prejudicing career progression (Australian Human Rights Commission, 2011: 72–83). It also found that the existence of a 'drinking culture' was clearly associated with 'unacceptable behaviour, including sexual misconduct' (p 45). As mentioned, the Commission's review report observed that these features were not necessarily unique to ADFA and had broader application to other universities (p 34). It also noted the potential utility of developing its survey in collaboration with other universities and colleges, 'in order to provide meaningful comparisons' (p xxv). This recommendation remained dormant until the release of *The Hunting Ground* in Australia in 2015 prompted a return to the recommendation and the subsequent design and implementation of the national student survey, which we discuss later on in this chapter.

The screening of the documentary across Australian university campuses in 2015 and 2016 also had broader effects beyond the development of the national survey. It generated a significant increase in Australian media reporting of incidents of sexual violence in university settings, many of which highlighted the frequently inept, deficient, often dismissive and damaging responses from universities which highlighted the critical need for transformation. The three recent incidents below (all of which were covered in the media) highlight the patterns of these responses which were reinforced by responses to the national student survey. When a male student who was allegedly sexually assaulted by another male 'classmate' in 2016, the University of Wollongong advised the complainant to 'change his own behaviour' when he requested that the alleged perpetrator be moved from his tutorial group. Shifting responsibility for preventing further incidents from the alleged offender to the complainant, the university provided the complainant with a 'safety plan' which included advice on minimising contact with the alleged perpetrator and recommended that he '[w]alk in groups of two or more after dark' (Funnell, 2016), reinforcing the myth that a perpetrator is more likely to be a 'stranger' than known to a victim (see End Rape on Campus Australia, 2017: 6). In the absence of appropriate university action, the student secured an apprehended violence order against the alleged perpetrator and eventually withdrew from the university, observing that his sexual assault and the response from the university were 'equally despicable. There is a shocking correlation between someone (the perpetrator) not listening to you say "stop" and an organisation (the university) not listening to you scream "help"'(Funnell, 2016).

Six months after a woman student was sexually assaulted in her room in a residential college at the University of Sydney in 2016, she was still awaiting the outcome of the university's investigation, filled 'with anxiety constantly that I may see him (her alleged perpetrator)'. A week after reporting the incident to her university, she was requested to complete a generic online form to explain why she had 'not taken steps to resolve the matter'. The student had to actively seek out any information relating to the procedures employed to determine her complaint and its progress and when she did ascertain details, she was directed by the university to keep the matter 'confidential' (Rooke, 2016).

A third example concerns a staff member at James Cook University (JCU) in northern Queensland who was charged with the rape of a woman student in 2015 (Chen, 2017). Following his arraignment, the alleged perpetrator was promoted from a research officer to an academic advisor in a university research centre and after pleading guilty to the charge, he remained in the role for three months. Despite the university's assertions that they were unaware of the charge or conviction, a member of university staff provided a character reference for the convicted perpetrator in mitigation of his sentence.

While *The Hunting Ground* depicts cases of university cover-ups in relation to claims of sexual assault and harassment at American universities, this problem does not appear to be widespread in the Australian context, despite allegations that universities have 'played down' the significant numbers of 'official complaints of sexual assault and harassment' (Bagshaw, 2017). However, as the above case studies and the subsequent national students survey data illustrate, the response of Australian universities has been deficient in other ways. In particular, 'first responders' to complainants of sexual assault, including security staff, academic staff, and campus counsellors, did not always refer students to the appropriate reporting channels and support services, and following questioning, students were sometimes made to feel that they are to blame, or that their experience has been trivialised. In addition, where students reported sexual harassment to university staff, they were told that the alleged perpetrator 'might just fancy you', to 'take [the conduct] as a compliment', or that it was 'just the culture ... get used to it' (Australian Human Rights Commission, 2017: 148; see also NUS, 2016: 26).

Strengthening Australian university responses: initial steps

A key response to the increasing accounts of university sexual violence, largely triggered by screenings of *The Hunting Ground* documentary at universities across Australia and the work of The Hunting Ground Australia Project, was the development of the *Strengthening Australian Responses to Sexual Assault and Harassment* research project, launched in September 2015 by the Australian Human Rights Centre (AHRCentre) at the University of New South Wales. The main aims of the project were to:

- identify the extent and nature of sexual assault and harassment in Australian university campuses;
- evaluate the experiences of students who report sexual violence to their university; to identify any barriers to reporting;
- highlight institutional responses that may entrench or prolong a culture where sexual violence is normalised, silenced, or excused; and,
- drawing on empirical data and comparative international research, provide a guide to Australian universities of good practice policies and procedures for their adaptation and application.

Throughout the project, we sought to amplify the voices of students from diverse backgrounds, including female students, international students and students who identify as LGBTIQ. While the project drew on comparative international research in identifying models of good practice, this foregrounding of Australian student voices ensured that the project conclusions and recommendations were directed to meet their needs.

Taking our lead from the student surveys conducted by the NUS in 2011 and 2015, as well as the Commission's ADFA survey, our initial task was to partner with the Commission to design the first national student survey (the national survey) on responses to sexual harassment and sexual assault in Australian universities. Through working with student representatives, the NUS, and sexual violence experts in developing the survey, we also sought to encourage sector-wide dialogue on responses to sexual misconduct in university settings, identify weaknesses in university procedures and practices, and build their capacity to prevent and respond to these behaviours.

The national survey, which secured ethics approval from the University of New South Wales Human Research Ethics Committee in August 2016, was sent to a randomly-selected cohort of 60,000 students across all 39 universities on an anonymous, confidential and voluntary basis. The Commission's analysis of survey responses from 30,000 students and qualitative data contained in over 1,800 written submissions received by the Commission from students and organisations during the period 23 August 2016 to 2 December 2016 (see, for example, The Hunting Ground Australia Project, 2017b), formed the basis of the public report, Change the Course, released in August 2017. Individual university reports were made available to each university on a confidential basis. Following interest in individual university results from media and student representatives, and encouragement from Australia's Sex Discrimination Commissioner, all 39 universities agreed to release their respective survey results (for example, Clure, 2017; Wahlquist, 2017). The Change the Course report revealed indicative data on the prevalence of sexual assault and harassment among Australian university students in 2015 and 2016, the characteristics of victims and perpetrators of sexual assault and sexual harassment, the sites or settings at universities where sexual assault and harassment occurred, the adequacy of reporting channels and support services and students' recommendations for change.

In analysing this prevalence data, the Commission observed that the 'prevalence and nature' of sexual assault and harassment in a university setting primarily corresponded with figures relating to sexual violence in the broader Australian community (Australian Bureau of Statistics, 2015), and that women aged between 18 and 24 (the age group largely reflective of the university student cohort) experienced sexual assault and harassment 'at over twice the national rate' (Australian Human Rights Commission, 2017: 4). The Commission also identified a number of factors that contributed to the perpetration of university sexual assault and harassment, including discriminatory attitudes towards women, the excessive use of alcohol, the abuse of a position of power by perpetrators, and 'easy access to bedrooms' in residential settings including colleges and university camps (p 5).

The report's other key findings include that: university colleges, grounds, teaching spaces, social events and transport to and from universities were the primary sites of sexual assault and harassment (p 8); women 'were almost twice as likely to be harassed' and 'more than three times as likely to be sexually assaulted' than men (p 7); and 'overwhelmingly, men were the perpetrators of both sexual assault and sexual harassment reported in the survey' with a 'significant proportion' of student victims knowing the perpetrator, who was 'most likely to be a fellow student from their university' (p 4). The report also found that 'the vast majority of students who were sexually assaulted [87%] or sexually harassed [94%] in 2015 and 2016 did not make a formal report or complaint to their university'. Their reasons for not reporting included a fear that they would not be believed by the university, a perception that the conduct was 'not serious enough' to warrant making a report, a lack of confidence in their understanding of the concepts of sexual harassment and sexual assault, and concerns that the reports would not be treated confidentially and that that no action would be taken (pp 140–45). Additional reasons included a fear of being victimised or discriminated against (for LGBTIQ students), and a confusion about whether the experience was 'just part of Australian culture' (for international students) (p 146). These responses suggest several concerning findings: a lack of trust by student victims in institutional procedures and practice; an acceptance or normalisation of conduct which is degrading, potentially unlawful, and frequently damaging and enduring in its impact; and additional reporting barriers for marginalised or vulnerable groups. The report further noted that both 'structural and attitudinal barriers' prevented students from reporting or seeking support, and that 'students who did report were often unsatisfied with the response of their university' (p 4).

The *Change the Course* report contains nine recommendations directed at universities and university colleges:

- the development of communication and educational strategies to prevent discriminatory conduct and sexual violence;
- dissemination to staff and students of internal and external reporting processes and support services;
- training of 'first responders' to disclosures of sexual assault and harassment and the provision of specialist support by expert practitioners;

- confidential collection and storage of reports of sexual assault and harassment and regular reviews of the effectiveness of university reporting procedures and support services;
- an independent expert-led review of the factors underlying the prevalence of sexual violence in residential colleges; and
- the conduct of the national student survey every three years to track progress in reducing university sexual violence.

Soon after the release of *Change of the Course*, the AHR Centre published its two project reports. The first report, *Local Perspectives: A case study on responses to sexual violence in a university setting,* presented the findings of a localised qualitative study of our own university, based on an initial review of its policies covering the management of sexual assault and harassment, and interviews with a sample of relevant individuals including university staff, student representatives and a former state Director of Public Prosecutions. A key reason for undertaking the *Local Perspectives* case study was to look critically at our own institutional policies and practice before tackling the need for change more broadly. It highlighted a number of weaknesses within a specific university framework that were similarly revealed in the national student survey, such as the need for a clear and accessible stand-alone policy on sexual violence and express institutional statements prohibiting sexual violence; disincentives to reporting incidents of sexual assault and harassment; a lack of clarity about the relationship between internal disciplinary mechanisms and external criminal justice proceedings; and deficient support services.

Our second report, *On Safe Ground: A good practice guide for Australian universities,* sought to provide Australian universities with a conceptual framework and practical recommendations for preventing and responding to sexual harassment and assault. It was informed by the Commission's report on the national survey and comparative international research on university good practice in addressing and preventing reports of sexual assault and harassment. The report details six foundational principles that should underpin all Australian university policies and procedures and argues that without visible senior university leadership, meaningful and formalised engagement with students and sustained, long-term institutional commitment, any policies adopted by universities will be of limited value, particularly if the institutional culture that enables sexual assault and harassment goes unchallenged (Australian Human Rights Centre, 2017a: 63–8).

The report's ten chapters include a comparative analysis of the legal and policy frameworks that govern university sexual assault and harassment in a number of countries (for example, the US, the UK, Canada, India and South Africa; pp 33–51) which underscores Australia's distinct lack of an explicit legislative framework and highlights the comparatively weak institutional arrangements at Australian universities for managing and preventing sexual violence (p 10). *On Safe Ground* makes 18 recommendations, including proposals for government and regulatory intervention, as well as recommendations to universities in relation to the implementation of accessible and consistent reporting processes, the enforcement of disciplinary action and sanctions, the provision of specialised and properly resourced student support services, and the delivery of evidence-based sexual violence prevention and bystander programmes.

The commitment by all 39 Australian universities to participate in the national survey was a significant demonstration of a collective imperative to address the 'concerning picture of the nature and prevalence of sexual assault and sexual harassment experienced by Australian university students' painted by the Commission's analysis of the survey data (Australian Human Rights Commission, 2017, p 3). The section below considers some of the responses to the national survey and the reports and recommendations outlined above.

Towards institutional change: recent developments

Until recently, many Australian universities have expressed ambivalence about their role in addressing assault and sexual harassment (Funnell, 2016; End Rape on Campus Australia, 2017; Rooke, 2016). At a broad level, there has also been a reluctance by universities to acknowledge the prevalence of sexual assault and harassment on university campuses, and therefore to provide sufficient training and resources for support services, and to improve processes for lodging and resolving complaints. While the reasons for this apparent disavowal of responsibility to proactively address campus sexual assault and harassment vary, they suggest a discomfort with regulating student (and staff) conduct 'beyond the ivory tower' (Bok, 1982) and a failure to acknowledge that the responsibilities of a university extend into areas of human interaction beyond the purely 'academic' sphere. Other contributing factors may include a concern with protecting institutional reputation and limiting legal liability.

At the launch of the national survey in August 2016, the then Chair of Universities Australia and Vice-Chancellor of Western Sydney University, Barney Glover, spoke of the 'damage caused by sexual harassment and sexual assault [that] cannot be undone' (Maniaty, 2016).

Professor Glover acutely observed that this harm may have an impact beyond the serious physical and emotional consequences for a student, prejudicing their capacity to learn, achieve academic progression and participate in university life – and even triggering a withdrawal from a course or their degree. Perhaps this public acknowledgement of the long-term harms of sexual violence – and a recognition of a university's duty of care towards its students and the potential exacerbation of harm by insensitive or dismissive management of incidents of student sexual assault and harassment – has seen the incremental development of institutional initiatives by some Australian universities aimed at more effective and sensitive management of reports of sexual violence, and its prevention.

Given that the reports discussed above were released in August 2017, it is premature to expect any major developments from universities in response in the short to medium term. However, some initial indications have seen a commitment to implement the recommendations made in the various reports referred to above, as well as attitudinal adjustments within the university sector which acknowledge that their responsibility to prevent and respond to sexual assault and harassment also ties in with a university's broader commitment to equity, diversity, and inclusion. As detailed in the *On Safe Ground* report, legal and regulatory obligations require universities to provide inclusive and non–discriminatory learning environments (Australian Human Rights Centre, 2017a: Chapter Three). Given findings by the Commission that victims of sexual assault and harassment in university settings are predominantly female, and that international and LGBTIQ students are also at increased risk of experiencing these behaviours and/or having negative reporting experiences, these obligations may now assume greater significance.

In addition to the campus screenings of *The Hunting Ground* documentary, the increased public affirmations by universities to actively prevent and respond to sexual harassment and assault were also influenced by the launch of the *Respect. Now. Always* campaign by Universities Australia in February 2016 (Universities Australia, 2016) and the implementation of the national survey. In the period between the release of the documentary and the publication of the various reports referred to above The Hunting Ground Australia Project surveyed a number of different universities and tracked their activities which they published in two Progress Reports in 2016 and 2017. These activities have included the drafting of stand–alone sexual assault and harassment (or sexual misconduct) policies; enhanced signposting of student misconduct policies and support services on their websites to provide clearer access to relevant information; training of staff and students who may receive initial disclosures or reports of incidents of sexual assault and harassment; the development of educational resources about what constitutes unacceptable behaviour and key bystander actions; and the introduction of a sex and ethics training programme for residential assistants and college social coordinators and student leaders from academic, sporting and cultural bodies with a view to embed aspects of the training 'into orientation and induction briefings for students each year'. (The Hunting Ground Australia Project, 2016: 6–11; The Hunting Ground Australia Project, 2017a: 12–18).

As an initial response to the release of *Change the Course*, Universities Australia announced the establishment of a '10-Point Plan Action Plan' which outlined some broad prevention, awareness and support initiatives, including the establishment of an interim 24/7 specialist support line for student victims and survivors that would operate for a few months following the release of the national survey. (Universities Australia, 2017: 19). While these ten broad actions reflected many of the recommendations detailed in the reports referred to above, to the disappointment of some student advocates, the Plan made no mention of the importance of rigorous disciplinary procedures and sanctions for students found to have breached university policies relating to sexual assault and harassment (Funnell and Hush, 2017) or the 'effective enforcement of policies' and the 'dissemination of disciplinary outcomes within the university community' as key components of a viable prevention strategy (see Australian Human Rights Centre, 2017a: 80).

At a regulatory level, the Australian Tertiary Education Quality and Standards Agency (TEQSA), an independent statutory authority, responded almost immediately to a recommendation by the AHR Centre (see Australian Human Rights Centre 2017a: 48–9). TEQSA requires universities to meet certain Threshold Standards relating to student equity, wellbeing and safety, grievance and complaints procedures, and monitoring and accountability compliance. Failure by universities to meet these standards can result in TEQSA revoking their registration. While university management of sexual violence was not initially referenced in these standards, a proposed revision of certain Threshold Standards by TEQSA subsequent to the release *On Safe Ground* incorporates reference to sexual assault and harassment as a distinct proposed focus of university management and reporting responsibilities (Australian Government, 2017). In addition, soon after the release *Change the Course*, the Federal Minister for Education and Training, Senator Simon Birmingham, wrote to each university to seek their response to the Commission's findings and recommendations 'given their legal obligation to provide a safe learning environment'. The Minister undertook 'to work with universities to ensure they address the findings and recommendations' of the Commission's report and 'implement changes that will make them safer and more inclusive environments in the future' (Birmingham, 2017).

In the past few years, the issue of weak institutional responses to sexual violence in universities has finally secured national attention, driven by the Australian release of *The Hunting Ground,* along with the national student survey, campaigns by NUS, The Hunting Ground Australia Project, and Universities Australia, increased media reporting and calls for the implementation of recommendations contained in reports by the Australian Human Rights Commission and the AHRCentre. The decision by some students to discuss their experiences of sexual harassment and sexual assault on social media, and/or to reach out to journalists, has further drawn attention to this issue. Although universities have begun to take practical steps to address this issue, a number of more long-term challenges that are far more difficult to address – such as entrenched attitudes that contribute to sexual assault and sexual harassment, the risks posed by the shift to online learning and social media, limitations imposed by the conventional 'victim narrative', the preservation of key institutional interests and a deference to the criminal justice system – may remain extant, especially in the absence of a sustained national focus on the issue and student activism (despite annual student turnover) that continue to hold universities to their commitments.

Key challenges

Ambiguities under dual systems of investigation of sexual misconduct

Unlike the criminal justice system, which is directed at the determination of culpability and sentencing in accordance with established criminal law criteria and standards, the internal disciplinary procedures that universities (and their residential colleges) employ to address allegations of sexual assault or harassment are primarily aimed at breaches of university policy and the moderation of institutional risk, with internally devised procedures and sanctions ranging from expulsion from a university (or college) and removal from leadership roles, to suspension from particular classes. The existence of these dual processes and procedures with their differing rationales can give rise to ambiguities in applicable standards of proof, procedures for complaint evaluation and outcome: the criminal justice system requires the prosecution to prove an offence beyond reasonable doubt, whereas the university's disciplinary system will usually have a lower standard of proof and 'less adversarial adjudicative processes' (Sheehy, 2017: 37). More importantly, as the surveys by the Commission and the NUS have made clear, the often opaque administrative disciplinary processes developed by universities lack clarity, consistency and certainty, often exacerbated by the absence of stand-alone policies on sexual assault and harassment which are merely embedded in generic student misconduct provisions. This creates confusion for those tasked with managing complaints, can potentially deter students from making a complaint in the first place, and may exacerbate harm by requiring victims to narrate their experience multiple times (Australian Human Rights Centre, 2017a: 48, 53–54).

In Australia, the disincentives underlying student reporting of cases of sexual assault are further complicated by a statutory obligation arising in most states to refer such reports to the police. For example, under New South Wales (NSW) criminal law, sexual and indecent assault constitute a 'serious indictable offence' and any person who fails to report information relating to such an offence 'without a reasonable excuse' may face a term of imprisonment. This provision goes further than requiring those who receive information on sexual assault to contact the police; it makes criminal a failure to report such information (Australian Human Rights Centre, 2017b: 23). This offence was introduced in 1990s, along with several other offences aimed at preventing interference with the criminal justice system (NSW Parliamentary Debates, 1990: 3691). In 1998, in response to concerns expressed by the NSW Law Reform Commission, the provision was amended to specify that certain persons, including healthcare providers, could not be prosecuted under this provision without the approval of the Attorney General. This amendment did not satisfy the Law Reform Commission, which recommended that the provision be repealed because it might prevent victims from seeking care because they feared police involvement (NSW Law Reform Commission, 1999). Despite this concern, the provision remains in place.

Students may therefore also be reluctant to report cases of sexual assault if university staff are legally obligated to refer these to the police, potentially with adverse consequences for the complainant (for example public exposure, protracted and invasive police investigations). In order to respect victims' agency, and enable them to make an informed choice about which details (if any) to disclose, it is essential that university policies clearly articulate the relationship between the university's disciplinary process and the criminal justice process and that first responders and those responsible for managing complaints, demonstrate clarity to complainants about their role and obligations vis-à-vis the police. In addition, where victims are adamant that a university staff member does not convey the information to the police, the university may require that provider to take a written statement from the victim to this effect, in order to respect of the victim's wishes while protecting the university staff and the university itself (Australian Human Rights Centre, 2017b: 24).

Online learning, social media and the regulation of 'technology-facilitated sexual violence'

As new technology accelerates access to online university education, the risk of 'technology-facilitated sexual violence' increases with corresponding imperatives for universities to develop effective institutional responses to this form of sexual assault and harassment (Henry and Powell, 2016). Examples of technologically facilitated sexual violence include 'threats of rape and virtual rape, online sexual harassment and cyberstalking, the use of Facebook groups to promote rape-supportive attitudes, the posting of degrading, sexually based comments about female students and teachers' (Henry and Powell, 2016: 84–5). The case that largely triggered the ADFA Review mentioned above concerned the covert filming and distribution via Skype of consensual sex by a male cadet (with a female cadet) to his colleagues in a neighbouring room, without the woman's knowledge or consent. In the criminal proceedings brought against the male cadet (on charges of sending offensive material over the internet without consent and committing an act of indecency) (Willis, 2013), the complainant stated that she 'had been offered no support by the Defence Force, … that she was told police did not regard the incident as a crime under ACT (local) law' and that the matter would not be investigated internally 'as it was not serious enough' (Knaus, 2013). After being sentenced to two 12-month good behaviour bonds, the perpetrator was permitted to resume his studies at ADFA; however, following an internal inquiry (and significant media attention on the Defence Force) he was expelled from the Academy a month later, his conduct viewed as 'inconsistent with the Army's values and the standards expected of a member of the Defence Force' (ABC News, 2013).

As mobile and online technology provide new modes for perpetrating sexual misconduct, universities face the challenge of capturing behaviour within their own policies that may not necessarily align with definitions of sexual violence but has similarly deleterious consequences. In addition, they will need to determine how to respond to forms of 'cyber-sexual violence and online sexual assault' (Sheehy, 2017: 37) by devising processes of investigation, accountability and sanctions that are suitable support services and reflect legal and policy developments in a relatively new area of regulation. Equally, universities face the challenge of assessing the nature and impact of the harm caused by technologically facilitated sexual violence in order to implement or adjust suitable support services and fashioning online prevention strategies.

Limitations of the conventional 'victim narrative' in designing and revising models of institutional response

As noted above, the *Change the Course* report indicated that many Australian university students who experienced sexual assault and sexual harassment do not report this conduct to their university. This issue was also addressed in *Local Perspectives* which indicates that students feared they might not be taken seriously or have their experience minimised because they failed to 'fit' or correspond with an assumed victim stereotype; or might attract shame from family or community due to 'cultural barriers that prevent them being able to talk about it' (Australian Human Rights Centre, 2017b: 12). These concerns are perhaps more acute when the sexual assault is incurred by an individual other than the mythologised 'real' rape victim, namely 'the morally upright White woman who is physically injured while resisting' (Du Mont et al, 2003). In particular, concerns about being believed may be heightened for men who experience sexual violence, students of colour, students from minority religions, students with disability or those who identify as LGBTIQ.

Addressing this challenge requires remedial and therapeutic services that are directed to the needs of specific student cohorts, and are clearly advertised to those cohorts in a language and format that they understand. This should include a reassurance that the service is inclusive, such as by displaying a visible statement or symbol of non-discrimination on the service website or at its premises. In addition, it requires consideration at the reporting and investigative stages of incidents of sexual assault and harassment. For example, providing students whose first language is not English with the option to provide an initial account of a sexual assault in writing (Australian Human Rights Centre, 2017a: 58–9). Sensitivity to the needs and experiences of a diverse student community is also fundamental in the design and delivery of any meaningful prevention training programmes. The engagement of students with diverse experiences in shaping these processes and programmes will serve to make them resonant and effective.

Conclusion: from risk management to harm prevention

Concerns about the impact of reports of sexual assault or harassment and misogynist practices at universities on a university's reputation and standing, or apprehension about possible claims by alleged perpetrators of university breaches of due process or procedural fairness can drive a defensive institutional response that focuses on liability (Australian Human Rights Centre, 2017a: 117).

In 2011, Sydney journalist and member of the NSW Premier's Council on Preventing Violence against Women, Nina Funnell, wrote that although the NUS *Talk About It* survey identified sexual assault and harassment as a 'real and serious problem' on university campuses, the online self-selecting methodology employed meant that the results were open to question. Funnell concluded that given the clear manifestation of sexual violence on university campuses, 'rigorous, methodologically sound, comprehensive research' was required that would 'stand up to scrutiny'. 'But to do this,' she continued, 'universities will have to get on board. This, I suspect, will be a whole different challenge, given the continuing resistance, from colleges especially, to proper research into the vulnerability of young women on campuses' (Funnell, 2011).

Despite pockets of ongoing resistance to decades of students' activism on the issue and a tendency at times for universities to invoke 'administration by incantation' (Powell, 2014) in response to this 'real and serious problem', it is, in our view, significant that all 39 Australian universities participated in the national student survey. In addition, prior to the release of the analysis of the survey data many universities had already taken steps to evaluate, redraft or revise relevant policies, facilitate student accessibility to services, and introduce prevention training. However, the nature of sexual violence, the harm it generates and the slow progress of change, demands that Australian universities commit to a long-term approach to address sexual assault and harassment by continuing to give visibility to the issue, adapt and enhance their responses and services, monitor and evaluate policies and processes and resource a sustained programme of intervention and prevention.

Importantly, the authenticity and potential utility of this work requires the formal engagement of student leadership in the formulation and application of policies and procedures (for example via properly resourced university advisory committees with representation from the senior university management, the student body, and academics with appropriate expertise), the assessment of support services, and the design of training programmes and campaigns if it is to yield enduring institutional impact. And equally, the doubts and discomfort often displayed by decision makers and service providers in Australian universities about their role in addressing 'the undeniable realities' (Maniaty, 2016) of sexual harassment and sexual assault require a fundamental shift and recognition that the systemic social and economic origins of this harm are reinforced by institutional culture.

At the 2016 Universities Australia conference, the former Australian Chief of Army, David Morrison, who oversaw the *Review into the Treatment of Women in the Australian Defence Force Academy*, noted that 'more often than not, domestic and family violence grows out of gender inequality' and a culture that embeds male dominance and entitlement. A change of this culture, said Morrison, requires 'leadership ... you need to stand next to this issue; if you don't you will find that the status quo quickly reasserts itself.' Standing next to this issue requires that universities 'bring [it] out into the open, place [it] under the strongest spotlight, confront [it], and develop effective strategies to tackle [it]' (Maniaty, 2016). Following the national student survey and research undertaken by the NUS, End Rape on Campus Australia, The Hunting Ground Australia Project, the Commission and the AHRCentre, Australian universities are now on notice to name, own and rectify the problem of campus sexual assault and harassment. What is now critical is genuine and comprehensive follow-through by universities which sees them implementing improved mechanisms for reporting and addressing these behaviours, and changing a culture that enables their repeated occurrence.

References

ABC News (2013) 'ADFA cadet Daniel McDonald sacked over Skype sex scandal', 8 November, www.abc.net.au/news/2013-11-09/adfa-cadet-sacked-over-skype-sex-scandal/5080834

Australian Bureau of Statistics (ABS) *Recorded Crime – Victims, Australia, 2015*, cat no 4510.0 (13 July 2017), www.abs.gov.au/ausstats/abs@.nsf/mf/4510.0

Australian Government (2017) 'Sector guidance to ensure safe campuses', https://www.teqsa.gov.au/latest-news/media-releases/sector-guidance-ensure-safe-campuses

Australian Human Rights Centre (2017a) *On Safe Ground: Strengthening Australian University Responses to Sexual Assault and Harassment*, www.ahrcentre.org/sites/ahrcentre.org/files/AHR0002%20On%20 Safe%20Ground_Good%20Practice%20Guide_online.pdf

Australian Human Rights Centre (2017b) *Local Perspectives: A Case Study on Responses to Sexual Violence in a University Setting*, www. ahrcentre.org/sites/ahrcentre.org/files/mdocs/AHR0001%20 Local%20Perspectives_Case%20Study_online.pdf

Australian Human Rights Commission (2011) Review into the Treatment of Women in the Australian Defence Force Academy, Phase 1.

Australian Human Rights Commission (2017) *Change the Course: National Report on Sexual Assault and Sexual Harassment at Australian Universities*, www.humanrights.gov.au/sites/default/files/document/ publication/AHRC_2017_ChangeTheCourse_UniversityReport. pdf

Bagshaw, E. (2017) '"Devastating" report shows universities are "failing" students"', *Sydney Morning Herald*, 22 February, www.smh.com.au/ national/education/devastating-report-shows-universities-are-failing-students-20170222-guj84k.html

Birmingham, S. (2017) 'University sexual assault and sexual harassment', media release, 1 August, www.senatorbirmingham.com. au/university-sexual-assault-and-sexual-harassment/

Bok, D. (1982) *Beyond the Ivory Tower: Social Responsibilities and the Modern University*, Cambridge, MA: Harvard University Press.

Chen, D. (2017) 'James Cook University staffer promoted after student rape', ABC News, 24 January, www.abc.net.au/news/2017-01-23/university-staffer-student-rape-james-cook-university-promoted/8203976

Clure, E. (2017) 'Human Rights Commission's university sexual harassment survey 'may let down students, victims"', ABC News, 4 April, www.abc.net.au/news/2017-04-04/human-rights-commission-report-on-sexual-harassment-questioned/8413418

Commonwealth of Australia, Department of Social Services (2016) *Third Action Plan 2016–2019 Of the National Plan to Reduce Violence against Women and their Children 2010–2022*, www.dss.gov.au/sites/ default/files/documents/10_2016/third_action_plan.pdf

Du Mont, J., Miller, K. and Myh, T. (2013) 'The Role of "Real Rape" and "Real Victim" Stereotypes in the Police Reporting Practices of Sexually Assaulted Women', *Violence Against Women*, 9(4): 466–86.

End Rape on Campus Australia (2017) *Connecting the Dots: Understanding Sexual Assaults in Australian University Communities*, https://static1. squarespace.com/static/5762fc04f5e231826f09afae/t/58b3d08ddb2 9d6e7a2b8271d/1488179368580/Connecting+the+dots.pdf

Funnell, N. (2011) 'Claims of uni rape need proper research', *Sydney Morning Herald*, 17 June.

Funnell, N. (2016) 'The shocking way sexual violence is handled at Australian universities' news.com.au, 29 June, www.news. com.au/lifestyle/real-life/news-life/the-shocking-way-sexual-violence-is-handled-at-australian-universities/news-story/ fdb2f5d827ee8f6f4c124af11847aa25

Funnell, N. and Hush, A. (2017) 'Unis dodge action on sexual assault offenders in 10-point plan', *Sydney Morning Herald*, 1 August, www. smh.com.au/comment/unis-dodge-a-crackdown-on-sexual-assault-offenders-20170801-gxn4jl.html

Henry, N. and Powell, A. (2016) 'Sexual Violence in the Digital Age: The Scope and Limits of Criminal Law', *Social and Legal Studies Journal*, 25(4): 397–418.

Hunting Ground Australia Project, The (2016) *Progress Report – July 2016*, www.thehuntinggroundaustralia.com.au/wp-content/ uploads/2015/12/Progress_Report_The_Hunting_Ground_ Australia_Project_July2016_e.pdf

Hunting Ground Australia Project, The (2017a) *Progress Report – July 2017*, www.thehuntinggroundaustralia.com.au/wp-content/ uploads/2017/07/Progress_Report_The_Hunting_Ground_ Australia_Project_July2017_e.pdf

Hunting Ground Australia Project, The (2017b) *Submission to the Australian Human Rights Commission's University Sexual Assault and Harassment Project – February 2017*, www.thehuntinggroundaustralia. com.au/wp-content/uploads/2017/06/The-Hunting-Ground-Australia-Project-submission-to-AHRC-University-Sexual-Assault-and-Harassment-Project.pdf

Johnston, S. (2016) Speech by former President, UNSW Student Representative Council delivered at a screening of *The Hunting Ground* at UNSW, Sydney, 2 May.

Knaus, C. (2013) 'Skype sex victim 'had to go public', *Canberra Times*, 20 August, www.canberratimes.com.au/act-news/skype-sex--victim-had-to-go-public-20130820-2s8is.html

Maniaty, T. (2016) 'Today we say with one voice: One incident is one too many', UNSW Sydney Newsroom, 23 August, https:// newsroom.unsw.edu.au/news/general/today-we-say-one-voice-one-incident-one-too-many

National Union of Students (NUS) (2011) *'Talk About It' Report 2011*.
NUS (2016) *'Talk About It' Report 2015,* https://d3n8a8pro7vhmx.
cloudfront.net/nus/pages/144/attachments/original/1454369041/
Talk_about_it_Survey_Report.pdf?1454369041

NSW Family & Community Services (2017) 'Minister joins university students for sexual assault consultation session', media release, 7 June, www.facs.nsw.gov.au/about_us/media_releases/minister-joins-university-students-for-sexual-assault-consultation-session

NSW Law Reform Commission (1999) *Report 93: Review of Section 316 of the Crimes Act 1900 (NSW)*.

Powell, D. (2014) 'The Australian Defence Force Academy "Skype sex scandal": lessons on leadership and ethics', lecture presented to the 8th Triennial Meeting of the Colleges and Universities of the Anglican Communion, Seoul.

Rooke, D. (2016) 'Campus Assault', *Saturday Paper*, No. 125, 10–16 September, www.thesaturdaypaper.com.au/news/education/2016/09/10/campus-assaults/14734296003720

Sheehy, E. (2017) 'Making Universities Safe for Women: Sexual Assault on Campus' in W. Antony, J. Antony and L. Samuelson (eds) *Power and Resistance: Critical Thinking About Canadian Social Issues*, sixth edition, Black Point, NS: Fernwood.

Steinem, G. (2016) *My Life on the Road*, Random House: New York.

Universities Australia (2016) *Respect. Now. Always*, www.universitiesaustralia.edu.au/uni-participation-quality/students/Student-safety#.WLlaCSN97aZ

Universities Australia (2017) '10 Point Action Plan: An initial response from Australia's universities to the national student survey on sexual assault and sexual harassment', https://www.universitiesaustralia.edu.au/uni-participation-quality/students/Student-safety/Respect--Now--Always-#.WoZiFCVua70

Wahlquist, C. (2017) 'Human Rights Commission defends survey on university sexual assaults', *Guardian*, 4 April, www.theguardian.com/australia-news/2017/apr/04/human-rights-commission-defends-survey-on-university-sexual-assaults

Willis, L. (2013) 'ADFA Skype sex scandal: Daniel McDonald, Dylan Deblaquiere avoid jail time', ABC News, 23 October, www.abc.net.au/news/2013-10-23/sentence-expected-in-adf-skype-sex-case/5039296

5

Preventing gender based violence in UK universities: the policy context

Anni Donaldson, Melanie McCarry and Aimee McCullough

Since the turn of the millennium across the UK, increased public and political awareness of the nature, extent and impact on women of all forms of gender based violence (GBV) has led to a significant expansion of the national policy framework and of funding for GBV prevention and specialist service provision. GBV occurring in higher education contexts has also gained attention among researchers, the government, the media and higher education institutions (HEIs) in recent years (see for example, National Union of Students (NUS) 2011, 2012; Jackson and Sundaram, 2015). Notably, national and international media coverage has highlighted universities as 'sites of violence' against women, with particular emphasis on sexual violence and harassment (Fenton et al, 2016: 5).

Research into campus-based GBV in the UK has tended overall to reflect experiences within English HEIs. In the 2011 National Union of Students UK survey *Hidden Marks* (NUS, 2011) on campus-based sexual violence, harassment and stalking, of the 2,058 responses, 88% were UK students and 12% from overseas students. Responses from students across the four home nations broadly reflected the distribution of student numbers across the four home nations (England: 85%; Wales: 10%; Scotland: 5%; Northern Ireland: 2%). Of the 62 institutions that contributed to the Universities UK Task Force's consultation on violence against women, harassment and hate crime in 2016, the vast majority were from England with five from Scotland, three from Wales and one from Northern Ireland. In 1998 the national governments of Northern Ireland, Scotland and Wales assumed responsibilities for a range of devolved matters (Home Office, 2013). Political and policy priorities emerged which were distinct from each other and from those in England meaning it is no longer accurate to refer to a UK response without reference to the differences between the four nations, as illustrated through the evolution of GBV policy in each of the home nations. GBV is a policy area that shows a degree of variation across the UK and merits examination for the impact this may have on how universities address this issue on campus sexual violence. This chapter will begin by outlining the current situation facing UK universities as they develop their responses to GBV. It will then contextualise this by examining the key factors influencing GBV policy in each of the home nations using a three point conceptual framework. The chapter will then summarise current developments in universities' approaches to the issue in their national context. The chapter will conclude by offering some observations on the opportunities and challenges facing the UK higher education sector as it develops its approach to GBV prevention.

Gender based violence in UK universities

In 2014–15 there were 2.3 million university students in the UK, of whom 56% were female and 44% male, with 45% of all students aged under 21 years. The distribution of UK university students across the four home nations during that period was 81% in England, 10% in Scotland, 5.9% in Wales and 2.5% in Northern Ireland . UK universities employ a total of 410,130 staff, of whom 54% are female and 46% male; while 55% of academic staff are men and 62% of non-academic staff are women (Universities UK, 2015). Despite the significance of these figures in relation to gender inequality there is a growing research base that points to concerns around women's wellbeing in the educational sector being traditionally 'marginalised' in research and policy (Phipps and Smith, 2012). National statistics show that gender and age are key determinants increasing the risk of experiencing GBV, with young women aged 16–25 more likely to be affected than other age groups (Rape Crisis Scotland, 2015). In the UK, one in seven women students have experienced serious physical or sexual assault; 84% knew their attacker; and 25% have experienced unwanted sexual behaviour (Phipps and Smith, 2012: 363). As a result, there has been increased scrutiny of the ways in which universities are responding to, and preventing, GBV, and in particular, sexual violence against, and by, students.

A growing body of work, including a number of high profile inquiries, have been influential in identifying best practice and providing recommendations to this complex issue in UK higher education contexts (Durham University, 2015; Bows et al, 2015). This developing field of research has also highlighted the often poor and inconsistent responses of HEIs, particularly surrounding reporting pathways (or lack thereof); inconsistencies in universities' approaches when dealing with victims/survivors of GBV; and gaps in students' knowledge of services available locally or on campus. As a distinct issue, GBV requires a distinct institutional response. Within UK higher education however, only a minority of institutions have specific GBV and/or sexual violence misconduct policies or procedures, though a growing number are beginning to implement such measures. Moreover, it has been argued that the primary concern of HEIs may be with the reputational and financial damage associated with reports of violence (Phipps and Young, 2015). There is growing acknowledgement that HEIs have a responsibility and duty of care to maintain the safety and wellbeing of the university, staff and student, community and by extension, to effectively address GBV. Institutions also have a role to play in challenging the attitudes that underpin GBV, as the harassment, abuse and violence on university campuses and education contexts both reflect and influence those of wider society.

A gendered framework

During the 1970s and 1980s, preventing violence against women (VAW) became a progressive social policy issue in the UK, Europe and the US as a result of feminism and women's social activism (Htun and Weldon, 2012). This drew public and political attention to the physical and sexual abuse of women (Dobash and Dobash, 1992; Hanmer and Maynard, 1987), deepened knowledge of women's lived and common experience of violence, and offered directions for prevention strategies (Walby, 2011; Walby et al, 2014). Feminist research looked beyond individual pathology and scrutinised VAW in its wider social and historical context. Definitions of violence derived directly from women's lived experience were developed, forms of VAW were reconceptualised as gendered phenomena and reframed within a matrix of embedded public and private social controls which maintained women's historic social subordination (Hanmer, 1978, 1996; Littlejohn, 1978).

In the 21st century VAW has been described as a 'concrete manifestation of inequality between the sexes' (Garcia-Moreno et al, 2005: 1282) which presents a significant impediment to women's equality. There is also recognition that most women experience more than one form and that the negative and cumulative impact can reach beyond the home, across social space, and throughout the lifespan (Scottish Government, 2009). Research on VAW policy development worldwide has shown that the most effective strategies are those that adopt an ecological perspective to instruct action across society at macro and micro levels and that interact with levels of power in society both vertically and horizontally and across public and private space (Heise, 1998; Samarasekera and Horton, 2015; Stockdale and Nadler, 2012). Hearn and McKie (2008) suggest a three point gender framework for examining VAW policy development which includes: a gendered definition and analysis of violence and abuse in all its forms; a recognition of the social norms and material conditions that facilitate the exercise of male power and privilege; and acknowledgement of the varied locations and context where such violence occurs. The extent to which VAW policy developments in the UK since the late 1990s have adhered to this conceptualisation in current UK frameworks will be examined. These will be contextualised within the constitutional changes which have taken place in the UK since 1998.

UK GBV policy

The majority New Labour administration which came to power in the UK in 1997 stressed its commitment to being 'tough on crime and the causes of crime' (Home Office, no date). The policy rested on reforming the criminal justice system, reducing offending and developing police and public sector partnership approaches to crime prevention. Phipps (2010) and others have noted that this approach to VAW policy individualised criminal behaviour in order to improve detection and prosecution rates, and it also led to increased reporting and better support for women crime victims (Ball and Charles, 2006; Phipps, 2010). This focus on the criminal aspects of VAW and on improving criminal justice responses was welcomed by the women's movement and feminist campaigners. However, the crime prevention focus depoliticised the issue and diverted attention from women's wider experiences of gender power relations, structural inequalities and the links to the pervasive continuum of gendered sexual violence which women faced in public and private life (Kelly, 1988; Stark, 2007). According to Phipps' research, this reframing of women's experiences of sexual and domestic violence in discourses of crime and victimhood was still evident in the Labour government's approach ten years later despite a more overt acknowledgement of the wider structural roots of VAW in women's social inequality in the 2007 cross government *Action Plan on Sexual Violence and Abuse,* for example (Phipps, 2010). While the Conservative/Liberal Democrat coalition government elected in 2010 continued to emphasise crime and community safety in its approach to VAW, there was an acknowledgement by the then Home Secretary, the Right Hon. Theresa May, that 'For too long government has focused on violence against women and girls as a criminal justice issue – dealing with the fallout of these terrible crimes' and that it was necessary to work on measures to prevent violence from happening in the first place (HM Government, 2010: 3).

In its 2010 *Call to End Violence Against Women and Girls*, the coalition government adopted the definition of violence against women and girls (VAWG) outlined in the United Nations Declaration of the Elimination of VAW (1994), noted the UK's ratification of the UN Convention on the Elimination of all Forms of Discrimination against Women (CEDAW) and acknowledged that this was the first time the government had agreed to work to a single definition. The Conservative government elected in 2015 published its *Ending Violence Against Women and Girls Strategy* for the period 2016–20 and committed £80 million to the *Violence Against Women and Girls Service Transformation Fund* for the period (HM Government, 2015). On a more regressive note, the single UN definition outlined in the coalition strategy was omitted and replaced by a gender-neutral working definition and new measures and legislation were introduced. Paradoxically, the new measures covered specific offences which all disproportionally affect women and are clearly gendered phenomena, such as stalking, forced marriage, FGM, and revenge pornography. The new domestic abuse offence captured coercive or controlling behaviour in an intimate or family relationship; and the Strategy also referred to the Modern Slavery Act; Domestic Violence Protection Orders (DVPOs), the national Domestic Violence Disclosure Scheme (DVDS), FGM Protection Orders and an FGM mandatory reporting duty. Again, somewhat paradoxically, there was an acknowledgement of the need to change attitudes through prevention work across society and especially with young people. While commitments to improving criminal justice responses aimed at apprehending and prosecuting offenders remained, wider work to prevent and address offending or abusive behaviour was not emphasised. Ishkanian (2014) argues that Conservative notions of the 'Big Society' and neoliberal policies have continued the depoliticisation of VAW by maintaining the emphasis on crime prevention and value for money. Service commissioning strategies, together with austerity economics, encourage the marketisation of civic society through the expansion of voluntary sector service provision and the commission of services that lack the expertise and feminist analysis of GBV (Berry et al, 2014; McCarry et al, 2017). This threatens to neutralise the ability of longstanding feminist-inspired VAW voluntary organisations such as Rape Crisis and Women's Aid to provide specialist local services, and contribute to progressive policymaking aimed at reducing women's inequality (Ishkanian, 2014). In a more recent development, The Preventing and Combating Violence against Women and Domestic

Violence (Ratification of Convention) Bill received Royal Assent on 27 April 2017 and is now an Act of Parliament in the UK. This ratifies the Council of Europe Convention on Preventing and Combating Violence Against Women and Domestic Violence 2011 (also known as the Istanbul Convention) in UK law. The Convention recognises the links between structural inequalities and VAW and commits signatories to creating coordinated national responses. The Act commits the UK to creating minimum enforceable standards to protect victims/survivors and a comprehensive legal and policy framework for preventing VAW (UK Parliament, 2017).

Since devolution, the national VAW strategies of Wales, Scotland and Northern Ireland have shared a focus on improving the criminal justice response to VAW, in line with that in England. However, distinctions in the way the issue has been conceptualised are evident. The genesis of these devolved nations' strategies lay in civic and political campaigns for increased women's representation in the proposed new national parliaments in the 1990s. The opportunity to develop political systems and structures in the new governments which supported equal representation of women was seized upon by feminist and women's organisations, politicians and trade unionists. The introduction of quotas and other measures to support the increased participation of women in the new political structures resulted in what has been described as the 'feminisation' of politics, whereby women's increased participation also promoted the advancement of issues affecting women's lives in the political agenda (Lovenduski, 2012; Mackay and McAllister, 2012). Women's political representation in the new Welsh and Scottish parliaments exceeded that of Westminster and Northern Ireland: in 1997, women were 18% of Westminster MPs, while 37% of those elected to the new Scottish Parliament and 40% of those taking their seats in the National Assembly of Wales were women. These improvements in gender parity have been attributed to the application of gender quotas, particularly in the Labour Party (Ball and Charles, 2006; Mackay and McAllister, 2012). The changing gender landscape in the political life of Scotland and Wales has been credited with achieving a new emphasis on the mainstreaming of equality and in the development of national policies on domestic abuse and VAW (Ball and Charles, 2006; Breitenbach and Mackay, 2001; Mackay, 2010). The role of feminist campaigning and service providers such as the established network of Women's Aid and Rape Crisis organisations have also had a significant impact on the development of GBV policy in Scotland and Wales through closer access to the policymakers and the development of successful lobbying strategies. Consistent and careful management of the tension between crime prevention focused strategies, survivor-informed approaches, and clearly linked strategies to structural gender inequality has resulted in the gendered framework adopted by Wales and Scotland (but which is lacking in the gender-neutral approach of Northern Ireland).

Northern Ireland

Despite a strong women's movement in Northern Ireland and clear statements of the need for a more equal society in the Good Friday Agreement, the progress of gender equality and gender mainstreaming in Northern Ireland has been slow (Brown et al, 2002; Gray and Neill, 2011). Only 15% of those elected to the new Assembly were women and the low numbers, in comparison to those of the new Scottish and Welsh parliaments, have been attributed to the more varied political landscape where 'political priorities are informed by ethno-national differences' (Ward, 2004: 1; see also Connolly, 1999). Northern Ireland's seven-year strategy *Stopping Domestic and Sexual Violence and Abuse in Northern Ireland,* published in 2016, for example, adopts a gender-neutral definition. Replacing the existing 'Tackling Violence at Home' and 'Tackling Sexual Violence and Abuse' strategies, this new overarching framework has the strategic vision of 'a society ... in which domestic and sexual violence is not tolerated in any form, effective tailored preventative and responsive services are provided, all victims are supported and perpetrators are held to account' (DHSSPSNI and DoJNI, 2016: 34). The Strategy does not highlight, however, that most victims are women and girls and most perpetrators are men. This gender-neutral approach is reflected in the emphasis that domestic and sexual violence 'affects all members of society', that 'it knows no boundaries with regard to age, gender identity, marital status, race, ethnicity or religious group, sexual orientation, social class, disability or geography' and that '*anyone can be a victim*' (DHSSPSNI and DoJNI, 2016: 7, 20, emphasis added). Statistics are provided on the incidence and prevalence of crimes and offences but not on the gendered nature of victimisation and perpetration. Women are rendered somewhat invisible within this strategy as a result, and domestic and sexual violence and abuse is not contextualised within wider structural inequalities. Overall the strategy takes a crime prevention approach similar to that in England and makes clear links to other NI Executive strategies and policy areas including the *Building Safer, Shared and Confident Communities – A Community Safety Strategy for Northern Ireland 2012–2017*, published in July 2012, and the 2013 *Making a difference to victims and witnesses of crime – Improving access to justice, services and support – a five-year Strategy*. Moreover, the wider backdrop for the *Stopping Domestic and Sexual Violence and Abuse* strategy is the Northern Ireland Executive's Programme for Government 2011–15, with priorities in crime prevention, and improvement planning focused on community safety, access to justice and safeguarding outcomes for children and vulnerable adults (DHSSPSNI and DoJNI, 2016).

Within the new strategy for *Stopping Domestic and Sexual Violence and Abuse* and its implementation plan there are five key strands: Cooperation and Leadership, Prevention and Early Intervention, Provision, Support Protection and Justice. Overall, the strategy emphasises the importance of collaborative approaches with prevention described as 'fundamental' to reducing incidence, promoting increased knowledge and understanding, and in changing societal attitudes. The implementation plan emphasises the key role of schools, supports the development of effective educational programmes and partnership working between local councils, employers and health and social care services, including a preventative school curriculum centred on encouraging healthy relationships. This involves providing teachers with the necessary skills and resources to teach about issues of violence and abuse, as well as training to support and respond appropriately to pupils in distress. The national strategy makes no reference to the contribution of further and higher education to wider implementation.

Wales

Under the terms of The Government of Wales Act 1998, devolution was limited to health, education and local government services, with responsibility for policing and criminal justice retained by the UK government. The Welsh Assembly recognised its statutory duties under the Equality Act 2010 to promote equality of opportunity and established structures to ensure these were met (Ball and Charles, 2006). The first Welsh strategy published in 2005 – *Tackling Domestic Abuse* – adopted a rights based framework and, in 2010, *The Right to be Safe Strategy* set out an integrated, cross government programme of action to tackle all forms of VAWG. Moreover, in 2015 the Welsh Government passed two pieces of legislation with significance for addressing GBV: the Violence Against Women, Domestic Abuse and Sexual Violence (Wales) Act 2015 and the Well-being of Future Generations (Wales) Act 2015. These set out the Welsh Government's vision and goals for Wales and place clear legal requirements on public bodies to ensure their strategic planning, actions and outcomes contribute to the wider wellbeing of the population in the long term across a number of areas, and make clear provision for their accountability to the Welsh Government. In this legislation, the Welsh Government has recognised the gendered nature of VAW as well as acknowledged that it is a cross-cutting issue which requires action across a number of policy and service areas. The 2015 Violence Against Women, Domestic Abuse and Sexual Violence (Wales) Act, for example, highlights 'gender-based violence, domestic abuse and sexual violence as mostly perpetrated against women and girls by men, and ... is both a cause and consequence of gender inequality' (Welsh Government, 2015: 10).

The overall aim of the new legislation is to improve the public sector response to GBV and make prevention of VAW a measurable priority. It places a legislative requirement on public bodies to produce national and local strategies for tackling GBV, and in doing so attempts to promote awareness of GBV and improve consistency and quality of service provision in Wales. Moreover, the Act confers Welsh Ministers with powers to issue guidance to public bodies, including local education authorities and further and higher education institutions, on how they might contribute to the pursuit of the purpose of the Act. The Act also provides for the appointment of a national VAW Adviser to the Welsh Government to drive improvements in planning and delivery of services for victims and survivors of GBV. Within this role, the Adviser will brief Ministers, improve joint working among public bodies and, most importantly, measure accountability (Welsh Government, 2015).

The Welsh Government's *National Strategy on Violence against Women, Domestic Abuse and Sexual Violence 2016–2021*, which sets out what the Welsh Government will do to contribute to the pursuit of the purpose of the 2015 Act, aims to improve prevention, protection and support for people affected by GBV. Three of the six main strategic objectives focus on prevention and include increased awareness and challenging attitudes of GBV across the Welsh population; increased awareness in children and young people of the importance of safe, equal and healthy relationships; and increased focus on holding perpetrators to account and providing opportunities to change their behaviour (Welsh Government, 2016a: 20). The *Good Practice Guide: A Whole Education Approach to Violence against Women, Domestic Abuse and Sexual Violence in Wales*, published in 2016 and developed in conjunction with Welsh Women's Aid, provides a guide for schools and FEIs (further education institutions) on how to develop and deliver a whole education approach to challenging GBV, including ways to integrate this into existing practices and by providing examples of effective practice. This guide highlights the importance of education settings as environments where positive attitudes towards gender equality may be fostered and acknowledges that in the prevention of GBV, a focus on raising awareness among children is central. In recognition that children and young people are educated within other learning settings, guidance for HEIs will be issued separately (Welsh Government, 2016b: 2). The Welsh Government also works with schools, local authorities and regional education consortia to implement and evaluate the implementation of the *National Training Framework on Violence against Women, Domestic Abuse and Sexual Violence*, which outlines the government's requirements for training on these subjects across the public service and specialist third sector. Published in 2016 and one of the key mechanisms for delivering the 2015 Act, the Framework aims to create 'a consistent standard of care' and an 'unfailing standard of service' for victims/survivors of GBV through high quality, standardised public sector training (Welsh Government, 2016c: 5, 6). This ensures that teaching professionals, alongside other service professionals, are aware of the signs of GBV and can respond appropriately, and that effective safeguarding procedures and support services are in place (Welsh Government, 2016a). Overall, the progressive legal framework adopted by the Welsh Government provides a basis from which GBV can be addressed in the round and is an approach unique in the UK.

Scotland

The Scotland Act 1998 gave the Scottish Parliament power to encourage equal opportunities and to ensure the observation of equal opportunity requirements and also the power to impose duties on Scottish public authorities and cross border public bodies operating in Scotland. The Scottish Government's statutory obligations in relation to gender equality derive from the UK Human Rights Act 1998, the Equality Act 2010, the Public Sector Equality Duty 2011 and the more specific requirements of the Gender Equality Duty 2007 (Engender, 2014). VAW is listed as a Ministerial priority in Scotland under the *UK Gender Equality Duty* (Scottish Government, 2010). The Scottish Government has articulated an aspiration to achieve true gender equality in society and to address deep-rooted structural inequalities that prevent women and girls thriving as equal citizens.

Towards this aim, inequality and VAW are addressed through the National Outcome Framework (Scottish Government, 2016b) using a national strategic approach to VAW outlined in *Equally Safe*, the Scottish Government's national strategy for tackling VAWG (Scottish

Government, 2016a). In *Equally Safe*, the Scottish Government and the Scottish Convention of Local Authorities (COSLA), acknowledge the significant individual and social costs of VAWG and the extensive benefits to wider society of effective prevention strategies, and the direct links to gender inequality. From the outset, the Scottish Government policy framework incorporated the UN's gendered definition of VAWG and utilises a gendered analysis of abuse, emphasising the inter-play between gendered power relations and inequalities. In *Equally Safe*, the Scottish Government conceptualises GBV as both a cause and consequence of gender inequality:

> By referring to violence as 'gender based' this definition highlights the need to understand violence within the context of women's and girls' subordinate status in society. Such violence cannot be understood, therefore, in isolation from the norms, social structure and gender roles within the community, which greatly influence women's vulnerability to violence. (Scottish Government, 2016a: 10)

The Scottish Government identifies a broad range of public and private forms of gendered interpersonal violence and abuse including physical, sexual and psychological violence. *Equally Safe* maintains this gendered analysis and articulates a pivotal emphasis on institutionalising its national approach across the country. This national approach has been recognised as a progressive and identifiably 'Scottish Model' for the prevention and elimination of GBV (Coy et al, 2008; Coy and Kelly, 2009). The approach stresses partnership working and outlines medium- and long-term goals for achieving gender equality through primary and secondary prevention, early intervention and a robust criminal justice response to perpetrators. For the period 2016–17 the Scottish Government committed over £30 million of central funding to support the implementation of *Equally Safe*. This continues its longstanding commitment to provide central funding for specialist domestic abuse and rape crisis services, national helplines, VAWG prevention and research, and reforming the justice system.

GBV in UK universities: current developments

The prevalence and impact of GBV experienced by women and girls in UK higher education contexts has remained a neglected topic until very recently (Bows et al, 2015). Due to increasing national and international attention focused on the issue of sexual harassment and violence in recent years, alongside a growth in student campaigning, there is growing pressure on UK universities to respond to GBV and increasing scrutiny of the ways in which they are currently doing so (Goldhill, 2015). In 2015, Durham University's Sexual Violence Task Force examined existing policy and practice in relation to sexual violence prevention and response, while the University of Sussex recently published an independent review into a high profile domestic abuse case between a student and member of university staff (Westmarland, 2017). With a broader remit, the 2016 *Changing the Culture* report published by Universities UK scrutinised VAW, as well as harassment and hate crime, affecting university students and its findings support a crime prevention focus. Collectively, this work marks a turning point in HEIs attention to GBV. Though the primary focus has been sexual violence among student populations, sexual violence interconnects with, and influences, other forms of gendered violence, harassment and abuse (Stockdale and Nadler, 2012) and is not limited to students. University staff are also affected by such violence as both victims and perpetrators (Westmarland, 2017).

This growing body of work has also revealed that, all too often, universities lack a consistent, effective and systematic response to incidents of GBV. Issues of sexual harassment and violence tend to be dealt with within broader and more general harassment policies (Bows et al, 2015). Without specific codes for sexual misconduct, evidence suggests that students are often unaware of the correct procedure to report incidents or how universities will manage them, placing a significant barrier to seeking help (Universities UK, 2016a). Furthermore, how HEIs manage issues of sexual misconduct under internal regulations has also been subject to criticism, as there have been ongoing concerns about the contemporary relevance of what is commonly known as the Zellick guidelines. Created in 1994 by the Council for Vice-Chancellors and Principals (CVCP, now Universities UK) in a response to a high profile case rape case, it provided advice to HEIs on handling alleged student misconduct which may also constitute a criminal offence. One of the most contentious issues in relation to the Zellick guidelines was the recommendation that rape and sexual assault should never be investigated via internal disciplinary procedures until the complaint is formally reported to the police (NUS, 2015). While not strictly legislation, these non–statutory guidelines are what some universities continue to use as a basis for internal disciplinary procedures (Universities UK, 2016b). However, due to increased criticism, including a campaign by the NUS launched in November 2015 (#StandByMe) which called upon HEIs to reject the Zellick guidelines and called for the creation of new robust reporting and disciplinary guidelines and survivor support, these original Zellick guidelines have recently been updated, as detailed below (NUS Connect, 2015; Universities UK, 2016b).

A further rationale for the update was that there has been tremendous social, cultural and technological developments since 1994, including the role and use of social media in contemporary society, specifically in relation to online abuse and harassment, as well as significant legislative changes, such as the Human Rights Act 1998 and Equality Act 2010. The recommendation that HEIs should never investigate or conduct internal disciplinary procedures until an incident has been reported to the police and outcomes are concluded could be classed as discrimination under the latter, in which universities are required to give 'due regard' to advancing equality of opportunity and to eliminating discrimination, harassment and victimisation (Equality and Diversity Forum, 2010). A ruling under the Equality Act 2010 confirmed that this includes HEI decisions about their policies and practices on VAW (which includes bullying and harassment), governance of student societies and sports teams, campus security, housing, bars and social spaces. The duty applies to decisions on individual cases, as well as policy decisions.

The 1994 Zellick recommendations also demonstrated a lack of understanding of the nature of GBV and the different forms which may affect students, including partner violence/abuse, revenge porn, commercial sexual exploitation and forms of violence such as FM (forced marriage) (Chantler et al, 2017). Evidence shows that the vast majority of incidents or experiences of sexual violence are not reported, and those that are reported can involve protracted and often distressing legal proceedings (NUS, 2015). Under the original Zellick guidelines, the majority of victims of sexual violence could expect no action by their institution if they did not report to the police. The outcome of this approach is that the victim becomes responsible for managing any potential and ongoing risk posed by the alleged perpetrator. By failing to respond effectively, or at all, HEIs are also leaving other students and staff potentially at risk (NUS Connect, 2016). Moreover, statistical and anecdotal evidence suggests that victims of sexual violence consider leaving and often do leave their studies: the NUS (2011: 4) found that 13% of victims of serious sexual assault reported that they considered leaving their course. When women and girls are denied access to education due to acts, or threats, of violence, this contributes to the maintenance of wider female equality (and is prohibited under UK law, see Whitfield, Chapter Seven in this volume). A further criticism of the original Zellick guidelines was that there seemed to be an emphasis on HEIs protecting themselves from legal challenges and reputational damage rather than recognising their duty of care to create a safe environment for students (and staff). This remains an important, and unresolved, issue in the context of the increasing marketisation and pursuance of a neoliberal agenda within the HEI sector (Phipps and Young, 2015) and the construction of students' rights as consumers under consumer protection law (HE Consumer Compliance Team, 2015).

In response to some of the criticism discussed above, Universities UK have reviewed the Zellick guidelines and issued new guidance for HEIs on handling alleged student misconduct which may also constitute a criminal offence, with some specific recommendations in relation to sexual misconduct (Universities UK, 2016b). Significantly, the new recommendations emphasise that universities have a duty of care to all students whether or not they choose to report to the police (Universities UK, 2016b). A clear distinction is drawn between internal university disciplinary processes and external criminal procedures and stresses that universities cannot determine criminality, but can invoke disciplinary procedures on the balance of probabilities (Universities UK, 2016b).

Concluding remarks

Theoretical frameworks

HEIs in the four nations of the UK are governed by both national and local policy guidelines. We recommend the adoption of the theoretical framework that conceptualises these forms of abuse/violence as gendered behaviours and manifestations of gender inequality, as that taken by the Scottish and Welsh Governments. Only a gendered analysis and a whole sector response can ever provide a truly effective response to both supporting victim/survivors and challenging perpetrators. Individual level change will be harder to achieve without wider attitudinal change and shifting of social norms and values to a truly inclusive society with genuine equality. We therefore endorse a gendered definition and understanding of GBV and argue that this must not be diluted in a misguided attempt at inclusivity.

It is apposite to be reminded that violence and abuse against women and girls continue because wider cultural beliefs support this behaviour and because in the majority of cases, perpetrators act with impunity. Therefore, universities must challenge wider sexist norms, problematic 'lad cultures' and gender inequality to send out a clear message that GBV is incompatible with these wider cultural norms. Furthermore, as Kelly (1988) argued, often these acts of abuse and or violence are not isolated or discrete events. HEI policies must genuinely cover the wider forms of GBV including, for example, intimate partner abuse, forced marriage, commercial sexual exploitation and homophobic violence in addition to the narrower focus on sexual violence (Stockdale and Nadler, 2012). HEIs must also be mindful that staff as well as students must be equally protected and have clear and supportive reporting pathways and institutional response.

Intervention

We suggest that universities must learn from good practice by becoming involved in local coordinated community responses to GBV. This ranges from ensuring that HEIs are involved in local VAWG partnerships and services; that the expertise of specialised services such as Women's Aid and Rape Crisis must be protected and supported and sought by universities; that the criminal justice model is mindful of the special dynamics involved in GBV, is supportive of victims and punitive towards perpetrators, and works with the local HEIs. Furthermore, HEIs must be proactive, rather than reactive, in developing progressive policy responses which involves strategic leadership. Equally, this must be joint activity with student and staff representatives and bodies. The ultimate aim is to have clear student and staff GBV misconduct procedures that are accessible to all staff to enforce. This is crucial as it is clear that a crime focused approach is not sufficient. On a contextual level, HEIs must address wider gender inequalities and culture/s which sustain GBV whether this is challenging problematic 'lad cultures' in the union bar or structural inequalities such as the lack of women in senior management positions and the gender pay gap.

Prevention

One of the positive prevention strategies being emphasised is the adoption of a whole systems approach to GBV. For example, the authors are currently working to implement *Equally Safe* in a higher education setting at the University of Strathclyde. This project will: develop research tools for investigating campus-based GBV in HEIs; review the extent of GBV prevention work in Scottish universities; identify examples of good practice and incorporate these into a national *Equally Safe in HE* Toolkit. This will be made freely available across

Scotland and has the potential to be adapted for use in further education and other organisational settings. This whole-system approach to prevention presents opportunities for curriculum-based GBV education and prevention work. Perhaps a more entrenched barrier to overcome is created by prevailing social norms which prevent a wider public recognition that GBV occurs across public and private space, across the life span and is pervasive and insidious.

Next steps

Within an emerging field of research into GBV on campus, the essential elements of an effective approach to preventing and responding to GBV in university settings is emerging. Fenton and Mott (2015), for example, argue that universities need to address policy, prevention and intervention; provide and signpost specialist support, and foster cultural change through training and bystander programmes, all in partnership with student unions, other student-led organisations and the VAW sector (Fenton and Mott, 2015; Fenton et al, 2015; Fenton et al, 2016). This might include a distinct policy that specifically addresses all forms of GBV, and that outlines reporting and recording procedures, support pathways and the sanctions perpetrators will face. Other strategies might include first responder training and support for all/relevant staff, and on campus specialist support. The *Changing the Culture* report likewise provided recommendations to support universities effectively and strategically in addressing sexual harassment and violence. Suggestions include a commitment from senior leadership and an institution-wide approach to addressing the issue, evidence-based bystander intervention programmes, clear and accessible disclosure responses, staff training, and partnerships with local specialist services. To respond effectively, universities are recommended to consider the various immediate and long-term support needs of reporting students and alleged perpetrators, and to ensure that their response is flexible and tailored to the individual and often complex circumstances of each case, irrespective of the age, gender identity, ethnicity and sexuality of the victim/survivor (Universities UK, 2016a). Overall, HEIs have a clear responsibility and duty of care to respond effectively and sensitively to any student or member of staff affected by GBV, and a systematic, all-encompassing and joined up institution-wide approach is recommended.

References

Ball, W. and Charles, N. (2006) 'Feminist social movements and policy change: Devolution, childcare and domestic violence policies in Wales', *Women's Studies International Forum*, 29 (2): 172–83.

Berry, V., Stanley, N., Radford, L., McCarry, M. and Larkins, C. (2014) *Building Effective Responses: An Independent Review of Violence against Women, Domestic Abuse and Sexual Violence Services in Wales*, Welsh Government Social Research, Number 45/2014. http://gov.wales/statistics-and-research/building-effective-responses-independent-review-violence-against-women/?lang=en

Bows, H., Burrell, S. and Westmarland, N. (2015) *Rapid Evidence Assessment of Current Interventions, Approaches, and Policies on Sexual Violence on Campus*, Durham: Durham University Sexual Violence Task Force, www.dur.ac.uk/resources/svtf/DUSVTFRAEfinalpdfversion.pdf

Breitenbach, E. and Mackay, F. (2001) *Women and Contemporary Scottish Politics: An Anthology*, Edinburgh: Edinburgh University Press.

Brown, A., Donaghy, T.B., Mackay, F. and Meehan, E. (2002) 'Women and Constitutional Change in Scotland and Northern Ireland', *Parliamentary Affairs*, 55 (1): 71–84.

Chantler, K., Baker, V., Mackenzie, M., McCarry, M. and Mirza, N. (2017) *Understanding Forced Marriage in Scotland*, Social Research. Edinburgh: Scottish Government.

Connolly, L. (1999) 'Feminist politics and the peace process', *Capital and Class*, 23 (3): 145–59.

Coy, M. and Kelly, L. (2009) *Map of Gaps 2; the Postcode Lottery of Violence against Women Support Services in Britain*, London: End Violence Against Women Equalities and Human Rights Commission, https://www.researchgate.net/publication/316789565_Map_of_Gaps_2_The_postcode_lottery_of_Violence_Against_Women_support_services_in_Britain

Coy, M., Lovett, J. and Kelly, L. (2008*) Realising Rights, Fulfilling Obligations: A Template for an Integrated Strategy on Violence against Women for the UK End Violence Against Women*, https://www.researchgate.net/publication/322421472_Realising_Rights_Fulfilling_Obligations_A_Template_for_an_Integrated_Strategy_on_Violence_Against_Women_for_the_UK

DHSSPSNI and DoJNI (2016) *Stopping Domestic and Sexual Violence and Abuse in Northern Ireland A Seven Year Strategy*, www.health-ni.gov.uk/sites/default/files/publications/dhssps/stopping-domestic-sexual-violence-ni.pdf

Dobash, R.E. and Dobash, R.P. (1992) *Women, violence, and social change,* London: Routledge.

Durham University (2015) *Durham University's Sexual Violence Task Force: A Higher Education Initiative to Address Sexual Violence and Misconduct on Campus – A Guide for Staff and Student HE Leaders in How the Issue of Sexual Violence and Misconduct May be Addressed in a University Environment,* www.neevawg.org.uk/sites/default/files/SVTF%20brochure%20PROOF%20(1).pdf

Engender (2014) *Gender Equality and Scotland's Constitutional Futures,* https://www.engender.org.uk/content/publications/Gender-equality-and--Scotlands-constitutional-futures.pdf

Equality and Diversity Forum (2010) 'Pieretti v Enfield Borough Council [2010] EWCA 1104', 12 October, www.edf.org.uk/blog/0080-pieretti-v-london-borough-of-enfield/

Fenton, R.A. and Mott, H.L. (2015) *Strategy for Addressing Sexual and Domestic Violence in Universities: Prevention and Response,* http://socialsciences.exeter.ac.uk/research/interventioninitiative/universities/violencepreventionstrategy/

Fenton, R.A., Mott, H.L. and Rumney, P.N.S. (2015) *The Intervention Initiative: Theoretical Rationale,* http://socialsciences.exeter.ac.uk/research/interventioninitiative/toolkit/

Fenton, R.A., Mott, H.L., McCartan, K. and Rumney, P.N.S. (2016) *A Review of the Evidence for Bystander Intervention to Prevent Sexual Assault and Domestic Violence in Universities,* London: Public Health England, www.gov.uk/government/uploads/system/uploads/attachment_data/file/515634/Evidence_review_bystander_intervention_to_prevent_sexual_and_domestic_violence_in_universities_11April2016.pdf

Garcia-Moreno, C., Heise, L., Jansen, H.A.F.M., Ellsberg, M. and Watts, C. (2005) 'Violence Against Women', *Science,* 310 (5752): 1282–3.

Goldhill, O. (2015) 'Sexual assault at university: MPs demand clearer policies to protect students', *Telegraph,* 15 January, http://www.telegraph.co.uk/women/womens-life/11343380/Sexually-assault-1-in-3-UK-female-students-victim-on-campus.html

Gray, A.M. and Neill, G. (2011) 'Creating a Shared Society in Northern Ireland: Why We Need to Focus on Gender Equality', *Youth and Society,* 43(2): 468–87.

Hanmer, J. (1978) 'Violence and the social control of women', in G. Littlejohn, B. Smart, J. Wakeford and N. Yuval-Davis (eds) *Power and the State,* California: Croom Helm.

Hanmer, J. (1996) 'Women and violence: Commonalities and diversities' in B. Fawcett and B. Featherstone (eds) *Violence and Gender Relations: Theories and Interventions*, pp 7–21.

Hanmer, J. and Maynard, M. (eds) (1987) *Women, Violence and Social Control*, London: Macmillan Press.

HE Consumer Compliance Team (2015) 'UK higher education providers – advice on consumer protection law: Helping you comply with your obligations', www.gov.uk/government/uploads/system/uploads/attachment_data/file/428549/HE_providers_-_advice_on_consumer_protection_law.pdf

Hearn, J. and McKie, L. (2008) Gendered policy and policy on gender: the case of 'domestic violence', *Policy and Politics*, 36 (1): 75–91.

Heise, L.L. (1998) 'Violence against women an integrated, ecological framework', *Violence Against Women*, 4(3): 262–90.

Home Office (2013) 'Devolution of powers to Scotland, Wales and Northern Ireland', www.gov.uk/guidance/devolution-of-powers-to-scotland-wales-and-northern-ireland

Home Office (no date) 'The Government's Approach to Crime Prevention – Home Affairs Committee', www.publications.parliament.uk/pa/cm200910/cmselect/cmhaff/242/24205.htm

HM Government (2010) *Call to End Violence Against Women and Girls*, www.gov.uk/government/publications/call-to-end-violence-against-women-and-girls

HM Government (2015) *Ending Violence against Women and Girls Strategy 2016–2020*, www.gov.uk/government/uploads/system/uploads/attachment_data/file/522166/VAWG_Strategy_FINAL_PUBLICATION_MASTER_vRB.PDF

Htun, M. and Weldon, S.L. (2012) 'The Civic Origins of Progressive Policy Change: Combating Violence against Women in Global Perspective, 1975–2005', *American Political Science Review*, 106 (3): 548–69.

Ishkanian, A. (2014) 'Neoliberalism and violence: The Big Society and the changing politics of domestic violence in England', *Critical Social Policy*, 34 (3): 333–53.

Jackson, C. and Sundaram, V. (2015) *Is 'Lad Culture' a Problem in Higher Education? Exploring the Perspectives of Staff Working in UK Universities*, Society for Research into Higher Education, Lancaster University and University of York, www.srhe.ac.uk/downloads/JacksonSundaramLadCulture.pdf

Kelly, L. (1988) *Surviving Sexual Violence*, Cambridge: Polity Press.

Littlejohn, G. (1978) *Power and the State*, Oxford: Taylor and Francis.

Lovenduski, J. (2012) 'Feminising British Politics' *The Political Quarterly*, 83 (4): 697–702.

Mackay, F. (2010) 'Gendering constitutional change and policy outcomes: substantive representation and domestic violence policy in Scotland', *Policy and Politics*, 38 (3): 369–88.

Mackay, F. and McAllister, L. (2012) 'Feminising British Politics: Six Lessons from Devolution in Scotland and Wales', *Political Quarterly*, 83 (4): 730–34.

McCarry, M., Larkins, C., Berry, V., Radford, L. and Stanley, N. (2017) 'The Potential for Co-production in Violence Against Women Service Provision: Combining Views from Users and Providers in Wales', *Social Policy and Society*, https://doi.org/10.1017/S1474746417000070NUS Connect (2015) '#StandByMe – Supporting Student Survivors', 23 September, www.nusconnect.org.uk/articles/standbyme-supporting-student-survivors--2

National Union of Students (NUS) (2011) *Hidden Marks: A Study of Women Students' Experiences of Harassment, Stalking, Violence and Sexual Assault*, www.nus.org.uk/global/nus_hidden_marks_report_2nd_edition_web.pdf

NUS (2012) *That's What She Said: Women Students' Experiences of 'Lad Culture' in Higher Education*, www.nus.org.uk/Global/Campaigns/That's%20what%20she%20said%20full%20report%20Final%20web.pdf

NUS (2015) *How to Respond to Complaints of Sexual Violence: The Zellick Report*, http://universityappg.co.uk/sites/default/files/field/attachment/NUS%20Zellick%20report%20briefing.pdf

NUS Connect (2016) 'Access Denied: Universities are failing survivors of sexual assault', 20 January, www.nusconnect.org.uk/articles/access-denied-universities-are-failing-survivors-of-sexual-assault

Phipps, A. (2010) 'Violent and victimized bodies: Sexual violence policy in England and Wales', *Critical Social Policy*, 30 (3): 359–83.

Rape Crisis Scotland (2015) 'Facts about Sexual Violence', www.rapecrisisscotland.org.uk/help-information/facts/

Phipps, A. and Smith, G. (2012) 'Violence against women students in the UK: time to take action', *Gender and Education*, 24 (4): 357–73.

Phipps, A. and Young, I. (2015) 'Neoliberalisation and 'lad cultures' in higher education', *Sociology*, 49 (2): 305–22.

Samarasekera, U. and Horton, R. (2015) 'Prevention of violence against women and girls: a new chapter', *The Lancet*, 385 (9977): 1480–82.

Scottish Government (2009) *Safe Lives: Change Lives: A Shared Approach to Tackling Violence Women in Scotland*, http://www.gov.scot/Publications/2009/06/02153519/0

Scottish Government (2010) *Equality Duty Detailed Proposals: Consultation on Public Sector Equality Duty Draft Regulations and Order*, www.gov.scot/Publications/2010/09/13094828/12

Scottish Government (2016a) *Equally Safe – Scotland's Strategy for Preventing and Eliminating violence against Women and Girls*, https://beta.gov.scot/publications/equally-safe/

Scottish Government (2016b) *The National Performance Framework*, http://www.gov.scot/About/Performance/scotPerforms/pdfNPF

Stark, E. (2007) *Coercive Control: The Entrapment of Women in Personal Life*, Oxford: Oxford University Press.

Stockdale, M.S, and Nadler, J.T. (2012) 'Situating Sexual Harassment in the Broader Context of Interpersonal Violence: Research, Theory and Policy Implications', *Social Issues and Policy Review*, 6(1): 148–76.

UK Parliament (2017) 'House of Commons Private Members' Bills: 24 February 2017', www.parliament.uk/business/news/2017/february/commons-private-members-bills-24-february-2017/

United Nations (1994) 'United Nations General Assembly RESOLUTION 48/104 20 December 1993 Declaration on the Elimination of Violence against Women', *International Journal of Refugee Law*, 6(4): 714–18.

Universities UK (2015) *Patterns and Trends in UK Higher Education*, www.universitiesuk.ac.uk/policy-and-analysis/reports/Documents/2015/patterns-and-trends-2015.pdf

Universities UK (2016a) *Changing the Culture: Report of the Universities UK Taskforce Examining Violence Against Women, Harassment and Hate Crime Affecting University Students*, www.universitiesuk.ac.uk/policy-and-analysis/reports/Documents/2016/changing-the-culture.pdf

Universities UK (2016b) *Guidance for Higher Education Institutions: How to Handle Alleged Student Misconduct Which May Also Constitute a Criminal Offence*, www.universitiesuk.ac.uk/policy-and-analysis/reports/Documents/2016/guidance-for-higher-education-institutions.pdf

Walby, S. (2011) 'The Impact of Feminism on Sociology', *Sociological Research Online*, 16 (3): 21.

Walby, S., Towers, J. and Francis, B. (2014) 'Mainstreaming domestic and gender-based violence into sociology and the criminology of violence', *The Sociological Review*, 62 (S2), 187–214.

Ward, R. (2004) 'Gender issues and the representation of women in Northern Ireland', *Irish Political Studies*, 19 (2): 1–20. Welsh Government (2015) Violence against Women, Domestic Abuse and Sexual Violence (Wales) Act 2015, www.senedd.assembly.wales/mgIssueHistoryHome.aspx?IId=10028&AIID=17668

Welsh Government (2016a) *National Strategy on Violence against Women, Domestic Abuse and Sexual Violence – 2016–2021,* http://gov.wales/docs/dsjlg/publications/commsafety/161104-national-strategy-en.pdf

Welsh Government (2016b) *Good Practice Guide: A Whole Education Approach to Violence against Women, Domestic Abuse & Sexual Violence in Wales,* http://gov.wales/docs/dsjlg/publications/commsafety/151020-whole-education-approach-good-practice-guide-en.pdf

Welsh Government (2016c) *The National Training Framework on violence against women, domestic abuse and sexual violence,* http://gov.wales/docs/dsjlg/publications/commsafety/160317-national-training-framework-guidance-en.pdf

Westmarland, N. (2017) *Independent Review into The University of Sussex's Response to Domestic Violence,* http://www.sussex.ac.uk/broadcast/read/38671

Section III
Challenges and interventions in the UK

6

Student feminist activism to challenge gender based violence

Ruth Lewis and Susan Marine

Introduction

In the midst of growing attention to and concern about gender based violence (GBV) in universities, a key piece in the jigsaw of responses to GBV are student activists who resist GBV and supporting cultures. This activism has attracted criticism from some quarters which caricatures students as delicate, precious and easily offended, resorting to silencing those they deem to cause offence, thereby threatening freedom of speech. In this environment where voicing resistance, silencing, and freedom of speech are coexisting realities, this chapter explores how feminist communities help young feminists to find their voice to say the unsayable and to speak out about GBV.

Universities, gender based violence and feminist activism

As established elsewhere in this book, GBV in universities has emerged as a social, policy and scholarly concern in the UK significantly later than in some other parts of the world. The advantage of this delayed attention is that we can learn from developments elsewhere. For example, while Title IX in the US may seem to provide a legal framework of accountability that UK activists can only dream of, recent commentaries identify the limitations of this approach (Harris and Linder, 2017; Marine and Nicolazzo, 2017). These include the mechanistic way that Title IX has come to be used in the context of campus GBV, by universities driven more by the desire to protect their status and reputation than their students. These mechanistic approaches are symptomatic of an 'audit culture' or 'compliance culture' which prioritises procedures and processes (have staff completed their allotted tasks?) rather than outcomes (are students safe?), and is characteristic of the galloping neoliberal encroachment of universities. Although universities are protected from some aspects of wider economic forces (for example, in the UK universities have not been as devastated by 'austerity measures' as have most other public sector bodies), they are by no means immune to neoliberalism's tentacles (McRobbie, 2009; Martínez-Alemán, 2014; Phipps and Young, 2015; Gill and Donaghue, 2016). The marketisation of universities and commodification of degrees come together with the deadening hand of audit cultures to interpret legislation such as Title IX in ways that arguably subvert its progressive potential. Moreover, the commodification of higher education generates an instrumental approach among students; there is a risk, familiar to many of us working in universities, that students do not engage with wider activities which seem not to directly improve grades and 'employability'. This risk may be sharper in the non–elite universities where the resources available to students are more limited and the financial pressures on students are greater. Witnessing such developments in the US must surely make us in the UK consider whether legalistic, administrative procedures can help us achieve our goal – freedom from GBV. In this chapter we argue that, in addition to developing effective systems of accountability, progressive responses also lie in student activism to resist GBV and create cultures which support freedom, resistance, and respect.

It is reassuring to see that, despite the challenges posed by mounting neoliberalism in universities, student activism is surviving and flourishing as part of a wider resurgence in feminism in and beyond the UK (Dean and Aune, 2015). A key focus of this activism is the drive to witness, name and challenge GBV, particularly as it is embodied in student communities. This manifests as what is often termed 'lad culture' (Phipps and Young, 2015), or 'rape culture' (Lazarus and Wunderlick, 1975). Students are coming together to form communities – typically called feminist societies – which are at the centre of principled resistance to sexist norms. Strengthened and informed by feminist communities, students resist and challenge the attitudes, behaviours and institutional practices that support GBV, develop their pragmatic and theoretical approaches to GBV, and hold universities and perpetrators to account. However, to date, more scholarly and media attention has been paid to the problem itself, rather than to resistance to it. To address this lacuna, this chapter explores how students come together in feminism to resist and challenge GBV, and the ways that community building and connection foster their work.

These resistive initiatives continue a long history of the university as a site for radical politics including feminism (Rhoads, 1998; Joseph, 2003; Naples and Bojar, 2013; Arthur, 2016). While universities are far from representative of class-diverse communities and so have been rightly criticised for generating an elitist form of politics, their position as sites of intellectual endeavour where political positions can be tried and tested in relative safety makes them an important source of social change, where new understanding, behaviours, identities and cultures can be imagined, developed and practised. However, Mohanty warns, in her critique of '"post" frameworks' (2013: 968) which privatise social divisions and individualise experience, that

> neoliberal intellectual culture may well constitute a threshold of disappearance for feminist, antiracist thought anchored in the radical social movements of the twentieth century. Radical theory can in fact become a commodity to be consumed; no longer seen as a product of activist scholarship or connected to emancipatory knowledge, it can circulate as a sign of prestige in an elitist, neoliberal landscape. (2013: 971)

Mohanty's call to arms to locate scholarship about activism in sites of activism guides our discussion of student activism against GBV.

Despite some media attention to contemporary feminist activism in universities (for example Pearce, 2014) and to the problems of GBV in universities (for example Younis, 2014) there has been relatively little scholarly attention paid to student activism against GBV, but we contend that it is important to document, understand and analyse this activism. The temporality of student activism makes it rather slippery to pin down; the student body regenerates every three or four years and students typically engage in extra-curricular activities such as feminist activism for only a fraction of their time at university, so the legacy of each generation is easily lost. Documenting each generation's work, in terms of community building and support for individuals to develop their politics, policy work, activities and campaigns, is essential to enable development from one generation to another. Without this sense of a legacy, of ongoing development and growth of the student activism between different cohorts, students can be easily 'bought off' by university administration who might provide superficial responses to student demands without committing to the longer-term, organisational and cultural change required to prevent GBV.

Moreover, documenting this activism is an important part of 'claiming' emerging discourses. Student activism against GBV is part of the discourse that is generated about and around GBV, although activists are themselves rarely in control of how they and their activism are recorded; the currency in stereotypes about feminists and feminist activism is testament to this (see, for example, Tomlinson, 2010). Gill (2016: 615) notes 'how different feminisms *materialise in media culture*' (emphasis in original), augmenting the presence of (neoliberal) 'feminism' in mainstream media, but argues that, with the exception of SlutWalk, contemporary feminist activism 'has generated relatively limited coverage' (p 616). She argues that the 'new feminist visibilities' appropriate concepts (such as 'empowerment' and 'choice') and symbols (such as the feminist 'fist') which resonate with feminism while promoting a distinctly anti-feminist ideology and, indeed, 'foment[ing] generational discord about feminism' (p 619). Similarly, we should be wary of discourses about GBV which are not embedded in student experiences of both GBV and of activism against it; instead, we contend that we should strive to put activists at the centre of our analysis of activism. However, some recent commentary has only added to these partial, problematic depictions of the feminist student, as we discuss in the following section.

The 'precious', 'protected' feminist student

Student feminist activity has been swept up in contemporary discussion about how we communicate in universities. Recent calls for trigger warnings and advocacy for safe spaces have been criticised as imposing limitations on intellectual freedom, including freedom of speech (McMurtrie, 2016). In some coverage of this debate (which rages particularly strongly in US media and scholarship; see for example, the collection of papers in *First Amendment Studies*, 30 (1)), contemporary students who call for teaching about trauma – such as sexual violence and racism – to be more sensitive to the effects on students have been depicted as 'coddled' (Lukianoff and Haidt, 2015), unable to deal with the harsh realities of life. Others express concern about the consequences of this development; although '[a]t first glance, these requests seem reasonable because at the core they are asking for a respectful atmosphere in which insults are not tolerated and student vulnerabilities respected', trigger warnings may keep students 'embedded in a culture of victimization' (Robbins, 2016).

In the UK, debates about freedom of speech in universities have highlighted the restrictive practice of 'no platforming' controversial speakers in university environments. Julie Bindel and Germaine Greer are infamous recent casualties of this practice which reflects how 'feelings have become a new political commodity ... in debates in which hurt feelings are used as currency' (Phipps, 2014: 15). Indeed, what some call causing offence is seen by others to be committing a microaggression (Sue, 2010), to which no platforming is a legitimate response. 'Traditionally about rejecting the rhetoric of violence; especially by far-right organisations, no-platforming is now used to avoid "offence"' (Ditum, 2014). Others have compellingly argued that 'no platforming' and other resistance strategies reveal the privileging of free speech at university as the domain of white men (Fenton, 2016).

These debates about trigger warnings and safe spaces, freedom of speech, and no platforming are complex, heated and polarised; there are no simple resolutions and a fuller discussion is beyond the scope of this chapter. We simply note that feminism has a long and proud history of saying the unsayable about 'offensive' things such as men's violence against women and girls, menstruation and childbirth, women's anger and their sexual desires – things that have been deemed 'shameful' and for which women have traditionally carried the burden of shame. Indeed, it is feminist work that has created a new vocabulary to name 'unsayable' offences against women, bringing them out from under the shroud of euphemisms such as 'domestic dispute', 'interfered with', 'seduction', to name them as 'intimate partner violence', 'child sexual abuse' and 'sexual assault'. While 'no platforming' and advocacy for safe spaces and trigger warnings can be valid and valuable in fighting oppression, we should also exercise caution in accepting simplistic narratives about 'taking offence', given that progressive social change has been achieved partly through 'offensive' speaking out by feminists.

It may be more fruitful to explore what purpose is served by these polarised public debates. Analysing 'the trope of the angry feminist', Tomlinson (2010: 33) argues that 'arguments about inappropriate affect are discursive technologies of power deployed strategically to suppress claims for social justice'. This analysis could equally apply to debates which emphasise the 'preciousness' of contemporary students, rather than their active engagement with and resistance to behaviours and cultures that inflict real harm. The attention to a particular range of activism (calls for no platforming, safe spaces and trigger warnings) focuses attention away from other forms of student activism against GBV (such as awareness-raising campaigns, demands for support services, fundraising for services) and simultaneously trivialises students' demands. Just as Gill (2016: 618) illuminates the media attention paid to 'celebrity and style feminism' at the expense of the myriad diverse topics addressed by contemporary feminist activism, and as Tomlinson (2010: 1) demonstrates that the trope of the angry feminist serves to 'foreclose feminist futures', the attention to trigger warnings and safe spaces in university environments serves to undermine the legitimacy of student activism against harms.

Contemporary student activism against GBV, then, occurs in a wider context of efforts to reconfigure the university environment. These efforts are subject to considerable critique, critique which sometimes has a patronising, dismissive tone, depicting young feminist sensibilities as 'precious'. While we share unease with some aspects of attempts to remove 'offence' from public debate, we also recognise that calls for greater sensitivity in how we communicate about traumatic experiences, such as sexual and domestic violence, reflect attempts to imagine cultures devoid of GBV and other forms of oppression.

Feminism in community

Activism happens in communities. Social movements thrive in and through communities of activists joined in struggle. Relationships, coalitions and connections have held a particular significance for feminist social movements. In universities, feminists are building communities of like-minded peers, coming together to develop their own and each other's understandings, identities, politics (we explore this in more detail in Marine and Lewis, 2017). Communities can help generate activist networks and collective identities (Taylor, Whittier and Morris, 1992; Hercus, 1999). They can be a source of emotional sustainability for activists and social movements (Brown and Pickerill, 2009). They can also 'reproduce sameness' as Rowe (2008) shows in her study of women academics whose differential investments in institutional power led white women to conceive of alliances with black women as 'difficult' and 'challenging'. Rowe's call for meaningful, authentic engagement with difference echoes Mohanty's (2013) warnings that a postmodern focus on difference distracts from radical critiques of power.

It is from feminist communities that much activism against GBV emerges, as individuals support each other to learn about GBV and about feminism, to change the normative narrative of blaming victims and exonerating perpetrators, to imagine worlds without GBV, and to experiment with small and large scale interventions to achieve those worlds on campus. In the midst of debates about the changing university environment, freedom of speech and the emergence of GBV as a matter of political, public and scholarly concern, this chapter explores how women students come together in feminist communities to challenge GBV in universities. The following section briefly outlines the research project from which findings are presented, and then analyses students' accounts of their feminist communities and of their activism.

Methods

The data discussed here are derived from a study about students' accounts of feminist identity, activism and community in UK and US universities. The participants in this study, 34 in total, represented a wide range of identities, including social class, racial/ethnic, sexual orientation, fields of study, years in school, and dis/ability statuses. Guiding questions shaping our inquiry included: how did you come to understand yourself as a feminist? What influences shaped your feminist identity? How do you live out feminism in your everyday life? Our sample was drawn from university students and recent graduates who self-identified as feminists, primarily through networks in feminist societies (in the UK) and women's centres (in the US). During the initial coding process of the in-depth interview data, 14 broad themes were identified and refined to make meaning of the students' perspectives. Key themes, explored in the following sections, were the importance of feminist space for exploring and refining one's ideas with like-minded others. For the purposes of this book's exploration of the current UK context with respect to GBV, we focus our discussion solely on the data yielded by the UK participants.

Findings

Students' resistance to GBV

In our research GBV was a common concern among participants, regardless of their own experiences. Some had experienced aspects of GBV before or at university, some were shocked to find 'laddish' cultures on campus, having expected university cultures to be more enlightened. As Laura, a white, straight-identified student bemoaned, "I thought it would be better here and I got to [university name] and it's really laddish". Similarly, Olivia, who identified as white and gay, found "this university is totally diabolical in terms of the rife sexism that is everywhere". Their experiences of the spectrum of GBV included: having drinks 'spiked' (presumably with the intention to commit sexual violence); sexual harassment by university staff and students; rapes and victim-blaming responses among their peer group; misogynistic and anti-feminist attitudes and behaviours among students and staff; and social pressures and surveillance of bodies, clothing and appearance.

However, their concern about and motivation to end GBV did not seem to be generated by their personal experiences alone; instead there was a sense in which GBV represents and reflects the state of gender relations and women's lives. While Ferrarro (1996) sees women's fear of sexual assault as a 'master offence' because it explains women's wider fear of victimisation, we suggest that GBV represents a master offence because it symbolises something fundamental about women's oppression and lack of freedom. When asked about her priorities for feminism, Katie, a white, straight woman, expressed this eloquently:

> 'I think the main ones that stand out for me are domestic violence and rape, obviously the most prominent and aggressive ones I think. But I think that's why they appeal to me because, you know, I feel like if you were sort of dropped on this world with no knowledge of society and you were suddenly told that women were married to these men who would constantly beat them and intimidate them and women would just walk the street at the risk of a man jumping out and raping them, you would think what the hell is going on?! How can that happen?'

As they expressed their deep anger and urgent concern about violence against women and girls in all its forms, the feminist student activists located GBV in its context of sexism, misogyny and men's oppression of women and girls. Perhaps reflecting the paucity of policy and scholarly developments about GBV in UK universities, the UK-based participants in this research referred less than the US participants to GBV *on campus*; UK participants spoke more often about the full spectrum – or 'continuum' (Kelly 1987) – of GBV, from the trafficking of women, through domestic violence and sexual harassment to sexual violence. Their orientation focused on their immediate environment in their university but also showed solidarity with women experiencing other forms of GBV. For example, Julie, a white, bisexual woman said "we were doing a campaign, it was about trafficking of women and we were trying to get the government to ratify this agreement to help support women who'd been trafficked to the UK".

Student activism against GBV takes various forms, few are entirely novel, having been used in activism about a range of issues over generations. Participants had been involved in: producing a zine presenting anonymous accounts of ideas and experiences about sex and sexuality, designed to challenge silences and dominant discourses about sex; producing performances of *The Vagina Monologues*; establishing, running and attending feminist groups on- and offline; holding discussion groups, book groups, film showings; joining local Reclaim the Night marches and SlutWalks. This activism aims to provide a counter-narrative to the existing lad culture on campus, and to amplify the voices of the silenced in order to build solidarity and community. Their activism involves saying things traditionally deemed 'unsayable', things that can offend mainstream society.

As they locate the roots of GBV in the attitudes and orientations of individuals and groups, the participants also focused on attitudinal change. They emphasised the importance of not only public campaigns and initiatives such as those listed earlier, but also more intimate, personal, small scale attempts to change attitudes. Many participants told stories of engaging friends, peers, teachers and strangers in discussions about their attitudes and behaviours. For some this one-to-one advocacy meant persuading friends of the importance of feminism. Sally, a white woman who preferred not to disclose her sexuality, took up this mantle gamely:

> 'I think you can choose to either kind of take on the world or take on the bit around you. I think I'm definitely that [the latter] kind of person so even just hearing one of my friends say "I see what you mean and I guess I would identify as one [a feminist]" is really kind of satisfying.'

This kind of one-to-one engagement provides the testing ground for many feminists, and an opportunity to practise one's developing ideas and arguments. It also exposes them to the stigma of being labelled feminist and carrying the burden of being the 'feminist killjoy' (Ahmed, 2010) or, as Olivia puts it, "the boring feminist":

> 'One of my really dear friends just doesn't feel that she can ... ever make those points because she doesn't want to be the boring feminist. And I think well you have to be the boring feminist! Because if you're not that person, if you don't keep making those points, if you just sit in the pub with men and allow them to make sexist jokes constantly, nothing changes. You know even if they think "she's really boring, let's not listen to her, she's very serious about life", then you know, I guess, putting your politics right at the front of your life and not just *thinking* about them but *doing* them in very small ways.'

The courage to 'do' their politics was enhanced by working in communities; resistance to GBV and the attendant attitudes and cultures happens, by and large, in and through feminist communities. Students come together with like-minded others to develop their understanding of gender and to participate in resistance to GBV among other forms of gender oppression. The next section explores their engagement with and creation of feminist communities.

Forging feminist student communities

Building feminist communities, networks and alliances has been an important part of the feminist movement, and of other social movements. Activists and scholars reflect on the joys as well as the tensions and challenges of forging activist friendships, (Rowbotham, 2001; Segal, 2007; DuPlessis and Snitow, 2007; Brown and Pickerill, 2009). Being part of feminist groups, in the wider context of cultures that demean women, particularly feminist women, can have positive impacts on self-esteem, confidence and happiness (Saunders and Kashubeck-West, 2006; Vaccaro, 2009). Indeed, in cultures where young women are constructed as the object of men's judgement, and hostility to feminism is widespread, the act of joining a feminist community is in itself an act of resistance.

While the concept of 'community' is not unproblematic and by definition involves exclusion as well as inclusion, a sense of community was a strong feature of participants' accounts. The experience of community helped them develop their feminist consciousness, politics, values and arguments. It provided an environment in which to pursue serious, informed exploration of feminist ideas, in contrast to the wider society where 'new feminist visibilities' (Gill, 2016) co-opt the language and concepts of feminism while expressing anti-feminist sentiments. Feminist communities can provide a network of like-minded individuals who come together inspired by shared values and dissent from cultural gendered norms. Participants, like Emma (who identified as white and straight), reflected on the value of "finding a group of people that you can talk to and communicate with, that is just a lovely thing, you can't put a price on that, I think that's really nice and having that community". Jess, a black, straight woman valued the fact of the network "just being there and feeling there's other people who feel like I do, and think like I do, that goes a long way, for me. Just that backing, I guess." For Lucy, a white lesbian, the action-orientation of her feminist community provides what she calls a "safe haven"; she notes "although you're sort of moaning about all these issues you feel there are people who are being positive and saying 'right, we do need to address this' and trying to do things about this."

Finding like-minded individuals plays an important role in validating one's subjectivity, including one's values and politics, which might be particularly longed for after the common experience of being a solitary 'feminist killjoy'. Katie was not alone among our sample in feeling solitary in her feminist identification before she came to university when she spoke of her first encounter with the feminist society:

> 'it was so interesting meeting other people who have the same views as you. And a lot of the time, especially before university, because obviously not that many people before the age of 18 class themselves as feminist, I possibly felt as though I was the only one [laughs]. And obviously it's, it's so lovely to meet these other people who have the same views as you and sort of understand your views and you're not alone in thinking that women and men are equal. It's really great to have people that you can talk to about these things and have these discussions about what so interests me and what obviously so interests other people. And it really, sort of, liberates your views and makes you look on a much wider scale of feminism.'

Rowe (2008: 57) describes this search for such connections as a 'yearning': 'each yearning arises from the author's desire to constitute her humanity.' This mutual validation can generate a sense of solidarity and, for some, such as Laura, a new experience of close relationships with women:

> 'So it's been finding women that I can relate to and who aren't going to grind me down in a popularity contest has been a revelation. That's something that I've really enjoyed about [the feminist society].'

While friendships were not an *essential* part of their feminist communities for all our participants, for some, the intersection of their activism and their friendships was an important experience. For example, Emma described an early encounter with what became her feminist network:

> 'I'd just moved to [city] and I didn't really have a group of friends so I met these girls and then I suppose the turning

point in my friendships with them was the SlutWalk – and it was a day like this [good weather], and we went and we made banners up at [neighbourhood] Park, and we had a barbecue and it was just really nice and really cool and we were just hanging out and talking with people who didn't care that I questioned things, and valued that in fact.'

Some participants reflected on these connections as life-enhancing. For example, Julie expressed this in her sense of validation when she found a group of people "who feel the same way about these things as me … It is really, really cool and totalling expanding my life and my knowledge." Feminist communities then, provide important affective benefits of validation, mutual care and friendship. They also enable members to expand their knowledge, understanding and skills, as we discuss in the following section.

Personal development in feminist student communities

Experiencing a feminist student community can provide a valuable opportunity for personal and intellectual development. Participants told us about several positive outcomes: improved self-confidence; enhanced powers of analysis and criticality; greater understanding of the complexities of feminist theory and politics; honed skills in arguing and debating. A very strong theme was the value of argument. In a society which has historically constructed the public domain, political engagement and the art of rhetoric as male (see Beard, 2014), there is a long history to women's silencing in the public sphere. This history clearly impacts on women even in education and even in the 21st century. It was not uncommon for participants to describe feeling close to tears when arguing with passion, a feeling that inhibited their engagement. Others described themselves as feeling unable to articulate an argument and learning from others whom they had encountered in feminist communities.Participants in our research valued the opportunity to engage in rhetorical debate, in order to develop their own understanding and powers of argumentation. For example, Ursula, a white, straight woman, reflecting on being part of a feminist society, said:

'For me it's a really important non-judgemental environment and you can say what you think about feminism, challenge, be challenged, but do so in a comfortable environment.'

A common outcome of engaging in such environments is that students feel bolstered in their feminist views; the combination of being validated by like-minded people and learning more about feminism strengthens their confidence in their politics. Liz, a white, straight woman, reflected on how engagement with a feminist community has strengthened her resolve to say the 'unsayable':

> 'So all of those kinds of issues I think I, I've become more interested in, and less, maybe, frightened to say so as well. Because I think there was a tendency for me when I spoke to people, which was quite rarely, about feminism, because I didn't have a feminist friendship group at all, to be quite careful about what I said for fear of being branded a little bit extreme or off my rocker type thing. And now it's a lot more like I don't mind talking to people about rape statistics, prevention, intervention and consequences and all those things. So I'm not so concerned about whether people think it's appropriate or not.'

Practising the art of argument develops a range of skills, which doubtless have an impact beyond their engagement in feminism. Several participants believed their ability to articulate their arguments had improved. For example, Katie said

> 'I feel as though I can explain what I think a lot better now. Before I came to university I was just like, well you know, women and men are equal and if people were like, well what do you mean by that or what d'you think about this? I was just like, well, I know what I mean but I can't really explain it. And I feel as though my thoughts are a lot more coherent now, with everything to do with feminism I think my views are possibly clearer than they were. So it has developed in that sense I think ... before university I would just get angry and be like well you're wrong! But yeah, now I'm a lot more able to argue my point.'

Discussion

Feminist communities, then, serve an important role in the struggle against GBV. They provide a network of like-minded individuals who, in their mutual validation and support, generate a collective voice that challenges GBV, among other forms of sexism, misogyny and oppression. They provide a testing ground for exploring and developing new ideas, values, and politics, as well as for practising the skills of argument and debate. These are precious sites of resistance for young women students, providing a 'safe haven' from mainstream society which can disparage, demean and objectify them. Such sites provide an opportunity for young women students to find their voice in resisting GBV on campus and beyond. In the flurry of activity at governmental and institutional levels, their role in changing cultures should not be overlooked.

However, galvanising the resistance generated in feminist societies presents some particular challenges. Student societies can be short-lived and leave relatively little trace, as most students complete their degree programmes within four years. Few youthful organisations prioritise documenting and recording their activities; their orientation is more likely to be forward-looking than concerned with leaving a legacy for subsequent groups, let alone for researchers to pore over. This chapter and our other work (Marine and Lewis, 2014, 2017; Lewis and Marine, 2015; Lewis et al, 2016) represents an attempt to record student feminist activism, to supplement the mainstream media accounts of feminism which, as Gill (2016) and McRobbie (2009) argue, appropriate feminist concepts and discourse while promoting anti-feminist ideology, distorting the very meaning of 'feminism'. In additional to scholarship, student bodies, such as the National Union of Students, also have an important role to play in recording contemporary student feminism, and ensuring its legacy survives for new generations of students who wish to resist the behaviours, attitudes and cultures associated with GBV.

By nature of their stage in life, student feminists tend to be relatively inexperienced in their feminism. Our observation in this research is that this inexperience was balanced by tremendous enthusiasm, heartfelt commitment to challenging GBV, among other issues, and excitement about the developing feminist communities they were creating. These emerging experiences of feminism as a movement and a community seemed as important as their developing politics of GBV. There was relatively little analysis of the complexities of different approaches to GBV or of the tensions inherent in feminist politics. Perhaps one-off interviews proved inadequate to explore these complexities. Perhaps our participants were keen to present a 'united front', knowing all too well the negative portrayals and stigma attached to feminism. As we discuss elsewhere (Marine and Lewis, 2017), this study suggests that student feminists' engagement with questions of power and difference, especially related to social identity, may be rather limited in comparison with more established groups of feminists. However, their role in forming feminist communities to challenge cultural and institutional scaffolding of GBV is vital and should not be overlooked by administrators and scholars in their work to dismantle this scaffolding.

Readers may note the lack of racial diversity in the voices represented in this chapter, and indeed, despite extensive efforts to recruit more students who identified as black and minority ethnic (BME) or of colour, we did not accomplish this goal. Given that, with respect to our positionality in this project, we functioned as etic (Creswell, 2013) researchers studying a phenomenon from the outside, we cannot presume that this means that minoritised students are not present or engaged in UK feminist societies or that they are not interested in collective resistance to GBV in universities. However, we can certainly presume that they are under-represented in these groups, as they are in this dataset, and that this lack of representation may reinforce a troubling and persistent concern that feminist communities and organising are often over-focused on white women's interests and concerns. GBV uncontestably affects women of all races, and strong arguments have been advanced that responses to GBV have historically suffered from centring whiteness, reinforcing racialised marginality (Crenshaw 1989). Our failing in this regard reminds us that it is incumbent on white feminists, young and seasoned alike, to consistently self-interrogate, and to examine the communities we create and in which we participate to be more accountable for this erasure.

If universities are serious about preventing GBV and changing the cultures which support it, they also have a role to play in facilitating feminist communities which can resist GBV. In contrast to the 'compliance culture' endemic in higher education institutions (HEIs) more widely, feminist student activism is directed at more profound cultural changes. It is through engagement in feminist communities that student activists develop their individual and collective 'voice' with which to challenge the norms and behaviours which support GBV, through activities designed to change campus cultures. However, the encroaching neoliberalism of HEIs threatens these communities as well as the very institutions of universities. 'Neoliberalism is a value system in which the economic has replaced the intellectual and political and in which the competitive, rational individual predominates over the collective' (Phipps and Young, 2015: 306). As universities are increasingly positioned as 'employability' machines, preparing students for the 'knowledge economy' rather than as sites of intellectual endeavour, and as students, perhaps particularly at non-elite universities, increasingly focus on instrumental education in order to position themselves for paid work, there is a risk these extra-curricular activities fall by the wayside or become attractive to students only for their CV-boosting potential. These threats come just at the moment when longstanding forms of sexism and problematic masculinity are injected with a new energy by the neoliberal values of individualism, competition, anti-intellectualism, and the commodification of sexual activity. In response, now is the moment for universities themselves, together with feminist scholars, to support the development of grassroots feminist organisations that can play an important part in challenging GBV and creating respectful campus cultures.

References

Ahmed, S. (2010) 'Killing joy: Feminism and the history of happiness', *Signs*, 35: 571–94.

Arthur, M.M.L. (2016) *Student Activism and Curricular Change in Higher Education*, London: Routledge.

Beard, M. (2014) 'The public voice of women', *London Review of Books*, 36 (6): 11–14.

Brown, G. and Pickerill, J. (2009) 'Space for emotion in the spaces of activism', *Emotion, Space and Society*, 2 (1): 24–35.

Crenshaw, K. (1989) 'Demarginalizing the intersection of race and sex: A black feminist critique of antidiscrimination doctrine, feminist theory and antiracist politics', *University of Chicago Legal Forum*, 1989 (1):139–67.

Creswell, J.W. (2013) *Qualitative Inquiry and Research Design: Choosing among Five Approaches*, Thousand Oaks, CA: Sage.

Dean, J. and Aune, K. (2015) 'Feminism Resurgent? Mapping Contemporary Feminist Activisms in Europe', *Social Movement Studies*, 14 (4): 375–95.

Ditum, S. (2014) '"No platform" was once reserved for violent fascists. Now it's being used to silence debate', *New Statesman*, 18 March, www.newstatesman.com/sarah-ditum/2014/03/when-did-no-platform-become-about-attacking-individuals-deemed-disagreeable

DuPlessis, R.B. and Snitow, A. (2007) *The Feminist Memoir Project: Voices from Women's Liberation*, New Brunswick, NJ: Rutgers University Press.

Fenton, S. (2016) 'The real enemies of free speech aren't the #RhodesMustFall campaigners – they're the privileged students who oppose them', *Independent*, 5 January, www.independent.co.uk/voices/in-defence-of-trigger-warnings-safe-spaces-and-no-platforming-the-tools-which-threaten-to-make-our-a6797681.html

Ferrarro, K.F. (1996) 'Women's Fear of Victimization: Shadow of Sexual Assault', *Social Forces*, 75 (2): 667–90.

Gill, R. (2016) 'Post-postfeminism? : new feminist visibilities in postfeminist times', *Feminist Media Studies*, 16 (4): 610–30.

Gill, R. and Donaghue, N. (2016) 'Resilience, apps and reluctant individualism: Technologies of self in the neoliberal academy', *Women's Studies International Forum*, 54: 91–9.

Harris, J.C. and Linder, C (eds) (2017) *Intersections of Identity and Sexual Violence on Campus: Centering Minoritized Students' Experiences*, Sterling, VA: Stylus Publishing.

Hercus, C. (1999) 'Identity, emotion, and collective feminist action', *Gender & Society*, 13 (1): 34–55.

Joseph, P.E. (2003) 'Dashikis and democracy: Black studies, student activism, and the black power movement', *The Journal of African American History*, 88 (2): 182–203.

Kelly, L. (1987) 'The continuum of sexual violence', in J. Hamner and M. Maynard (eds) *Women, Violence and Social Control*, Basingstoke: Macmillan, pp 46–60.

Lazarus, M. and Wunderlick, R. (1975) *Rape Culture*, Cambridge Documentary Films.

Lewis, R. and Marine, S. (2015) 'Weaving a tapestry, compassionately: towards an understanding of young women's feminisms', *Feminist Formations*, 27 (1): 118–40.

Lewis, R., Marine, S. and Keeney, K. (2016) '"I get together with my friends and I change it": Young feminist students resist "laddism", "rape culture" and "everyday sexism"', *Journal of Gender Studies*, 27 (1): 56–72.

Lukianoff, G. and Haidt, J. (2015) 'The Coddling of the American Mind', *The Atlantic*, September, www.theatlantic.com/magazine/archive/2015/09/the-coddling-of-the-american-mind/399356/

Marine, S. and Lewis, R. (2014) '"I'm in this for real": Revisiting young women's feminist becoming', *International Women's Studies Forum*, 47: 11–22.

Marine, S. and Lewis, R. (2017) 'Mutuality without alliance: the roles of community in becoming a college feminist', *Gender and Education*, http://dx.doi.org/10.1080/09540253.2017.1332342

Marine, S.B. and Nicolazzo, Z. (2017) 'Campus Sexual Violence Prevention Educators' Use of Gender in their Work: A Critical Exploration', *Journal of Interpersonal Violence*, doi: 10.1177/0886260517718543

Martínez-Alemán, A.M. (2014) 'Managerialism as the "New" Discursive Masculinity in the University', *Feminist Formations*, 26 (2): 107–34.

McMurtrie, B. (2016) 'U. of Chicago's Free-Expression Letter Exposes Fault Lines on Campus', *The Chronicle of Higher Education*, 2 September, www.chronicle.com/article/U-of-Chicago-s/237672

McRobbie, A. (2009) *The Aftermath of Feminism: Gender, Culture and Social Change*, London: Sage.

Mohanty, C.T. (2013) 'Transnational feminist crossings: On neoliberalism and radical critique', *Signs*, 38 (4): 967–91.

Naples, N.A. and Bojar, K. (2013) *Teaching Feminist Activism: Strategies from the Field*, London: Routledge.

Pearce, E. (2014) 'Surge in student feminism: Meet the new generation of "bold, hilarious feminists"' *Telegraph*, 3 January, www.telegraph. co.uk/women/womens-life/10548692/Student-feminist-societies-surge-Meet-the-new-generation-of-bold-hilarious-feminists.html

Phipps, A (2014) *The Politics of the Body. Gender in a Neoliberal and Neoconservative Age*, Cambridge: Polity Press.

Phipps, A. and I. Young (2015) 'Neoliberalisation and 'Lad Cultures' in Higher Education', *Sociology*, 49 (2): 305–22.

Rhoads, R.A. (1998) *Freedom's Web: Student Activism in an Age of Cultural Diversity*, Baltimore, MD: Johns Hopkins University Press.

Robbins, S.P. (2016) 'From the Editor—Sticks and Stones: Trigger Warnings, Microaggressions, and Political Correctness', *Journal of Social Work Education*, 52 (1): 1–5.

Rowbotham, S. (2001) *Promise of a Dream: Remembering the Sixties*, New York and London: Verso.

Rowe, A.C. (2008) *Power Lines. On the Subject of Feminist Alliances*, Durham, NC, and London: Duke University Press.

Saunders, K.J. and Kashubeck-West, S. (2006) 'The relations among feminist identity development, gender-role orientation, and psychological well-being', *Psychology of Women Quarterly*, 30 (2): 199–211.

Segal, L. (2007) *Making Trouble: Life and Politics*, London: Serpents Tail.

Sue, D.W. (2010) *Microaggressions in Everyday Life: Race, Gender, and Sexual Orientation*, Hoboken, NJ: John Wiley & Sons.

Taylor, V., Whittier, N. and Morris, A.D. (1992) 'Collective identity in social movement communities: Lesbian feminist mobilization' in P.M. Nardi and B.E. Schneider (eds) *Social Perspectives in Lesbian and Gay Studies*, New York: Routledge, pp 349–65.

Tomlinson, B. (2010) *Feminism and Affect at the Scene of Argument: Beyond the Trope of the Angry Feminist*, Philadelphia, PA: Temple University Press.

Vaccaro, A. (2009) 'Third wave feminist undergraduates: Transforming identities and redirecting activism in response to institutional sexism', *Journal about Women in Higher Education*, 2 (1): 1–25.

Younis, J. (2014) 'Rape culture at university needs urgent action', *Guardian*, 27 January, www.theguardian.com/education/mortarboard/2014/jan/27/rape-culture-campus

7

Using the law to challenge gender based violence in university communities

Louise Whitfield

Although laws do exist to protect women from violence against women and girls[1] (VAWG) on campus, they are rarely used by survivors and routinely ignored by the institutions. There have been very few cases in this area, making legal analysis difficult but this chapter looks at the existing law and how it could be used more to bring about much-needed change in the accountability of universities and respect for women's rights. The very small number of cases to date reflect both the cultural and legal landscape as well as the difficulties women face in bringing such cases. However, there is scope under existing law to hold universities to account and this chapter, authored by a solicitor who has used these laws in recent cases (including *R (Ramey) v Governing Body of the University of Oxford*), examines in detail the UK, European and international legislation available to survivors of gender based violence (GBV), their advocates and activists.

Introduction

Governing bodies of universities must comply with two key pieces of legislation in relation to the vast majority of their activities: the Human Rights Act 1998 on the basis that they are state bodies, and the Equality Act 2010 on the basis that they are education and service providers. This chapter looks at the legal obligations that universities have in terms of protecting the human rights of women students (and staff) in the education setting, alongside the legal obligations under the Equality Act 2010 not to discriminate or harass women in the provision of education.

The Human Rights Act 1998 codified and implemented the protections of the European Convention on Human Rights directly into UK law. All public bodies (and other bodies carrying out public functions) must comply with the Convention rights. The relevant rights in the context of VAWG in university communities include: Article 3 – the prohibition on inhuman and degrading treatment; Article 8 – the right to protection of one's private and family life; Article 14 – the prohibition on discrimination; and Article 2 of the First Protocol – the right to education.

The Equality Act 2010 prohibits discrimination on the grounds of sex in the provision of education, and services generally. The conduct prohibited under the Act includes direct and indirect discrimination as well as harassment. These concepts are explained further below along with the public sector equality duty under section 149 of the Act, which requires all public bodies in the exercise of any of their functions to have due regard to the need to eliminate discrimination and conduct prohibited under the Act, to advance equality of opportunity for those with protected characteristics[2] and to foster good relations between different groups. Thus the governing bodies of universities should not only behave in a way that ensures they do not discriminate against or harass women students when addressing VAWG in their institutions, but they must also be proactive in their policy development and decision making to ensure that they comply with this important statutory duty to have due regard to such matters to avoid women facing discrimination and disadvantage.

Both areas of law have the potential to be used in lobbying and campaigning on these issues as well as in litigation on behalf of survivors of VAWG, and examples of both are given in the final section of this chapter. Given the seriousness and prevalence of VAWG in university communities it may be somewhat surprising that the potentially powerful tools of the Human Rights Act and the Equality Act have not been used more but women students and staff face a number of barriers. Education for non-lawyers about human rights and equality protections is severely limited. There is also limited expertise in relation to discrimination law among lawyers themselves outside the employment field or disability discrimination in education for those under 18. There is limited scope for litigation in the higher education context given the severe restrictions on legal aid and the high cost and risk involved of bringing such cases.

A very significant barrier for many survivors of VAWG is the fact that the target of any court case is the very institution that they hope will be awarding them a degree. In addition, having survived the trauma of an assault few women will wish to face the additional trauma of a risky, high cost and very combative legal process. Strict court time limits also make bringing cases very difficult. In addition, strong cases settle at an early stage often with confidentiality clauses or non-disclosure agreements, meaning very few claims are heard by a court so no precedents are set and there is no publicity. There must therefore be increased commitment to and emphasis on legal education and a rights-based approach for both state bodies and women students and staff themselves so that human rights and equality protections are embedded in all policy development and decision making processes. The status quo will remain unchanged if existing legislation proves unenforceable due to lack of funding, expertise, knowledge or political will.

Domestic legislation: the Human Rights Act 1998 and the Equality Act 2010

The Human Rights Act 1998

The Human Rights Act 1998 is composed of a series of sections that have the effect of codifying the protections of the European Convention on Human Rights into UK law. The relevant Articles of the Convention are discussed below. The governing body of a university, which is a public authority for the purposes of the Human Rights Act (because it exercises functions of a public nature), must comply with these Articles.

A breach of a Convention right can render a decision unlawful and susceptible to challenge by way of judicial review,[3] and can form the basis of a claim for damages. However, any such claim for a breach of a Convention right can only be brought by the victim who has suffered the breach. This is in contrast to judicial review claims generally which can be brought by anyone with sufficient interest in the matter, often allowing organisations (such as campaign groups) not directly affected by an unlawful decision or policy to bring a legal challenge without involving an individual.

Article 3 of the Convention, known as the prohibition on torture, reads: 'No one shall be subjected to torture or to inhuman or degrading treatment or punishment'. This Article is not simply about prohibiting the state from subjecting someone to inhuman or degrading treatment. It also creates a positive obligation on state bodies to protect people from having this right breached, even by a private individual. Thus if a state body such as the police or the governing body of a university is aware of the threat to someone's safety (that they may be subjected to inhuman or degrading treatment for example), that public authority should take steps to protect the individual. Generally, the courts have set the threshold for a breach of Article 3 very high in that the ill-treatment must involve actual bodily injury or intense physical or mental suffering. However, in the context of the positive obligations on state bodies to protect people from such treatment, the failure by the police to protect people from a serious assault has been held by the courts to be a breach of Article 3.[4]

In certain situations, the positive obligations on state bodies under Article 3 may also include a duty to investigate alleged breaches. A failure to investigate such allegations properly can amount to a breach of the investigative duty under Article 3. Generally the litigation in this area is usually related to the failures of the police or other investigative bodies (such as coroners) and has involved the most serious of breaches, but there is arguably an analogous situation if educational institutions fail to investigate allegations of sexual assault, or have policies which specifically say they will never investigate such incidents. As discussed below, this was one of the problems with the Zellick guidelines which, until recently, many universities relied on to justify not dealing with allegations of sexual violence.

Article 8 of the Convention is the right to respect for private and family life. This is a qualified right in that Article 8(2) allows state bodies to interfere with the right in certain limited circumstances where it is justified (in the interests of national security, public safety or the protections of others' rights, for example). In terms of Article 8 it can be difficult to argue that public authorities have positive obligations to protect these rights, but this has been established in more extreme cases[5] and it can be a useful argument to raise in the context of policies and practices that educational institutions are adopting (or not, as the case may be) to protect women and girls from violence. The protection afforded by Article 8 includes protection of one's physical and psychological integrity. Thus a failure by a university to deal with repeated incidents of abuse or harassment in person or over the internet, when on notice of the harm this is causing a woman student, may breach Article 8.

Article 14 prohibits discrimination but only in the context of the other Convention rights. It is not a freestanding right, but can only be relied on in relation to the exercise of another Convention right (for example the right to access education). Article 14 provides:

> The enjoyment of the rights and freedoms set forth in this Convention shall be secured without discrimination on any ground such as sex, race, colour, language, religion, political or other opinion, national or social origin, association with a national minority, property, birth or other status.

Thus an individual can only rely on Article 14 if the discrimination relates to an issue which falls within the ambit of another Convention Article. Worth noting is the justification defence available to state bodies in relation to Article 14: if the discrimination is a proportionate means of achieving a legitimate aim, it will not amount to a breach of the Convention.

Article 2 of the First Protocol sets out the right to education: 'No person shall be denied the right to education.' The right to education is the right to access education being provided by the state, not a freestanding right to education per se. However, in the context of university education provided by state institutions, it is clear that when read with Article 14, any failure on the part of a university to provide the same access to women students as is provided to male students is likely to amount to a human rights violation.

The right to education is not limited to teaching in the classroom or instruction; it covers the whole social process whereby beliefs, culture and other values are transmitted. This broad definition is therefore wide enough to include the internal administration of education institutions and other activities ancillary to the teaching that is being provided. While there has been no litigation in this area in the UK as far as the writer is aware, there is clearly scope to argue that a failure to address VAWG that prevents women students from accessing not only their lectures but also any other university-based activities will constitute a breach of the right to education protected by Article 2 of Protocol 1.[6]

The Human Rights Act 1998 clearly provides potential to hold universities to account regarding their approach to VAWG although this potential has rarely been exploited. Similarly, the Equality Act 2010, discussed below, provides potential to protect women, to increase the accountability of universities and change the culture.

Equality Act 2010

Anti-discrimination provisions

The anti-discrimination provisions contained in the Equality Act 2010 prohibit various forms of discrimination including direct discrimination, indirect discrimination, harassment and victimisation, in the context of listed activities including the provision of education (Part 6 of the Act) and services (Part 3). Legal protection from discrimination is afforded on the basis of the 'protected characteristics'. The two forms of discrimination most likely to be relevant in the context of VAWG in university communities are indirect discrimination and harassment.

Direct discrimination (defined in section 13 of the Equality Act 2010) regulates less favourable treatment because of a protected characteristic, in this case sex. Direct discrimination can never be justified; there is no defence provided for in the legislation. Section 91 of the Act covers the provision of further education and states:

> The responsible body of such an institution must not discriminate against a student
>
> (a) in the way it provides education for the student;
> (b) in the way it affords the student access to a benefit, facility or service;
> (c) by not providing education for the student;
> (d) *by not affording the student access to a benefit, facility or service*;
> (e) *by excluding the student*;
> (f) *by subjecting the student to any other detriment*. (emphasis added)

This is clearly broad enough to prohibit discrimination and harassment in how a university addresses VAWG, arguments that formed the basis of the judicial review claim brought against the University of Oxford in 2015 and discussed below.

Indirect discrimination (set out in section 19) arises where an education provider (such as the governing body of a university) applies (or would apply) an apparently neutral practice, provision or criterion which puts either sex at a disadvantage, and applying the practice, provision or criterion cannot be objectively justified by the education provider. Thus, the situation where a university does not investigate an allegation of sexual assault, or has no policy for addressing sexual harassment of women students, can amount to indirect discrimination and be a breach of the Act. Indirect discrimination can be justified (and therefore is lawful) if it is a proportionate means of achieving a legitimate aim, but a failure to investigate sexual assaults is unlikely to be justifiable on any grounds, particularly in the light of the new guidance from Universities UK (2016a, b) on this issue (discussed in the final section of this chapter).

Harassment is defined in section 26(1) of the Equality Act 2010 as unwanted conduct related to a protected characteristic (such as sex) that has the purpose or effect of violating a person's dignity or that creates a degrading, humiliating, hostile, intimidating or offensive environment. The Act also specifically prohibits sexual harassment, under section 26(2); this is defined as any conduct of a sexual nature that is unwanted by the recipient, including verbal, non-verbal and physical behaviour, and which violates the victim's dignity or creates an intimidating, hostile, degrading or offensive environment for them. Ordinarily, a university would be liable for harassment of a student by a member of staff but not for harassment by a student.

In addition, section 26 includes a prohibition on 'third-party harassment', that is, harassment done by a person other than the person held responsible for it under the Act.[7] A failure to investigate an allegation of sexual harassment or violence may itself have the effect (particularly if the perpetrator is allowed to remain in the university) of 'creating an intimidating, hostile, degrading, humiliating or offensive environment', and thus amount to harassment, putting the institution in breach of section 91 of the Act, even if the original incident of harassment was perpetrated by another student (for which the university would not ordinarily be liable).

In summary, in the context of universities, if an institution has, for example, a blanket policy – or a practice – of not investigating sexual harassment or sexual violence and simply refers such gender based incidents to the police, this may amount to direct discrimination as female students are being treated less favourably than male students, that is, the university is refusing to investigate the complaint because the complainant is a woman, although it would be unlikely to spell it out in this way given that it could so easily be interpreted as discrimination. It is also likely to be indirect discrimination in that it is a provision, criterion or practice that puts women students at a particular disadvantage when compared to men and it cannot be justified in terms of being a proportionate means of achieving a legitimate aim. It may also amount to harassment. Similarly a failure to take steps to ensure women students can access all elements of their course and the other benefits, facilities and services that the university offers may amount to subjecting them to 'any other detriment' such as to be in breach of section 91 of the Act.

A claim for discrimination under the Act can be brought as a civil claim in the county or high court with remedies including declarations, damages and injunctive relief, such as an order forcing the other party to do something or to stop doing something in order to address the unlawful discrimination. This type of discrimination claim can also form a ground of challenge within a claim for judicial review brought in the Administrative Court, for example where an individual seeks to challenge a policy that is discriminatory *and* a specific incident in which they were discriminated against. Usually civil claims are about what has happened to an individual, and resolve a dispute between them and another party; most cases like this settle, but they can lead to changes in behaviour if institutions become increasingly concerned about the risk of litigation if they do not address particular problems. In contrast a judicial review may have more scope to consider wider issues, for example whether a policy that affects large numbers of people is discriminatory or not. In a judicial review, the Administrative Court is checking up on the behaviour of the public body in terms of whether they are acting lawfully or not.

The public sector equality duty

Under section 149(1) of the Equality Act 2010, when a public authority, such as a university, exercises any function, it is required to have due regard to:

- the need to eliminate discrimination and harassment of those with a protected characteristic (such as women);
- the need to advance equality of opportunity for people with particular protected characteristics (which includes sex); and
- the need to foster good relations between different groups (in this case between women and men).

The governing bodies of higher education institutions (HEIs) are public authorities for the purposes of the public sector equality duty. Examples of the relevant functions that they may be exercising on which the duty bites would include developing a policy as to how to investigate allegations of sexual harassment made by women students, or the decisions they take when dealing with individual allegations themselves. Thus when a university is making decisions about their policies and practices on violence against women and girls (which includes bullying and harassment), the governance of student societies and sports teams, campus security, housing, management of bars and social spaces, they must have due regard to the need to eliminate discrimination and harassment, and due regard to the need to advance equality of opportunity for women staff and students. The duty applies to decisions in individual cases, as well as policy decisions.

In practice this means that while there is no legal requirement on a university to carry out a specific equality impact assessment on its decisions or policies, the courts do expect them to have applied their minds specifically to the various parts of the duty when taking decisions or developing policies that are likely to affect people with protected characteristics, and to document this process. Guidance from the

Equality and Human Rights Commission (2014: 61, paragraph 5.51) and some court decisions[8] have pointed out that decision makers should record how they have assessed the impact of the proposed policy or decision on protected groups and, that without such a record, it will be difficult for the court to accept that the public authority in question has in fact had 'due regard' and met the duty.

The courts have repeatedly stated that the equality duty must be met in substance, with rigour and an open mind.[9] It must be integral to the decision making process and cannot be an afterthought. If public authorities do not have enough information or evidence to enable them to have due regard, they must obtain that evidence to ensure they can meet the duty properly. This might mean that a university has to consult women students, staff and those with particular expertise in VAWG on its proposals to ensure they have the right evidence about the potential impact on gender equality before a particular policy is introduced.

To have 'due regard', a university is also required to consider each part of the duty and the additional definitions contained in the relevant subsections of s.149. Section 149(3), about advancing equality of opportunity, stipulates that this involves having due regard to the need to: remove or minimise disadvantages (that women face); take steps to meet the needs (of women students and staff); and encourage women's participation in public life and any other activities in which their participation is disproportionately low. In addition, under section 149(5), having due regard to the need to foster good relations involves having due regard to the need to tackle prejudice and promote understanding.

The public sector equality duty is however only a procedural duty and does not require a particular outcome. It is not a duty to eliminate discrimination, but a duty *to have due regard to* the need to eliminate discrimination for example. It is unfortunately perfectly possible for a university to have due regard to the needs set out in section 149 of the Equality Act 2010, but reach a conclusion that any negative impacts (if they spot them in the first place) can be mitigated or are justified. However, the courts would expect an educational institution to be able to explain its rationale behind any decision to go ahead with the policy that appeared to have a significant adverse impact on gender equality, and that rationale would need to be recorded and in the public domain.

As part of the public sector equality duty, public authorities must also comply with the specific duties set out in the Equality Act 2010 (Specific Duties) Regulations 2011. This requires public authorities to publish information annually to show that they have complied with the duty (see Regulation 2(1)). This must include information on those with protected characteristics who are affected by their policies and practices: Regulation 2(4). Universities should have been doing this every year since January 2012. Under Regulation 3(1), every four years universities are also required to publish equality objectives that they think they need to achieve to meet the statutory needs set out in section 149(1), that is, the elimination of discrimination, advancing equality of opportunity and fostering good relations. These objectives must be 'specific and measurable' (Regulation 3(3)). However, in practice such objectives are often extremely vague and very general with no specificity or any sensible means by which they can be measured.[10] There also seems to be little consultation on the objectives and limited publication of either the objectives or the information required under Regulation 2.

Before the specific duties were watered down by the 2010 coalition government, their more robust forerunners (linked to the individual race, gender and disability equality duties) were more commonly used to establish a breach of the general equality duty in question.[11] If a specific duty had been breached, this could be used as evidence that the equality duty itself had been breached. However, the current version of the specific duties is now so vague and general – essentially a requirement to publish objectives and information with no enforcement mechanism – that while a breach may assist in providing evidence of a public authority's general attitude to equality, it is unlikely to assist in establishing the duty has been breached in relation to a specific decision or policy.

If it *can* be established that the public sector equality duty has been breached, this can render the policy or decision unlawful and susceptible to challenge by way of judicial review, the court having discretion whether to quash the non-compliant decision or policy. Fewer cases are now brought on this basis for a variety of reasons, not least the fact that more public authorities are properly complying with their duty, or settling claims before they are issued when it is pointed out to them that they have failed to have due regard as required in respect of a specific decision or policy. Judicial review is a remedy of last resort and should only be used when all else has failed, although the tight court deadline of issuing a claim within three months of the decision under challenge makes attempts at negotiation or pursuing complaints procedures problematic. Judicial review also only allows the judge to consider the decision making *process*, as opposed to the merits of the decision itself; the public authority can therefore go ahead and re-take the decision on an apparently lawful basis, complying with the equality duty but at the same time reaching the same conclusion – this latter decision then being very difficult to challenge if they have in fact had the due regard required.

European and international law and instruments

Notwithstanding the result of the 2016 referendum and the likelihood that the UK will leave the European Union, there are two significant pieces of European-based law that are relevant to decision making by UK state bodies in relation to VAWG in university communities. The first, the Istanbul Convention, is an international convention that is not in fact EU law but comes from the Council of Europe, a separate and distinct body from the EU. The second, the Victim's Directive, is an EU Directive but it has already been implemented in the UK in any event. These two legal instruments are therefore unlikely to be affected by withdrawal from the EU. In addition, the UN Convention on the Elimination of All Forms of Discrimination Against Women (CEDAW) has been ratified by the UK and can be used in a number of ways to combat VAWG. These three instruments are discussed in turn below.

Istanbul Convention

The Istanbul Convention is a Council of Europe Convention from 2011. It addresses violence against women through measures aimed at preventing violence, protecting victims and prosecuting perpetrators. The Convention recognises violence against women as a human rights violation. It aims to bring societal change by challenging acceptance or denial of such violence and gender stereotyping. Of specific relevance to universities seeking to address VAWG are the prevention obligations:

> Parties shall take the necessary measures to promote changes in the social and cultural patterns of behaviour of women and men with a view to eradicating prejudices, customs, traditions and all other practices which are based on the idea of the inferiority of women or on stereotyped roles for women and men. (Council of Europe, 2014: 7)

Specific obligations also include awareness raising, education, training of professionals, preventative intervention and treatment programmes, and participation of the private sector and media. This would easily cover obligations relating to training and education of all staff and students on campus.

Chapter IV covers protection and support including the general obligation to take necessary legislative or other measures to protect all victims of VAWG from any further acts of violence. Any such measures must be based on a gendered understanding of violence against women, and be based on an integrated approach which takes into account the relationship between victims, perpetrators and their wider social environment, arguably of particular relevance in the context of higher education. Such measures must allow for a range of protection and support services. The Istanbul Convention came into force in August 2014. To date it has been signed by 42 countries and ratified by 22. The UK has signed but not yet ratified the Convention, although ratification is edging closer after a widespread campaign by women's organisations with considerable support in Parliament. By ratifying the Convention, there would be a strong inference that UK law is compliant with the treaty. Upon ratification, the government would be undertaking to fulfil the Convention's positive obligations to exercise due diligence to prevent violence against women, to prosecute perpetrators and to protect victims (as set out above). While the Convention does not create enforceable rights for an individual woman (she cannot take the government to court over a breach of the Convention), once ratified, a failure to take the obligations into account in decision making may render any such decision unlawful and susceptible to legal challenge.

By signing the Convention the government has expressed its intention of abiding by it and it has already taken a number of steps to enable ratification (such as introducing new laws to criminalise coercive control and forced marriage). However, it will only become legally binding once ratified. Up until then, it can still be used in lobbying and campaigning.

EU Victims' Directive

Another piece in the jigsaw of law relevant to VAWG in university communities is the UK government's obligations towards victims of crime. The UK government has already set up a Code of Practice for Victims of Crime and this was amended to comply with the EU Directive on Victims of Crime, which came into force in November 2015. The aims and objectives of the Directive are to ensure that victims are recognised and treated with respect and dignity; are protected from further victimisation and intimidation from the offender and further distress when they take part in the criminal justice process; receive appropriate support throughout proceedings and have access to justice; and have appropriate access to compensation.

Thus when investigating and addressing VAWG in university communities, all state agencies must ensure that they comply with the EU Directive, as implemented by the Victims' Code. This includes for example the right to be offered the opportunity to have a person of the same sex conduct the police interview where someone is a victim of 'sexual violence, gender-based violence, or domestic violence' (see paragraph 1.8, Part A, of the Victims' Code). Paragraph 1.10 also states that victims of the most serious crime, those who are persistently targeted, vulnerable or intimidated, are entitled to additional support including special measures to give extra protection if giving evidence in court. They are also entitled to be referred to a specialist organisation (where available and appropriate) and to receive information on pre-trial therapy and counselling. These rights are likely to be highly relevant to survivors of VAWG and the Code requires all relevant state agencies to comply by providing the services in question. A failure to do so will be a breach of the Directive.[12]

CEDAW

This UN Convention has been both signed and ratified by the UK. The Convention defines discrimination against women as:

> any distinction, exclusion or restriction made on the basis of sex which has the effect or purpose of impairing or nullifying the recognition, enjoyment or exercise by women, irrespective of their marital status, on a basis of equality of men and women, of human rights and fundamental freedoms in the political, economic, social, cultural, civil or any other field. (CEDAW, Article 1)

The CEDAW Committee has made clear – in its General Recommendation no. 19 in 1992 (UN Women, 1992) – that 'gender-based violence is a form of discrimination that seriously inhibits women's ability to enjoy rights and freedoms on a basis of equality with men'. Thus the steps that the state must take to end discrimination against women include ending VAWG.

As explained above, a Convention, even when ratified, does not create rights that can be enforced through the courts by individual women, but they can rely on the Convention to argue how laws should be interpreted in the UK, and a failure to take the Convention into account, or to comply with it, could render a decision unlawful and susceptible to challenge. In addition, the Optional Protocol to the

Convention establishes a system whereby individual women or an organisation on their behalf can complain to the UN Committee if there has been a Convention breach by the UK government.[13]

As articulated above, domestic law, as well as European and international legal instruments, provide opportunities to hold universities to account in terms of how they deal with – or fail to deal with – VAWG. The following section sets out how those laws have been used in action by individuals and campaigning groups to improve university approaches.

Law in action

Campaigners began using legal arguments to address VAWG in universities in January 2015, when the End Violence Against Women Coalition produced a legal briefing entitled 'Spotted: Obligations to Protect Women Students' Safety and Equality'.[14] Its subtitle explained its intended role: 'Using The Public Sector Equality Duty & the Human Rights Act in Higher and Further Education Institutions to Improve Policies and Practices on Violence Against Women and Girls'. The briefing was aimed at women's organisations working in this area, and was increasingly used as a lobbying tool with state bodies. It formed a significant part of an important discussion in March 2015 with the then Minister for Business, Innovation & Skills, whose brief included higher education. Later the same year, at the request of the new minister, Universities UK (the umbrella body for HEIs) set up a taskforce to explore what more could be done to support the higher education sector to prevent and respond to incidents of violence and sexual harassment against women, hate crimes and other forms of harassment.

Also in early 2015, Elizabeth Ramey, a former postgraduate student of the University of Oxford, took that University's governing body to court over their failure to properly investigate her complaint that she had been raped by another student.[15] The judicial review claim argued that the University's new policy on investigating allegations of sexual violence discriminated against women students and was in breach of the public sector equality duty as well as the Human Rights Act. The new policy, which had been developed partly in response to Elizabeth Ramey's complaint to the Office of the Independent Adjudicator (OIA) over the University's handling of her complaint, continued to rely heavily on the Zellick guidelines which suggested that allegations of serious sexual assault should only be investigated if they had been reported to the police, and then only in very exceptional circumstances. For the reasons set out above this arguably amounted to unlawful indirect discrimination on the basis that women students would face a substantial disadvantage as a result of the policy, and that there could be no justification for such an approach. The policy would fail to protect women students adequately from inhuman and degrading treatment and there could be no justification for such interference with their right to protection of their private life. The University had failed to meet the public sector equality duty as there was no evidence that it had had due regard to the need to eliminate discrimination and harassment of women students when developing the policy.

The judicial review claim was unsuccessful, being dismissed at a relatively early stage on the basis that Ms Ramey was the wrong claimant for such a legal challenge as she was no longer a student at the University and therefore did not have standing to bring the case in those particular circumstances.[16] Although he held that the policy itself was not unlawful on the grounds alleged, the judge did indicate that he thought it could potentially be applied unlawfully in an individual case. The University continued to argue throughout the case that its policy and the Zellick guidelines were lawful, non-discriminatory and did not amount to a breach of the Human Rights Act (HRA).

Ms Ramey's case illustrates the barriers that individuals face in bringing claims and the limitations of judicial review challenges. It had taken her almost three years to find a solicitor with the necessary expertise to represent her. Although on a modest income at the outset of the case, she quickly became ineligible for legal aid; she was very lucky to secure funding for the claim from the Equality and Human Rights Commission but they fund only a handful of cases each year. She had to go through a tortuous internal complaint procedure and through the lengthy OIA process before she could embark on a legal challenge to Oxford's new policy. The original decisions taken by the University at the time of her complaint not to investigate further and to simply 'have a chat' with the perpetrator about his behaviour towards women, needed to be challenged within three months – an impossible feat for most rape survivors and very difficult indeed for those seeking to challenge the institution that they are currently studying with, which in many cases also provides their accommodation and funding.

However, Elizabeth Ramey's decision to waive anonymity led to considerable media coverage which significantly highlighted the problem (despite the preliminary hearing and judgment being on the day of the 2015 general election results). The case concluded two months after the End Violence Against Woman (EVAW) Coalition had met the relevant minister to lobby him on the wider issues. The

Taskforce was established in November that year, confirming in March 2016 that they intended to review the Zellick guidelines.

In October 2016, the Universities UK Taskforce produced its final report and new guidance for UK universities: *Guidance For Higher Education Institutions, How To Handle Alleged Student Misconduct Which May Also Constitute A Criminal Offence.* It is notable for what it left out: the Zellick guidelines have been largely abandoned. Universities are no longer advised to require complainants to have reported a matter to the police before they will investigate allegations of sexual assault, and they are no longer advised only to investigate such complaints in very exceptional circumstances. The new guidance has its flaws – most significantly that it fails to recognise GBV itself or that it requires a response that is compliant with the HRA and the Equality Act. There is nothing in the new guidance that refers to the fact that women are disproportionately the victims of sexual violence; there is no reference to gender discrimination in the context of sexual violence on campus, nor any guidance as to responding to it in terms of gender. There is one oblique reference to human rights but no analysis as to how to avoid a breach of students' human rights in dealing with allegations. The Universities UK (2016b) report published at the same time does attempt to focus on violence against women having a chapter devoted to responses to sexual violence, but its recommendations lump VAWG in with harassment and hate crime generally. Nor are the recommendations framed in terms of the institutions' duties under the HRA or the Equality Act 2010.

However, to some extent the new guidance and the report represent a step in the right direction following both a sustained campaign by the women's sector – using legal arguments – and Liz Ramey's legal challenge relying on submissions which revealed the inadequacy of the University's approach, summed up best in the advice in an internal document disclosed within the judicial review court case, and relied upon in the judicial review grounds of challenge:

> let him tell you what he wants to about his relations with Ms R and female students generally (so that you can form a view about whether he is in fact a risk to others); unless you have cause for concern, advise him to be more careful in the future about putting himself in situations with female students which are open to misinterpretation, and close the case on that basis.

While the new Universities UK (2016a) guidance is welcome, it was hard-fought and has its limitations. What it leaves out speaks volumes and its success depends upon HEIs' wholehearted and effective implementation of the recommendations. Although the current legal framework does allow for universities to be held to account, it remains the case that such action largely depends upon individuals bringing court cases – and fighting them all the way to trial. Legal interventions, then, can be only part of the strategy of holding universities to account and providing protection and justice for all women.

Notes

1   This is the term used by the End Violence Against Women Coalition, the leading UK coalition campaigning to end violence against women and girls, the work of which has informed many of the legal arguments explored in this chapter.

2   The protected characteristics of the Equality Act 2010 are: age, disability, gender reassignment, marriage and civil partnership, pregnancy and maternity, race, religion and belief, sex, and sexual orientation.

3   Judicial review is the court process by which an individual or a group can challenge the decision or policy of a public body; usually this consists of a review of the decision making process, not a merits review of the decision itself.

4   See, for example, the decision in *The Commissioner of the Police of the Metropolis v DSD & Another* [2015] EWCA Civ 646.

5   See, for example, the cases asserting positive obligations under Article 8 such as *Abdulaziz v United Kingdom* (1985) 7 EHRR 471 in the immigration context; or *Lopez Ostra v Spain* (1994) 20 EHRR 277 in the context of environmental pollution.

6   Women students in the US are using the equivalent laws there, known as Title IX – the prohibition on sex discrimination in education – to sue universities on the basis that when students suffer sexual assault and harassment, they are deprived of equal and free access to an education.

7   Although the specific prohibition on third-party harassment in employment has been scrapped, there is still case law that can be relied on to establish that a failure to treat sexual harassment in the education context may in itself create a hostile environment which is in breach of the anti-harassment provisions; see, for example, the decision of the 'Employment Appeal Tribunal Sheffield City Council v Norouzi' [2011] IRLR 897 in which the employer was liable for racial harassment of the claimant social worker by a resident in a care home in which the employee worked.

8   See the case of *R (Brown) v Secretary of State for Work & Pensions* [2008] EWHC 3158 (Admin) for example, where the court held that:

> it is good practice for those exercising public functions in public authorities to keep an adequate record showing that they had actually considered their [disability] equality duties and pondered relevant questions. Proper record-keeping encourages transparency and will discipline those carrying out the relevant function to undertake their [disability] equality duties conscientiously.

[9] The leading case on public sector equality duty is *R (Bracking & Others) v Secretary of State for Work & Pensions*, [2013] EWCA Civ 1345; see paragraph 26, which sets out the agreed principles in some detail.

[10] For example, it is common to see objectives such as, 'provide an excellent and inclusive educational experience' or 'raise awareness of and engagement with equality and diversity', with little detail as to how this will be achieved and making no reference to tackling sexual violence. As far as the writer is aware and having considered a sample of five institutions, no university has set a reduction in VAWG as an equality objective despite it being one of the most widespread and devastating problems facing half the student population.

[11] Before the Equality Act 2010 introduced the public sector equality duty covering all protected characteristics, the law imposed a general equality duty on public bodies in respect of race, gender and disability. These general duties were supported by specific duties, which included important requirements such as consulting stakeholders and assessing the impact of policies and practices on say, gender equality. However, these were replaced with far less prescriptive specific duties undermining the value and significance of compliance.

[12] As the EU Directive has been implemented via the Code which is a type of statutory guidance, the state agencies listed must also follow the Code (unless they have a very good reason not to) to avoid making an unlawful decision which could be challenged in the UK courts without reference to the EU Directive itself.

[13] See for example the complaint made by a Bulgarian woman on behalf of her daughter who had been a victim of sexual assault; the UN Committee made a series of recommendations to the Bulgarian government including amendments to the criminal code as to the definition of rape and covering healthcare protocols and procedures to address sexual violence against women and girls: www.ohchr.org/Documents/HRBodies/CEDAW/Jurisprudence/CEDAW-C-53-D-31-2011_en.pdf

[14] This legal briefing was co-written by the author of this chapter.

[15] The author of this chapter was the legal representative for Elizabeth Ramey.

[16] *R (Ramey) v Governing Body of the University of Oxford*, [2015] EWHC 4847 (Admin).

References

Council of Europe (2014) *Preventing Violence Against Women: Article 12 of the Istanbul Convention*, https://rm.coe.int/168046e1f0

Equality and Human Rights Commission (2014) 'Technical Guidance on the Public Sector Equality Duty: England', www.equalityhumanrights.com/en/advice-and-guidance/public-sector-equality-duty

United Nations Human Rights: Office of the High Commissioner (no date) 'Convention on the Elimination of All Forms of Discrimination against Women, New York, 18 December 1979', www.ohchr.org/EN/ProfessionalInterest/Pages/CEDAW.aspx

Universities UK (2016a) *Guidance for Higher Education Institutions: How To Handle Alleged Student Misconduct Which May Also Constitute a Criminal Offence*, London: Universities UK, www.universitiesuk. ac.uk/policy-and-analysis/reports/Documents/2016/guidance-for-higher-education-institutions.pdf

Universities UK (2016b) *Changing the Culture, Report of the Universities UK Taskforce Examining Violence Against Women, Harassment and Hate Crime Affecting University Students*, London: Universities UK, www. universitiesuk.ac.uk/policy-and-analysis/reports/Documents/2016/changing-the-culture.pdf

UN Women (1992) 'CEDAW General Recommendation No 19', www.un.org/womenwatch/daw/cedaw/recommendations/recomm. htm#recom19

8

The Intervention Initiative: theoretical underpinnings, development and implementation

Rachel A. Fenton and Helen L. Mott

Introduction

The bystander approach to prevention of violence against women is predicated upon empowering bystanders to intervene in a positive, pro-social way upon witnessing an event that they recognise to be problematic. The intervention made has potentially powerful social effects: it sends a clear message to the culprit about the social unacceptability of their behaviour, while concurrently alerting other bystanders to the appropriateness of challenging it. Constant and reinforced messaging about the unacceptability of behaviour within communities can thus shift social norms as to what constitutes desirable behaviour. While this narrative appears instinctive, bystander programmes are multi-faceted interventions underpinned by complex and sophisticated theory. The growing evidence base, predominantly from the US, indicates the aptitude of bystander intervention for university settings, its potential importance and promise denoted by legal and funding requirements for US universities (Campus SaVE Act, 2013; DeGue, 2014).

Aware of the promise of bystander interventions from the developing evidence base, and of the work done by the National Union of Students (NUS) and Alison Phipps (for example NUS, 2011) in exposing the problem of violence against women in UK universities, in late 2013 Public Health England commissioned an evidence review of bystander intervention for this setting (Fenton et al, 2016), to identify best evidence and practice from which to develop a public health intervention toolkit for all universities to use for the prevention of sexual and domestic violence (SDV), which became *The Intervention Initiative* (Fenton et al, 2014, hereafter referred to as TII).

The creation of TII at the University of the West of England was preceded by an intensive development period including the trialling of existing resources with student focus groups, and extensive consultation with an Expert Advisory Group (EAG) and a Student Bystander Committee (SBC). Our EAG comprised national and regional experts in SDV and our SBC was recruited from across the university and comprised students of different genders, sexualities, ethnicities, ages, years of study, disciplines and countries of origin. TII was published online in 2014,[1] becoming the first evidence-based bystander programme for the sector, and is available free of charge. It is an eight-hour facilitated intervention designed to be delivered to small groups over time. The research and programme have had significant impact on the higher education sector. Within six months of its publication, four government departments had written to all Vice Chancellors asking them to look at implementing TII, and from this point onwards – and particularly since Higher Education Funding Council for England (HEFCE) catalyst funding was made available with adherence to TII a condition of funding – a growing number of universities are implementing it in various ways. The results from a full statistical evaluation using a curriculum-based design with a cohort of students, funded by Public Health England, are promising (Fenton and Mott, 2018). Student evaluations showed excellent self-report learning outcomes (Fenton and Mott, 2015).

TII is predicated on bystander theories, social norms theory, the criteria for effective prevention programming (Nation et al, 2003) and Prochaska and DiClemente's (1983) transtheoretical model of behaviour change (TTM) as applied to bystander intervention by Banyard et al (2010). The TTM suggests that both communities and individuals pass though several stages – from precontemplation or denial of the problem, to contemplation or awareness of the problem, to preparation or intending to take action, to actual action through modified behaviour, and finally to maintenance or continued behaviour change (Banyard et al, 2010). TII is thus a complex model designed to have multi-faceted prevention capabilities, as illustrated by the theory of change (in Fenton and Mott, 2017), which sets out the internal processes participants will pass through to achieve behaviour change and the intermediate and distal outcome measures designed to evaluate this. TII aims to accomplish two core interwoven purposes in order to engender a reduction in violence at the community level: first, that potential bystanders will intervene to prevent problematic behaviours; and second, that it operates strategically to change a number of the attitudes, beliefs, social norms and peer group relationships which facilitate perpetration and impede bystander behaviour (Fenton et al, 2016: 20).

As detailed analysis of the evidence base for bystander programmes is available elsewhere (Fenton et al, 2016; Fenton and Mott, 2017), this chapter will concentrate particularly on the methodological and pedagogical application of the evidence to each session of TII, its overarching structure, and the relationship with the outcome measures, in order to substantiate that TII may genuinely claim to be evidence-based. This is important because in the current climate a multitude of interventions which are not necessarily evidence-based, nor tested, are available for the sector, some of which are marketed for a substantial fee.

Evaluations of bystander programmes for university settings

There is a methodological difficulty inherent in using reduced incidence of violence as the primary measure of success (see Fenton et al, 2016: 40 for a discussion) and thus it is not surprising that for bystander programmes rigorous evaluative/outcome evidence such as randomised control trials is limited. However, Coker et al (2016) do provide evidence of lower reported rates of victimisation and perpetration at campus-level. Considerably more significant evidence is available for proxy measures, such as decreases in rape myth acceptance, sexist attitudes, perceptions of peer sexist attitudes, denial of violence as a problem, actual and intended perpetration of violence, increases in empathy for rape survivors, confidence and intention to intervene, and knowledge about violence (see Fenton et al, 2016). These intermediate outcome measures correlate with those risk and protective factors which are agreed to be related to SDV victimisation and perpetration. They are important for evaluating prevention likelihood when incidence cannot be measured and additionally evaluate how and in what way the programme is working as participants pass through the necessary stages for intervening, as detailed later.

The development of TII: bystander theories

Perhaps the key to the promise of bystander intervention for this setting is that its very ethos – becoming a positive pro-social bystander – is intrinsically appealing, or at the very least, unobjectionable, and may engage men. Prevention efforts have shifted away from addressing men as potential perpetrators and women as potential victims which created resistance and were not effective (Flood, 2006; Powell, 2011;

Berkowitz, 2013). Efforts now focus on situating responsibility for ending violence within the community as a whole by engaging everyone as pro-social bystanders (Berkowitz, 2013). The underpinning approach of TII is thus the fostering of a *shared social identity* among students as 'students of X university', which transcends other identities. This does not diminish the importance of other social identities nor mean that violence and abuse is not differentially experienced by different individuals and groups but rather asserts that as 'a student of X university' they will act to prevent violence against others in this community.

In order to be able to act to prevent violence, bystanders must complete the stages required to move from inaction to action, as outlined by Latané and Darley (1970) in their organising framework for understanding bystander behaviour. Thus a bystander must notice an event, understand that it is problematic, decide that they are part of the solution thus assuming responsibility for helping and, finally, possess the skills to intervene effectively and safely (Banyard et al, 2009; Berkowitz, 2009; Powell, 2011). These four stages constitute the skeleton framework of TII and also map particularly well onto the ten processes of change of the TTM (Prochaska and DiClemente, 1983; Banyard et al, 2010; for a summary table see Fenton et al, 2016: 22). Of the eight hours of training which constitute TII, the first three stages for intervention are covered in sessions one to five, and the skills training (stage 4) is covered in sessions five to eight. The sessions are detailed later.

Sessions one to five of TII: from noticing the event to assuming responsibility

Noticing an event and interpreting it as problematic requires knowledge. Although knowledge by itself is not sufficient to produce behavioural change (DeGue et al, 2014), it is a crucial precursor to noticing a problematic event and key to the consciousness-raising process of the TTM. The knowledge required in the field of SDV relates to the recognition of: the risk factors for victimisation and perpetration; the impact on victims; behaviours along the continuum of sexual violence (Kelly, 1987) (for example, everyday sexism, hostile attitudes towards women, rape myth acceptance); the early warning signs of domestic abuse; and potentially dangerous situations (Fenton et al, 2016: 17). An increased sense of motivation or responsibility is essential to accompany knowledge and can be fostered through increasing empathy for victims (also a protective factor against perpetration), and through a gender-transformative approach which engenders a critical understanding of participants' own attitudes about gender equality and violence, such as those manifested by rape myth acceptance. There is strong evidence that bystander programmes are effective in generating positive attitudinal changes, such as significantly reduced rape myth acceptance and sexism and that knowledge, empathy, and attitudes and beliefs are related to intermediate outcomes for programme success (see Fenton et al, 2016).

In line with this, TII explores bystander theory, relevance of SDV to the student community, gender inequitable attitudes, empathy, and facts about SDV in sessions one to four. It is here, in the noticing stage, that deeper understandings about the intersection of social identities and differential experiences of SDV can be fostered. These sessions correspond with the consciousness-raising (information gathering), dramatic relief (being emotionally moved, empathy), environmental re-evaluation (understanding harms caused in the environment and one's own role in this), social liberation (realising that it would be liberating and empowering to be free of the problem), self-re-evaluation (acknowledgement of previous unsafe practices), and stimulus control (thinking of how to divert risks for problematic behaviour) processes of the TTM (see Fenton et al, 2016: 31). As noted earlier, bystander approaches seek to engage everyone as part of the community in preventing violence and abuse. Engaging men has proven particularly challenging because, in critically exploring gender roles, gender equality and masculinity, men may perceive interventions as blaming of men or labelling them as perpetrators (Casey et al, 2012). While situating men as pro-social bystanders is an important and potentially effective theoretical means to deflect defensiveness and hostility, the content of any intervention must simultaneously be mindful of the role of gender in violence perpetration and victimisation. This tension between recognising that men are more frequently the perpetrators of violence on the one hand, and not generating resistance on the other will need to be constantly negotiated. The bystander framework operates like a masquerade: what is seen and experienced by participants is the outward guise of becoming a bystander – which is inclusive and non-gendered – but underneath the mask the intervention is acknowledging and addressing the gendered nature of violence, and aiming to reduce actual and intended perpetration.

Following extensive consultation with our SBC, TII introduces bystander theory in a neutral context (not related to SDV) to engage participants' interest in bystander intervention as a social phenomenon per se in the opening session of TII. In recognition of the importance of the first session for student engagement and 'buy-in', the sensitivity of the topic of SDV, and the importance of engaging men from the outset, the session facilitates discussion and debate about students' own previous bystander behaviour, and encourages the processing of emotions about when and why they may, or not, have intervened and the consequences of doing or not doing so. The session subsequently introduces the extent of SDV within student communities as an issue directly relevant for the participants for which participants can be 'part of the solution' (Berkowitz, 2011, 2013).

Session 2 aims to shift attitudes supportive of gender based violence (GBV) by critically exploring norms surrounding masculinity and femininity, and gender inequality (the most commonly identified attitudinal risk factor for men's violence against women; Ricardo et al, 2011). In taking this gender-transformative approach, the input of our SBC and further male student feedback was crucial in addressing the engagement of male participants. Of particular note was the advice not to mention feminism or use any words associated with feminism perhaps because of the social undesirability and stigma associated (or perceived to be associated) with the label 'feminist' (Roy et al, 2007). While universities may offer young feminists spaces for engaging with feminism and resisting sexism (Lewis et al, 2016), we were mindful that TII needs to be applicable across the board and that some disciplines are almost exclusively male-dominated. Thus for example, we instruct facilitators not to use language that might be associated with feminism but to wait for the language to come from participants themselves. The session gives men space to explore and process how they feel when confronted with the reality of GBV and with some examples of 'lad culture' – which are used as a springboard to launch discussion of male peer group behaviours. Facilitators are instructed that maintaining positivity is crucial, and to reiterate throughout the session that male participants are not being blamed for violence against women and that most men do not perpetrate, and to emphasise that men have a powerful role in ending other men's violence. The session seeks to generate a critical understanding of the continuum of sexual violence and the importance of intervening to prevent underlying sexist behaviour within this. This is indicated because studies show that college students may have trouble identifying 'low and no risk' situations for intervention, be less willing to intervene to prevent everyday sexist behaviour, and less likely to refuse to participate in sexist activities not explicitly related to sexual violence (McMahon, 2010; McMahon et al, 2011; McMahon and Banyard, 2012). We use a clip from a UK television documentary *Blurred Lines: The New Battle of the Sexes* (2014) which engagingly sets out the results of a psychological study demonstrating the effects of sexist humour on the social attitudes of sexist and non-sexist men. Although all sessions in the first half of the programme work to increase empathy, session 2 also incorporates a specific empathy exercise (adapted from Plante, 2002 in Banyard et al, 2005) to enable participants to process the significant life changes which might follow assault or abuse.

Sessions 3 and 4 explain the nature of SDV within the framework of the first three steps of bystander intervention. We do not discuss the low reporting rates for violence (descriptive norms) to guard against discouraging reporting and encouraging a sense of impunity on the part of any potential perpetrators. Presenting information about injunctive norms is likely to be more effective, such as about the strength of social disapproval of sexual violence (see Paul and Gray, 2011). Session 3 examines the law on rape and sexual assault in detail; imperative for knowledge in order to be able to notice the event and for consciousness-raising. We seek to draw participants' attention to male sexual victimisation within a gendered understanding of sexual violence. While there is only limited evidence that knowledge of law may have some positive effect on behavioural intent (Withey, 2010) it is nonetheless an important component of the intervention. From a criminological standpoint, a more definite understanding of the behaviours which constitute criminal offences can increase conditions for decreased motivation to perpetrate and increased capable guardianship, including increased potential confidence to intervene and the increased likelihood of reporting (Fenton et al, 2016). A good example of this would be the recognition of behaviours now recognised to be commonplace and normalised in UK student populations such as unwanted groping (NUS, 2011) actually constituting a sexual offence in criminal law (in this case a sexual assault under s.3 of the Sexual Offences Act 2003). This session challenges, and seeks to reduce, rape myth acceptance (RMA) which serves to legitimise sexual aggression by men and downplay their responsibility for it, and is a predicting factor for perpetration (McMahon, 2010). RMA is recognised in the literature as an important attitude indicator and potential impediment to bystander intervention (McMahon, 2010). RMA is important not only as an attitudinal outcome measure per se but because lower RMA is associated with lower denial (precontemplation) and increased responsibility (contemplation) and action in the stages of change (Banyard et al, 2010). McMahon (2010: 9) also found that those students who endorse more rape myths are less likely to intervene as bystanders. Reducing RMA is thus a potentially important component in increasing bystander programme effectiveness. Law also serves as a useful springboard; for example, examination of the law on consent in this session facilitates wider discussion about what consent means – particularly in circumstances of incapacity (such as through intoxication) – and how it can be communicated.

This session brainstorms potential situations appropriate for intervention by asking participants about the kinds of situations they might now notice and in which they might be motivated to take responsibility for action. One technique that TII adopts is to increase recognition of the negative consequences for an offender, as men may be more likely than women to intervene with perpetrators (Banyard, 2011). Thus TII aims to increase the responsibility and motivation of men to intervene by suggesting that they can be a friend by stopping a friend from 'doing something stupid'.

Session 4 examines coercive and controlling behaviour in the many forms that it can manifest, including stalking (a particular problem in universities) and online abuse, within the bystander framework. The session begins with an interactive empathy exercise scripted by a public health specialist from our EAG. The exercise solicits an understanding of what life would be like if they lived on an island controlled by a dictator, the risks involved in planning to leave the island, and how coercion and control can be subtly expressed. The session strongly promotes the message that domestic violence can affect anyone regardless of age, sexuality, ethnicity, gender, background and religion, to increase inclusivity. It simultaneously ensures that understandings are positioned against an awareness of the gendered aetiology, prevalence and impact of domestic abuse. There is far less literature on the application of bystander prevention to domestic violence and little that evaluates prevention in universities. Coupled with the dearth of quantitative data about domestic violence in student populations from student surveys (which have concentrated far more on sexual violence), the input of the SBC and national data became particularly important in designing this session. Focus on recognising the early warning signs of domestic violence was identified as key for this population, and as key for intervention strategies. In order to combat resistance and to continue to engage men, we consciously 'de-gendered' the early warning signs while ensuring that students were nevertheless made aware of the very gendered nature of domestic abuse. Key messages for participants centre on not influencing a victim's decision to leave a relationship and referring a victim to specialist services (provided online and in a handout). The session also seeks to dispel myths about the ease of leaving an abusive relationship and fosters a non-judgemental approach. The technique of understanding consequences for perpetrators, couched as 'being a friend' (outlined earlier for session 3) is also adopted here in terms of noticing, and being motivated to act against a friend's problematic behaviour towards a partner.

At this stage, participants should be assuming an increased willingness, motivation and responsibility to act, in readiness for skills training in the second half of the programme. It is also important to note that a further outcome of these attitudinal and cognitive shifts for participants will be a contemporaneous decrease in their own likelihood to perpetrate violence (Fenton et al, 2016: 23) and this lends weight to the multi-faceted theoretical promise of bystander approaches to prevent violence.

Social norms theory

Social norms theory can be integrated into bystander programming to mitigate some of the barriers to bystander intervention (Berkowitz, 2009, 2013), and accordingly, is incorporated throughout TII. In relation to bystander intervention, the mutually reinforcing interaction of pluralistic ignorance and false consensus (Berkowitz, 2013) is key. Pluralistic ignorance denotes the misperception of others' desire to intervene, which prevents intervention – which, in turn, leads the wrongdoer to suffer from false consensus, the incorrect conviction that others are like oneself when they are not (Berkowitz, 2009, 2013).

The social norms approach to behaviour change is a theory and evidence-based approach aimed at correcting the misperceptions which influence behaviour (Berkowitz, 2003, 2013). In this context, the social norms concern norms which scaffold violence against women, such as peer support for violence which can facilitate men's violent behaviour (Schwartz et al, 2001; 12; Gidycz et al, 2011; Berkowitz, 2013; Witte and Mulla, 2013) and misperceptions that inhibit bystander intervention (Brown and Messman-Moore, 2010).

An understanding of social norms theory opens session 2 of TII and here we introduce the emblem and logo of TII: the red and green people, which denote, respectively, problematic behaviour and healthy, positive behaviour. The emblem is used as an illustrative and visual pedagogical device for understanding social norms and the effects of positive intervention. The visual reappears in sessions 3 and 4 to demonstrate the connections between misperceptions of norms and perpetration of SDV, and the negative link with willingness to intervene, as evidenced in the literature. The emblem is intended to be associated with social norms and trigger these associations whenever they return throughout the programme. While we recognise that the idea of red and green behaviours is simplistic and risks interpretation as dividing society into 'good' and 'bad' people, rather than behaviours exhibited by people which vary across time and situation, TII is designed for all students regardless of academic background and our SBC advised on the effectiveness of the design for understanding key messages, particularly for students with no social science background.

Rather than rely purely on second hand messages about other people's social norms misperceptions from reported studies, even where participants were college students and therefore similar to TII participants, it was theorised that maximal effectiveness is likely to be achieved by correcting participants' own norms. Thus at the start of the first session, students are asked to complete a social norms questionnaire which asks questions relating to their own norms and their perceived peer norms (of students of the same sex as themselves) about SDV (Witte and Mulla, 2013). For example, participants are asked how likely they would be, and how likely they think people in their peer group would be, to 'Do something to help a very intoxicated person who is being brought upstairs to a bedroom by a group of people at a party' on a scale of 'not at all, rarely, neither likely/unlikely, likely, extremely likely'. Direct feedback is given to students during session 5 about their own misperceptions via slides which illustrate the percentage differences between their own norms for individual questions and their perceived norms. The difference in these percentages is then discussed and peer participants are invited to recollect the importance of these misperceptions in terms of willingness to intervene. Participants are shown that their misperceptions map onto those found by other studies, evidenced in sessions 3 and 4. Again the red and green people visuals are used to reinforce the social norms data. The critical message for participants is that it is far safer to intervene than they thought: far more people share their positive, healthy beliefs than they had thought and they are therefore in the majority. Thus the facilitator is able to correct the misperceptions of the social norm held by TII participants and participants' barriers to intervention will be lowered.

Sessions five to eight of TII: possessing the skills to act

The final stage for being able to intervene to prevent violence is possessing the requisite skills for safe and effective interventions in a comprehensive array of situations. Assuming responsibility is not sufficient: programmes that equip participants with situation-specific skills for intervening are more likely to be successful (Banyard, 2011). A perception of having a 'skills deficit' has been found to be a significant barrier to intervention, particularly for women (Burn, 2009 cited in

Banyard, 2011) and thus confidence in one's skills and self-efficacy are key. The literature indicates significantly increased efficacy (confidence to intervene) scores for bystander intervention programmes (Banyard et al, 2009). Thus, sessions 5 to 8 of TII are based on the acquisition of relevant and specific skills, confidence to intervene and intervention strategies and these sessions relate to the counter-conditioning (acquisition of new skills to replace old strategies), social liberation (realising that it would be liberating and empowering to be free of the problem), helping relationships (social support for helping is available), reinforcement management (social rewards for prevention behaviour) and self-liberation (belief in own ability and commitment to carry out prevention behaviour) processes of the TTM (see Fenton et al, 2016: 31). Participants are taught to strategise and consider relevant intervention options for 'in the moment' interventions which require very different skills to supportive interventions post-disclosure.

Session 5 begins the transition from didactic to experiential learning by utilising a film from the New Zealand campaign 'Who are you?' which is designed specifically for young adults to discuss who could have intervened in a scenario which, devoid of intervention(s), ultimately ends in the rape of an intoxicated young woman. The film rewinds to show concrete examples of different potential bystanders and their actions that could have prevented the rape. We then move to exploring intervention strategies and introduce a chart derived from the literature (Berkowitz, 2009, 2013) illustrating intervention methods, which reappears through the next sessions. The work by Berkowitz (2009, 2013) constitutes the mainstay of the teaching and theoretical strategising on interventions, and in producing handouts with tips and phrases and examples of interventions we have adapted best examples from bystander programmes worldwide for UK language and contexts.

During sessions 6, 7 and 8, role play is introduced. The sessions transition from reading already-scripted dialogue to participants scripting their own. Role play develops communication skills and research suggests that the very act of role playing may itself contribute to opinion change in the direction espoused by the role play (Janis and King, 1954). Role plays may also operate as a potential vehicle for understanding intersectionality, such as the experiences of women and men who identify as LGBT. The role plays thus constitute a multi-faceted way of facilitating intervention. In session 6 we adopt a script from a real-life scenario which is based on male-on-male violence, both to ensure continued relevance to, and engagement of, men, and because male participants are likely to have many opportunities to practice bystander intervention yet concurrently be less committed to intervening (Brown et al, 2014). The role play scenarios were developed with extensive consultation with our EAG and an emergency (999) phone call script was written for us by an Avon and Somerset Constabulary call handler, and one script on disclosing a rape to a friend was provided by a student rape survivor based on her own experience. Many scenarios were provided by Somerset and Avon Rape and Sexual Abuse Services. Thus authenticity was ensured. We also used scenarios from existing programmes worldwide where they could be adapted linguistically and contextually to suit a UK audience. The role plays included in TII are a starting point and we encourage facilitators in different parts of the UK to develop their own scenarios to reflect the experiences of their own demographics and audiences and to further explore intersectionality.

Crucial to the success of role play is that it reflects not only real-life situations and contexts but is written in the language used by participants (McMahon et al, 2011). Thus, once we had scripted our scenarios to incorporate different intervention strategies and techniques, they were re-scripted by our SBC into what they termed (UK) 'student-speak', to ensure salience for our participants.

In addition to taking participants through the stages for bystander intervention so as to effect internal change as described above, there are several important features, which scaffold effective prevention programming, to which TII adheres, as discussed in the following section.

Effective prevention programming criteria

Successful prevention programming should adhere to the well-established criteria for effective behaviour change set out by Nation et al (2003). There are three categories: the characteristics of effective prevention programmes; principles matching programme to target population, and principles related to implementation and evaluation. These categories and how bystander interventions should adhere to them have been discussed elsewhere (Fenton and Mott, 2017). We suggest that the criteria can be discussed under the broader terms of pedagogy, and design and implementation. The criterion that interventions should be theory-driven has been discussed in relation to TII at length earlier.

Pedagogy (sociocultural relevance, varied teaching methods and fostering relationships)

TII adopts a multiplicity of pedagogical techniques, such as presentation of material by facilitators via on-screen slideshows, whole and smaller group discussion and group work, interactive exercises and role play skills training. We consulted extensively with our SBC on use of materials. Participant interaction is key as this in itself may result in social norms corrections as well as security in participation, the building of enduring relationships and the heightening of positive group norms. As visual and engagement aids TII uses a variety of YouTube clips, prevention videos, excerpts from documentaries, posters from prevention campaigns and the recurring emblem of red and green people, to reinforce messaging. Given that it is crucial for a prevention programme to be directly relevant to the lives of its participants, each session of TII utilises quantitative and/or qualitative data which are taken from UK student surveys to ensure that the problem of SDV is conveyed as proximal and salient to participants' lives and lived experiences, fostering a social norm that places responsibility firmly on them, as part of their community, to prevent violence. For example, in session 2, we use the testimony of a student (NUS, 2011) who was sexually harassed by a group of male students and then sexually assaulted by one of the group as a springboard to discussing male peer group norms and social identity, 'lad culture', empathy for the victim and escalation. Where possible we use YouTube and video clips that are in UK, as opposed to US, English and we adapted resources from the US into UK English. In addition, students also made their own motivational bystander film, which was filmed in various parts of the university in which students of a mix of genders, ages, ethnicities, courses of study and countries of origin talk about being an active bystander and pledge to be active bystanders. The film is played at the end of session 1 to facilitate motivation and 'buy-in' for the programme. While there are many such US films it was felt vitally important to script a specific culturally-relevant UK film with which participants could identify. TII also gives space to participants to air their feelings about the material by confronting any potential disconnect or resistance to ensure that the programme remains relevant to them. In session 2, when confronted with data evidencing the gendered nature of SDV, male participants are given space to talk about, and process, how they feel, whether they feel angry or annoyed or defensive or blamed so that their feelings are acknowledged and reassurance can be given. This space is of course also open to women to process their reactions to the

181

gendered nature of violence, as women may also be resistant. However, at this precise point in the intervention, particular attention is paid to men because if they feel blamed for perpetration, they may not return to the programme. Women's resistance is unlikely to manifest as feeling blamed. Discussing resistance is built in to the programme throughout. For example, in session 3 when we discuss RMA and victim-blaming, we address resistance using just-world theory and defensive attribution theory – and examine how defensive attribution may operate differently for men and women. The programme intends to create a 'safe' learning environment where feelings can be acknowledged and discussed and this is created not just by the materials but through the establishment of 'ground rules' for the sessions at the start between the participants and the facilitator which include how to talk about feelings, how to respect each other and about confidentiality within the group.

Design and implementation (comprehensive, dosage, timing, well-trained staff and outcome evaluation)

The evidence suggests that longer programmes appear to have more impact (Banyard et al, 2007) and that single-session interventions 'are not effective at changing behaviour in the long term' (DeGue, 2014: 1). As a complex intervention TII thus requires time: TII is designed as eight 1-hour sessions that can be delivered in this format or in others, such as four 2-hour sessions, and delivered to small (mixed or same sex) groups of seminar or tutorial size (10–25 participants) by (ideally) the same facilitator per group to foster ongoing relationships. TII was designed to be placed within student timetables and potentially feature within curriculum design backed up by visible affirmative institutional messaging about expected attendance. This model has been successfully trialled (Fenton and Mott, 2015, 2018) both at UWE and elsewhere. We suggest that required attendance at all sessions is the preferred approach in order to have the greatest reach, because those who need to be exposed to the message may strategically evade attending (Rich et al, 2010). However, we recognise that some institutions do not mandate attendance and so institutions will have to decide on how they implement in accordance with their own attendance rules, and, of course, provide other options for victims/survivors who may feel unable to participate. Institutions might make module credits available, for example, when they cannot mandate attendance. The careful positive and inclusive framing of TII is designed to deflect any resistance which may be provoked by expected or required attendance. The programme is cumulative and sequential, intended to be delivered at intervals, for example, spaced out across semesters, thus repeating and reinforcing the message over time. We suggest that maximal effectiveness will be achieved by delivery from the very start of entrance to university in order to set the tone for appropriate behaviour throughout students' university careers.

The arguments as to whether interventions should be delivered by peers or by professional facilitators/university staff have been discussed elsewhere (Fenton and Mott, 2017). We strongly suggest that the use of highly-skilled professional facilitators who have undergone disclosure training is the appropriate university-led response because TII is a complex intervention and facilitators must navigate the sensitive social environments that the subject matter engenders.

A self-report learning outcome questionnaire is included in TII for students to fill in anonymously at the end of TII. It includes 15 questions on learning outcomes and five questions on the structure and flow of the programme (measured on a scale of 1 to 5), and space for qualitative commentary on the programme and its facilitation. This gives facilitators a good measure of how, and if, the programme is meeting its learning objectives, its acceptability to students, and facilitates ongoing review of the programme. This evaluation is important for university managers and for sustainability. However, some interventions are in fact harmful, achieving the opposite effect to that intended (Hilton et al, 1998; Hilton, 2000; Flood, 2006) and thus any potential 'backlash' – which may ultimately lead to a potential increase, as opposed to decrease, in violence – must be assessed. Thus, in order to measure the effects and success of the programme, a pre and post evaluation using appropriate measures for attitudinal and behaviour change should be conducted.

Conclusion

The introduction of fees and league tables have rendered students consumers, and universities businesses. University reputation, student recruitment, teaching excellence, graduate employability and the student experience are high on the agenda for UK universities at the current time. The introduction of an evidence-based bystander programme aligns perfectly with this agenda. This is because lower perpetration and victimisation levels should equate with less opportunity for reputational damage to the university and more opportunity for an enhanced student experience. Together with the acquisition of professional and leadership skills in sessions 5–8 which support graduate employability and teaching excellence, these advantages of TII, if marketed correctly, could positively impact student recruitment.

The work done by activists, academics, journalists, the third sector, and latterly Universities UK and HEFCE in establishing tackling violence against women as a priority for universities has meant that at this moment in history UK universities are ready to act and resistance to acknowledging the problem for fear of reputational damage has been, for many senior managers, overcome. However, potentially effective programming, such as TII, costs time and money because there is no quick 'tick box' solution to violence against women. A strategy consisting solely of individual-level interventions, such as one-off workshops, cannot expect to make an impact on prevalence of SDV and, as the White House Task Force points out, 'continuing to invest scarce resources in low- or no-impact strategies detracts from potential investments in more effective approaches and may be counter-productive' (DeGue, 2014: 8). Although all the resources are free and available online as a public health intervention, TII nonetheless requires resourcing. The positive recommendation for bystander programming in *Changing the Culture* (Universities UK, 2016) refers to *evidence-based* bystander programming and thus senior managers should beware implementing programmes that cannot demonstrate a theoretical and pedagogical adherence to the research literature including the criteria for effective programming, and which have not been evaluated for negative effects.

Acknowledgements
We are grateful to our colleague Phil Rumney for his input into session 3 of TII.

Note
[1]   www.uwe.ac.uk/interventioninitiative

References
Banyard, V.L. (2011) 'Who will help prevent sexual violence: creating an ecological model of bystander intervention', *Psychology of Violence*, 1 (3): 216–29.

Banyard, V.L., Eckstein, R.P. and Moynihan, M.M. (2010) 'Sexual violence prevention: the role of stages of change', *Journal of Interpersonal Violence*, 25 (1): 111–35.

Banyard, V.L., Moynihan, M.M. and Crossman, M.T. (2009) 'Reducing sexual violence on campus: The role of student leaders as empowered bystanders', *Journal of College Student Development*, 50 (4): 446–57.

Banyard, V.L., Moynihan, M.M. and Plante, E.G. (2007) 'Sexual violence prevention through bystander education: An experimental evaluation', *Journal of Community Psychology*, 35 (4): 463–81.

Banyard, V.L., Plante, E.G. and Moynihan, M.M. (2005) *Rape Prevention Through Bystander Education: Bringing a Broader Community Perspective to Sexual Violence Prevention*, Document No. 208701, Washington, DC: US Department of Justice, www.ncjrs.gov/pdffiles1/nij/grants/208701.pdf

Berkowitz, A.D. (2003) 'Applications of social norms theory to other health and social justice issues', in H. Wesley Perkins (ed) *The Social Norms Approach to Preventing School and College Age Substance Abuse: A Handbook for Educators, Counselors, and Clinicians*, San Francisco: Jossey-Bass, pp 259–79.

Berkowitz, A. (2009) *Response Ability: A Complete Guide to Bystander Intervention*, Chicago: Beck and Co.

Berkowitz, A. (2013) *'A Grassroots' Guide to Fostering Healthy Norms to Reduce Violence in our Communities: Social Norms Toolkit*, Atlanta, GA: CDC, www.alanberkowitz.com/Social_Norms_Violence_Prevention_Toolkit.pdf

Berkowitz, A.D. (2011) 'Using how college men feel about being men and "doing the right thing" to promote men's development', in J.A. Laker and T. Davis (eds) *Masculinities in Higher Education: Theoretical and Practical Implications*, New York: Routledge, pp 161–76.

Blurred Lines: The New Battle of the Sexes (2014) TV Programme, BBC 2, Hornsby, G. (dir.), Friday 23 May.

Brown, A.L. and Messman-Moore, T.L. (2010) 'Personal and perceived peer attitudes supporting sexual aggression as predictors of male college students' willingness to intervene against sexual aggression', *Journal of Interpersonal Violence*, 25 (3): 503–17.

Brown, A.L., Banyard, V.L. and Moynihan, M.M. (2014) 'College students as helpful bystanders against sexual violence: Gender, race, and year in college moderate the impact of perceived peer norms', *Psychology of Women Quarterly*, 38 (3): 350–62.

Campus SaVE Act (2013) Violence Against Women Reauthorization Act of 2013, pub. L. 113-4, §4, 127 stat. 54, (2013).

Casey, E.A., Carlson, J., Fraguela-Rios, C., Kimball, E., Neugut, T.B., Tolman, R.M. and Edelson, J.L. (2012) 'Context, challenges, and tensions in global efforts to engage men in the prevention of violence against women: an ecological analysis', *Men and Masculinities*, 16: 228–51.

Coker, A.L., Bush, H.M., Fisher, B.S., Swan, S.C., Williams, C.M., Clear, E.R. and DeGue, S. (2016) 'Multi-college bystander intervention evaluation for violence prevention', *American Journal of Preventive Medicine*, 50 (3): 295–302.

DeGue, S. (2014) *Preventing Sexual Violence on College Campuses: Lessons from Research and Practice. Part One: Evidence-based Strategies for the Primary Prevention of Sexual Violence Perpetration*, Washington DC: White House Task Force to Protect Students from Sexual Assault, https://endingviolence.uiowa.edu/assets/CDC-Preventing-Sexual-Violence-on-College-Campuses-Lessons-from-Research-and-Practice.pdf

DeGue, S., Valle, L.A., Holt, M.K., Massetti, G.M., Matjasko, J.L. and Tharp, A.T. (2014) 'A systematic review of primary prevention strategies for sexual violence perpetration', *Aggression and Violent Behavior*, 19 (4): 346–62.

Fenton, R.A. and Mott, H.L. (2015) *The Intervention Initiative: Student Feedback February 2015*, Bristol: University of the West of England, http://socialsciences.exeter.ac.uk/media/universityofexeter/collegeofsocialsciencesandinternationalstudies/research/interventioninitiative/resources/Student_Feedback_report.pdf

Fenton, R.A. and Mott, H.L. (2017) 'The Bystander Approach to Violence: Considerations for Implementation in Europe', *Psychology of Violence*, 7(3): 450–58.

Fenton, R.A. and Mott, H.L. (2018) 'Preliminary Evaluation of The Intervention Initiative, a Bystander Intervention Program to Prevent Violence Against Women in Universities', *Violence and Victims,* forthcoming.

Fenton, R.A., Mott, H.L., McCartan, K. and Rumney, P.N.S. (2014) 'The Intervention Initiative toolkit and website', http://socialsciences.exeter.ac.uk/research/interventioninitiative/

Fenton, R.A., Mott, H.L., McCartan, K. and Rumney, P.N.S. (2016) *A Review of Evidence for Bystander Intervention to Prevent SDV in Universities* (No. 2016011), London: Public Health England, www.gov.uk/government/uploads/system/uploads/attachment_data/file/515634/Evidence_review_bystander_intervention_to_prevent_sexual_and_domestic_violence_in_universities_11April2016.pdf

Flood, M. (2006) 'Changing men: Best practice in sexual violence education', *Women Against Violence*, 18: 26–36.

Gidycz, C.A., Orchowski, L.M., and Berkowitz, A.D. (2011) 'Preventing sexual aggression among college men: An evaluation of a social norms and bystander intervention program', *Violence Against Women*, 17 (6): 720–42.

Hilton, N.Z. (2000) 'The role of attitudes and awareness in anti-violence education', *Journal of Aggression, Maltreatment and Trauma*, 3(1): 221–38.

Hilton, N.Z., Harris, G.T., Rice, M.E., Smith Krans, T., and Lavigne, S.E. (1998) 'Antiviolence education in high schools: Implementation and evaluation', *Journal of Interpersonal Violence*, 13(6): 726–42.

Janis, I.L. and King, B.T. (1954) 'The influence of role playing on opinion change', *The Journal Of Abnormal And Social Psychology*, 49(2): 211–18.

Kelly, L. (1987) 'The continuum of sexual violence' in Hanmer, J., and Maynard, M. (eds) *Women, Violence and Social Control*, UK: Palgrave Macmillan, pp 46–60.

Latané, B. and Darley, J.M. (1970) *The Unresponsive Bystander: Why Doesn't He Help?* New York: Appleton-Century Crofts.

Lewis, R., Marine, S. and Keeney, K. (2016) '"I get together with my friends and I change it": Young feminist students resist 'laddism', 'rape culture' and 'everyday sexism"', *Journal of Gender Studies*, 27 (1): 56–72.

McMahon, S. (2010) 'Rape myth beliefs and bystander attitudes among incoming college students', *Journal of American College Health*, 59 (1): 3–11.

McMahon, S. and Banyard, V.L. (2012) 'When can I help? A conceptual framework for the prevention of sexual violence through bystander intervention', *Trauma, Violence and Abuse*, 13 (1): 3–14.

McMahon, S., Postmus, J.L. and Koenick, R.A. (2011) 'Conceptualizing the engaging bystander approach to sexual violence prevention on college campuses', *Journal of College Student Development*, 52 (1): 115–30.

Nation, M., Crusto, C., Wandersman, A., Kumpfer, K.L., Seybolt, D., Morrissey-Kane, E. and Davino, K. (2003) 'What works in prevention: Principles of effective prevention programs', *American Psychologist*, 58 (6–7): 449–56.

NUS (National Union of Students) (2011) *Hidden Marks: A Study of Women Students' Experiences of Harassment, Stalking, Violence and Sexual Assault*, London: NUS, www.nus.org.uk/Global/NUS_hidden_marks_report_2nd_edition_web.pdf

Paul, L.A. and Gray, M.J. (2011) 'Sexual assault programming on college campuses: using social psychological belief and behavior change principles to improve outcomes', *Trauma, Violence and Abuse*, 12 (2): 99–109.

Powell, A. (2011) *Review of Bystander Approaches in Support of Preventing Violence Against Women*, No. P-052-V B, Carlton, VIC, Australia: Victoria Health Promotion Foundation.

Prochaska, J.O. and DiClemente, C.C. (1983) 'Stages and processes of self-change of smoking: toward an integrative model of change', *Journal of Consulting and Clinical Psychology*, 51 (3): 390–95.

Ricardo, C., Eads, M. and Barker, G. (2011) *Engaging Boys and Young Men in the Prevention of Sexual Violence*, Pretoria, South Africa: Sexual Violence Research Initiative and Promundo, http://www.svri.org/sites/default/files/attachments/2016-03-21/menandboys.pdf

Rich, M.D., Utley, E.A., Janke, K. and Moldoveanu, M. (2010) '"I'd rather be doing something else": male resistance to rape prevention programs', *The Journal of Men's Studies*, 18 (3): 268–88.

Roy, R.E., Weibust K.S. and. Miller C.T. (2007) 'Effects of stereotypes about feminists on feminist self-identification', *Psychology of Women Quarterly*, 31: 146–56.

Schwartz, M.D., DeKeseredy, W.S., Tait, D. and Alvi, S. (2001) 'Male peer support and a feminist routine activities theory: Understanding sexual assault on the college campus', *Justice Quarterly*, 18 (3): 623–49.

Universities UK (2016) *Changing the Culture, Report of the Universities UK Taskforce Examining Violence Against Women, Harassment and Hate Crime Affecting University Students*, London: Universities UK, www.universitiesuk.ac.uk/policy-and-analysis/reports/Documents/2016/changing-the-culture.pdf

Withey, C. (2010) 'Rape and sexual assault education: where is the law?', *New Criminal Law Review*, 13 (4): 802–25.

Witte, T.H. and Mulla, M.M. (2013) 'Social Norms for Intimate Partner Violence', *Violence and Victims*, 28 (6): 959–96.

9

Understanding student responses to gender based violence on campus: negotiation, reinscription and resistance

Ana Jordan, Sundari Anitha, Jill Jameson and Zowie Davy

This chapter presents findings from the 'Stand Together' action research project at the University of Lincoln (UOL), one of the first bystander intervention (BI) programmes designed to challenge gender based violence (GBV) in a UK university. The research accompanying this project investigated student attitudes to GBV and the potential of prevention education. The focus of this chapter is on two sites which emerged in student accounts as key spaces where acts of GBV occur, as well as where sexist and heteronormative gender norms are re-inscribed, negotiated and resisted: social media and the night-time economy (NTE).

The bystander intervention model at the University of Lincoln

Based on the recognition that there is a continuum between acts of GBV and problematic gender norms, BI programmes seek to foster a community response to shifting the dominant cultural norms that underpin GBV (Banyard et al, 2007). They seek to equip men and women with the skills and confidence to recognise gendered, violence-tolerant norms and situations where acts of GBV may take place, and to intervene effectively and safely (Moynihan and Banyard, 2008). US programme evaluations have evidenced attitudinal change, such as increased willingness to intervene (Ahrens et al, 2011), (self-reported) actual intervention behaviour (Casey and Lindhorst, 2009), and decreases in (reported) levels of GBV perpetrated (Potter et al, 2009). However, there remains a gap in understanding the nature, contexts and meanings of any intervention behaviour in relation to broader social norms around gender and sexuality.

The programme at UOL – funded by UOL – was implemented by academics (supported by the students' union), who collaborated with three voluntary sector groups: Scottish Women's Aid (SWA – a charity working to prevent domestic violence), the White Ribbon Campaign (WRC – the England branch of the global campaign to ensure that men take responsibility for reducing GBV) and Tender (which uses theatre to work with young people to address GBV). All partner agencies involved in delivering the programme operated with a feminist understanding of GBV. Though relatively short-lived (although aspects continue through student activism), the BI programme at UOL involved a combination of activities, including social marketing through the dissemination of student-designed posters, peer education and a theatre project.

The peer education/support model using the 'Get Savi' resources (see Hutchinson, Chapter Ten in this volume) to support a train-the-trainer approach was central to the UOL programme and was delivered by SWA and WRC. SWA and WRC delivered a total of four half-day training sessions to 14 (out of 27) student volunteers enrolled in the programme (hereafter 'programme volunteers'), who went on to cascade the training to successive groups beyond the life of the project. The programme volunteers also created and implemented awareness-raising campaigns throughout the academic year. For example, when a domestic abuse conference was organised for students across different subject areas, they encouraged passers-by and conference participants to write personalised anti-violence messages to complete the statement, 'Let's "Stand Together" against gender based violence because …' These messages were displayed to create a visually powerful 'wall of voices'.

The theatre project was part of an optional 'Forum Theatre' module in the School of Performing Arts run by a member of the research team, in conjunction with Tender. Theatre students created short performances on GBV which utilised techniques such as 'red-flagging' by the audience to stop and discuss an act/expression of violence as it unfolds (Mitchell and Freitag, 2011). The scenarios were performed on campus over two evenings and selected aspects of their performances were also enacted across the campus for passers-by.

Research methods

This chapter draws on semi-structured interviews and, to a lesser extent, on observations recorded during the project. Twenty-six qualitative interviews were conducted with students aged 18–25 (seven core BI programme participants – composed of two theatre student volunteers, and of five programme volunteers who completed the

'Get Savi' training – and 19 non-participants). There were seven men and 19 women in the sample, with no-one identifying as neither male nor female, or as having a gender identity different to that assigned at birth. Most of the men/women answered that they were either 'only or mostly attracted to' women/men respectively, with one woman stating that she was 'equally attracted to females and males', and another woman that she was 'mostly attracted to females'. Eighteen participants identified as 'White British', two as 'Asian/Asian British', three as 'Black/African/Caribbean/Black British', two as 'Mixed/Multiple Ethnic groups' and one as 'Other' – a relatively diverse sample compared to the student intake at UOL. Interviews lasted between one and two hours and were audio-recorded and transcribed. Qualitative data analysis software (NVivo 10) was used to organise and facilitate thematic analysis of the interview transcripts and fieldwork notes.

Vignettes were used in the interviews to probe students' perspectives on, and experiences of, GBV, and the practicalities and challenges of intervention behaviour in their everyday social interactions. The vignettes drew upon insights from previous research findings, issues raised by the programme volunteers, and media reports about GBV in UK universities, and were piloted to ensure that they 'rang true' for students. Ethical approval was provided by the University Research Ethics Committee.

The data do not suggest a clear-cut difference in attitudes to GBV between programme participants and non-participants. This is likely to be for a number of interrelated reasons. First, participants may not necessarily identify as feminist – violence/abuse may not be conceived of as a gendered issue. Although the 'Get Savi' materials aimed to challenge this gender neutral perspective, the training was relatively brief and may not have created feminist understandings of GBV as programme volunteers may receive/interpret information in unintended ways. Second, the range of activities on campus meant that non-participants might have encountered elements of the programme in ways which possibly influenced their views. Finally, the research topic itself might have encouraged students who previously identified as feminist, but were not programme volunteers, to sign up for interviews. Due to the lack of an overall pattern of difference between the two groups, we do not present the data analysis below in terms of a direct comparison between participants and non-participants. The purpose of this chapter is therefore not to evaluate the programme itself (which would require systematic comparison between the two groups), but to explore the complex nature and perceptions of GBV and of resistance to it in university communities.

Gender based violence and social media: student experiences of online 'lad culture'

Social media is a key site through which young people negotiate gender norms and relationships (Renold and Ringrose, 2011) and a space where 'lad culture' is enacted and resisted (García-Favaro and Gill, 2016). Interviewees recognised 'lad culture'[1] as ubiquitous in university settings and were often critical of such behaviours: "just lads being lads [...] lads want to be the guy that sleeps with most women and can drink the most and do the stupidest stuff. It's all just hypermasculine. It's so ridiculous" (Isabelle, white woman).

Women are simultaneously objectified and subjected to policing of their sexuality on social media through gendered shaming practices such as the 'rating' of women's appearance and/or sexual performance: "oh god, there used to be a [Facebook] page called rate your shag [...] all about like lads on the pull" (Naila, Asian woman). Similar Facebook pages were mentioned by several interviewees, including one called "biggest sluts" where "people were taking terrible pictures of girls and posting them" (Molly, white woman). A social media application aimed at students, 'Yik Yak'[2], was identified as especially problematic due to its anonymity. Users frequently 'name and shame' individuals and target people in a manner that renders them recognisable, while remaining cloaked by anonymity themselves. A programme volunteer described Yik Yak as "an absolute gift to people who want to abuse anyone" (Ryan, white man). Programme volunteers mentioned a specific incident of abuse aimed at a university women's sports team: "they are writing vile things about them [...] they're easy, they'll go with anyone, they've got STIs, like don't go near them" (Leila, white woman, programme volunteer).[3]

'Slut-shaming' practices were noted as being frequent on Yik Yak: "one I have seen is like who is the biggest slut on campus and you have to put people's names under it" (Molly). Interviewees condemned these practices as "outrageous"; "awful", and "disgusting", often using explicitly feminist language to name them as "sexist"; "misogynistic"; "degrading [to] women"; and "objectifying". Alongside this disapproval, there was a general acceptance of such behaviours as regrettable but 'normal' and just a part of life: "as awful as it is, people do stuff like that" (Zoe, white woman); "unfortunately, that's just the way it is" (Elizabeth, white woman).

The problem was conceived by some interviewees in an individualised way, as a private problem for the person abused, and as gender neutral, rather than reflecting harmful gendered structures of violence. When asked if rating of women on social media is 'sexist', one participant commented:

> 'I'd say most of this is sexist, but the rate your shag thing, [...] it's just as bad either way, it's just as much objectifying males "shags" [...] it seems quite balanced, the play on like the sexy thing [...] the rugby team did like the naked photoshoot thing for the leaflets, I thought that was hilarious, but's that because it balances it out.' (Zoe)

This response mirrors a dominant 'postfeminist' perspective in which the language of feminism is taken for granted but gender is simultaneously depoliticised, rendering feminism 'an individual lifestyle choice rather than a focus for collective politics' (Jordan, 2016: 32). In postfeminist narratives, 'residual' sexism may still exist in a largely gender–equal society, but sexism affects women and men equally rather than being more harmful to women overall. In this case, male rugby players choosing to pose naked is seen as directly equivalent to the public rating of women's appearance without their consent. This resonates with the common idea that men are just as objectified as women (Gill, 2011). Postfeminism reflects neoliberal discourses which position the individual as genderless, raceless, classless, and so on, shifting focus away from social structures of power and onto simplistic notions of individual choice and empowerment (Gill, 2007; McRobbie, 2009; Connell, 2011; Scharff, 2012). While postfeminist perspectives are distinct from 'backlash' politics, they may in some ways be even more difficult to challenge than overt anti-feminism due to their depoliticising effects (Jordan, 2016).

Everyday sexism was frequently dismissed in interviews as trivial, and as personal rather than political. Objectifying language used privately between friends was seen by some as harmless: "I know people use that sort of language just to describe people. And it's never in a malicious, harmful way" (Jake, white man).In contrast, a programme volunteer who identified as "quite a bit of a feminist", suggested that the "it's just banter" (Lily, white woman) response serves to legitimise sexist behaviour, which has implications for broader gender equality. Others recognised the continuum of GBV, linking casual sexism with more obvious violence:

> 'It might seem quite small to a lot of people but it can have quite serious detrimental effect and then where do you draw that line exactly. It's just the start of this "lad culture". Girls

are asking for it – girls leading men on [...] It leads to quite serious consequences.' (Isabelle)

Some interviewees stated that women are more often objectified than men, and criticised sexual double standards: "it's always been seen as a good thing if like men have a lot of sex [...] But if a woman does that, they will say, oh god, she's such a slag [...] it makes me think we haven't really got much equality" (Rebecca, white woman, theatre student). When probed further, many interviewees who initially saw the issues as gender neutral, reflected that women are more likely to be harmed by public objectification/shaming due to this gendered context. For example Jake, the man who saw rating as essentially harmless, later recognised that when "girls" are "branded as the village bike" it is "more negative than being called a player". For prevention education, it may be possible to use this familiarity with problematic gender norms as a starting point for raising awareness of how they scaffold GBV. However, it is crucial that this awareness be grounded in analysis of gendered power structures (Coker et al, 2011; Katz et al, 2011).

Responses to objectification, sexism and rape culture on social media

For those who saw the issues as individualised/private, the most appropriate responses to online shaming were similarly seen as individual – for example, targets of abuse should report behaviour to social media sites. In addition, perceptions of 'lad culture' as normal were connected with a general unwillingness to challenge it as such behaviour was seen as too dominant/embedded to be worth contesting, even if it were desirable to bring about change.

Nonetheless, 'lad culture' was seen by some as a public/community problem, rather than just a private issue. There was a corresponding sense that it was students' responsibility to intervene and that resistance is possible. Several interviewees mentioned calling people out on using sexist language. One woman noted the dominance of 'lad culture' but at the same time suggested there was a clear 'backlash' among some students and collective action: "friends are saying on Facebook, being a lad isn't cool, it's not funny, it's not clever and it's just really stupid and sexist" (Isabelle). Others were less optimistic about challenging attitudes, commenting on the exhausting nature of constantly battling embedded norms:

> 'It is difficult because it happens quite a lot [...] the word slag was thrown around [...] at the beginning, you say something like you shouldn't call her that [...] But I think it's like common practice that you just think well – you can't just keep telling people not to say it because they're just going to keep saying it anyways [...] So admittedly I think you do get quite immune to it and you just think well, it's always going to be like that.' (Rebecca, theatre student)

Interviewees reported that the idea of 'banter' was used as a strategy to close down resistance: "I was only joking, why can't you take a joke [...] what's wrong with you today" (Sophie, white woman). Some of the men interviewed also commented on the difficulty of speaking out as they would be told not to be boring, to have a sense of humour. They also noted the gendered nature of the response to them as men challenging 'laddishness':

> 'you're not seen as a lad, are you, a 'lad' in inverted commas if you don't like talk about it [sex] all the time or behave in the stereotypical 'lad culture' way [...] I've even been called gay for expressing that it's wrong to call people sluts and stuff like that.' (Ryan, programme volunteer)

Men who do not conform to hegemonic masculinity may be penalised by being cast as unmasculine, frequently expressed as homophobic abuse which draws on notions of gay men as not *real* men (Connell, 2005). This policing of masculinity and sexuality may shed light on why many male students are complicit in hegemonic masculinity in HE settings, even where they may be critical of it (Dempster, 2011). Further, the importance of intersectional analysis is reinforced as this illustrates the complex interaction between dominant binary constructions of gender and heteronormativity in these settings. Attempts at resistance are constrained in these contexts. Below, two prominent incidents where programme volunteers attempted to intervene are analysed to illustrate the complexities of challenging dominant campus cultures and the difficulties of defining what counts as a successful intervention.

The first incident occurred when a series of rape 'jokes' were posted on Yik Yak, including: "I called a rape advice line earlier today, unfortunately it's only for the victims"; "no + rohypnol = yes" and "if rohypnol doesn't work use a brick". When two programme volunteers pointed out the harmful effects of such jokes, the perpetrators responded with further offensive comments: "But it's not rape if you leave a fiver"; "statistically 9 out of 10 people enjoy gang rape". The volunteers persisted in their attempts to intervene, but reported an emotional toll as they were subjected to a barrage of personal, gendered abuse, replicating precisely the attitudes they sought to resist:

> 'Oh just fuck off you dirty little sket [derogatory slang meaning 'slut'], your [sic] probably the type who leads guys on to the point they think they're going to have sex then decide last minute that all you wanted was them to walk you home.'

The more they highlighted the serious ramifications of the jokes, the more the young women were aligned with 'political correctness' and positioned as humourless feminists: "You femmy slags [...] the fact is the majority of punchline in jokes are offensive to somebody". Situating feminists as man-hating is a common discursive strategy which positions men as innocent victims of 'feminazis' (García-Favaro and Gill, 2016). Within postfeminist paradigms, pressures on young women to 'be cool' and to participate in 'lad culture' as 'honorary lads' (Gill, 2007; Scharff, 2012; Phipps and Young, 2015a, b) militate against their resistance being taken seriously. Young women (and men) who wish to challenge 'lad culture' have limited choices. Those brave enough to dissent are positioned as outsiders and their messages delegitimised, often in ways which perpetuate the very narratives they seek to alter (Phipps and Young, 2015b; García-Favaro and Gill, 2016). Ultimately, the programme volunteers were silenced by the apparent weight of dominant opinion.

During the exchange, a rape victim/survivor posted her distress at reading the jokes. The programme volunteers, having received information about sexual assault/rape services through the training programme, directed her to them. Although revealing her experiences was insufficient to silence the perpetrators, she expressed gratitude for the solidarity expressed by the volunteers. In these small ways, BI programmes may help to facilitate a more supportive culture for GBV victims/survivors, and to raise awareness of support services.

The second incident involved a more obviously 'successful' intervention by another programme volunteer. Two (women) lecturers used anonymous polling software to gain insight into students' understandings of criminological theories, whereby their responses appeared on a screen in the lecture theatre.[4] A few students persistently attempted to undermine the activity and, by extension, the lecturers. For example, when asked for their opinion on a minister's views, they responded: "He's a prick"; and "My cock". 'Laddish' behaviour in higher education is associated with the attitude that it is 'not cool' to take studying seriously (Jackson and Dempster, 2009; Jackson et al, 2015). When asked about types of sexual offences where reform might be feasible, one student replied: "Rape", which was quickly followed by other posts: "Don't be afraid to try anal"; "Doing anal". A programme volunteer challenged them, responding: "Making rape jokes is not cool and makes rape seem socially ok. Get savi, people". After her intervention, there were no more 'humorous' posts. In their feedback on the session via the software, a few students expressed their disapproval: "Really enjoyed it, shame some people had to ruin it."

The following factors may have increased the chances of an effective challenge in this case. First, although the attempts to undermine the lecturers could be read as gendered, the academics were nonetheless in a position of authority in that setting. The lecture was therefore a different kind of space to Yik Yak. Although challenging disruption is not without risk, other students are sometimes able to shut down behaviour which they perceive as immature and as impeding their learning (Jackson et al, 2015). Second, the comments were directed at specific individuals. This may have been seen by the majority as less acceptable than more generalised (but ultimately similar) behaviour. Given the representation of, for example, rape jokes, as victimless, this once again suggests the importance of BI campaigns/programmes communicating links between generalised sexism and other acts of abuse. Third, the reference to 'Get Savi', was perhaps an attempt to draw on a collective identity at a time when the BI programme was visible on campus and had institutional support. One of the lecturers was involved in the BI programme. This suggests that having a visible and semi-institutionalised presence on the campus can be a useful tool in legitimising resistance. Collaborations between students and lecturers are crucial to resisting 'lad culture' (Jackson and Sundaram, 2015) and programme volunteers commented on this in interviews. BI programmes in universities must also engage with gendered abuse directed at staff as gendered cultures within HE extend beyond the student body. Lectures and seminars are as much a site for GBV and of possible resistance as are halls of residence, nightclubs and social media.

Overall, the interviews suggest that social media is a contradictory site where 'lad culture' is enacted and where resistance is possible, although the latter is often constrained by dominant gendered constructions.

Students' experiences of sexual harassment in the night-time economy: "this is just what happens"

Spaces in the NTE are utilised by women in diverse ways as they negotiate fun, friendships and group identities through shared drinking, and make sexual connections (Griffin et al, 2013). While literature documents how women negotiate new feminine identities of empowerment and sexual agency through bodily presentation and new modes of alcohol consumption (Waitt et al, 2011), sociologists have also drawn attention to the convergence between the traditional and new gender scripts within these spaces, including sexual double standards (Griffin et al, 2013).Research suggests that 'microaggressions in everyday life' (Sue, 2010) such as non-consensual sexual attention and sexual harassment are particularly common in the NTE (Kavanaugh, 2013), particularly within student-frequented venues (Ronen, 2010; Graham et al, 2016). In comparison to research documenting the prevalence of sexual harassment in the NTE, there is comparatively less exploration of how these violences are inflicted, maintained and normalised, and the many ways in which young people account for, and resist, them (for exceptions, see Brooks, 2011; Waitt et al, 2011; Tan, 2014; Nicholls, 2015).

The NTE is overwhelmingly constructed to meet the desires of a particular idea of the heterosexual man by commodifying and capitalising on female bodies. Young people who inhabit this space spoke about the processes whereby this gendered construction is packaged and conveyed to consumers:

> 'You know how they promote these club things ... and it's like "oh, free drinks for you" – they target certain people. Like the women they put on leaflets most of the time – because I've walked past them; they've never offered [it to] me. The way they're dressed, kind of airbrushed celebrity, small figure and probably half-dressed or totally naked to be honest.' (Letitia, black woman)

This woman is aware of how, under a heterosexual male gaze, her body and appearance fall short of the standards of physical appearance that are deemed acceptable in certain nightclubs. Interviewees' descriptions of themed events such as 'doctors and nympho nurses' point to a hetero-pornified aesthetic of raunch culture represented by women with high heels, heavy make-up and scant clothes (Levy, 2005). The promotional literature and gatekeeping policies conform to a specific classed and racialised construction of an ideal bodily presentation which is not only problematic in contributing to the objectification/subjectification of all women, but particularly excludes those who are older, non-white, disabled or not slim (Gill, 2009; McRobbie, 2009).

A female interviewee who identified as 'equally attracted to both males and females', reported working with the LGBT society at her college to prevent nightclubs from circulating flyers using fetishised images of lesbian women. Representations of "girl-on-girl stuff" (Zoe) to promote events as sexy/glamourous rely on fantasies of lesbians as seen through a male gaze (Gill, 2009). As representations of gender are intertwined with constructions of sexuality, 'LGBT' women and men may experience 'lad culture' differently given the pervasive heteronormative culture of such spaces.

Interviewees described how men would routinely run their hands over women's backs, grab their bottom, and persistently invade their private space. Such harassment was seen as part of the minutiae of everyday life, as inevitable, and as something that must be tolerated by women, but simultaneously as morally unacceptable (Brooks, 2011; Graham et al, 2016; Tinkler et al, 2016). One interviewee articulated the dilemmas and contradictions in negotiating the boundaries of non-consensual sexual contact:

> Interviewee: 'It is accepted because nobody says anything about it, nobody really makes it a big enough deal.'
>
> Interviewer: 'What do you think would happen if they did make a big deal?'
>
> Interviewee: 'I don't know, but these kind of things, they seem harmless in a way. I don't agree with it. I think you should be able to say … people shouldn't have to have people slapping their bums and making them feel uncomfortable. But at the same time, it's like, oh, he only a touched a bum or he only put his arms around you, so what's the big deal … Because you just think, oh, well, did I really get harmed?' (Janice, black woman)

Paradoxical discursive strategies deployed by this young woman both normalise and minimise sexual harassment using words like "only", not a "big deal" and "did I really get harmed", but at the same time condemns it by signalling her disagreement with these narratives. Other interviewees framed their expectation of sexual harassment in the context of particular understandings of gender and sex, which accounted for men's actions:

> 'It's like the lads will be lads. It's not that I think that should be acceptable in society. It's basically lazy to say we don't want to deal with it, so you should just let it happen. But it shouldn't really be like that – I don't know, my flatmates think it's fine when they go out.' (Molly)

Such discursive strategies simultaneously condemn and re-inscribe gendered sexual scripts by drawing upon biological narratives about men's sexuality. These narratives suggest that simply appearing attractive – in a context where women's entry into nightclubs is premised upon a 'freely' chosen hypersexual mode of bodily presentation – encourages male sexual aggression because men's sexual appetites cannot be controlled. At the same time, traditional, as well as postfeminist, constructions of femininity commonly require women to take responsibility for managing male desire. Women may be subjected to blame if they are seen to have made themselves 'vulnerable' through ineffective gatekeeping of sexual advances (Nicholls, 2015) which 'let it happen'.Feminists have long argued that sexual harassment and violence reflects, creates and maintains, gendered and sexed hierarchies which secure relations of male domination and female subordination (MacKinnon, 1979; Sue, 2010). Our respondents utilised culturally available discourses relating to heteronormative sexual scripts to make sense of everyday harassment, violence, coercion and misogyny in the context of the NTE.

Responses to sexual harassment: building resilience, recuperating, evading and challenging

Despite the ubiquity of sexual harassment in the NTE, several interviewees reported that such behaviour seemed invisible to the bar staff and the bouncers.

> Interviewee: 'Things like that happen in front of security's eyes, but they just stand there doing nothing. If I've seen it and if I say something to them – they just turn around and laugh in my face. So it's like you just end up just keeping quiet [...] They probably think, 'I'm only here to protect people from getting harmed.'

Interviewer: 'So you don't think they see that as harm?'

Interviewee: 'Well, he hasn't fought with nobody. He hasn't punched nobody. So oh well, nothing we can do about it.' (Letitia)

This account does not mention just one incident, but describes a pattern of aggressions and help-seeking that has been ignored by bouncers who police physical conflicts between men, while seeing men's harassment of women as unproblematic (Tinkler et al, 2016). This invisibilisation of men's sexual harassment of women as a private and trivial matter between two people reiterates historic constructions of violence against women (Kelly and Radford, 1990). It was in this context that some women also viewed their experiences as 'not really harmful', even as they regarded such behaviour as unacceptable.

Programme volunteers felt that student union run venues were more cognisant of the potential 'risk' of sexual harassment and took measures to create safer drinking cultures, including having supportive bar staff. This highlights the importance for any BI programme of engaging with nightclubs in local communities – an uphill task where any such efforts may be seen as a challenge to their business model.

Most interviewees felt that the ephemeral nature of most microaggressions (a fleeting touch, an unseen hand grabbing a bottom) combined with the prevailing culture of NTEs made resistance fraught with difficulties. In particular, the gendered social scripts about making sexual connections – men as initiators and women as gatekeepers – meant that challenges were seen as risky and likely to be rebuffed with the assertion that men's 'normal' sexual advances had been misinterpreted by the women. In this cultural and institutional context, women were often forced to devise a range of strategies to inhabit these spaces of fun and pleasure while staying safe. A few women recounted going to nightclubs in groups to derive protection from each other's presence (Ronen, 2010; Graham et al, 2016). Other refusal strategies were reported. For example: "Me and my friend, we had two boys talking to us, and we felt that we couldn't leave really. So I went to the toilet and then like waited until she joined me. You shouldn't have to do that" (Rebecca, theatre student).

Feeling unable to openly challenge the persistent and unwelcome attention, this young woman and her friend felt that avoidance was the safest and most effective way out. Research indicates that such avoidance behaviour – ignoring initial sexual advances and aggressions, moving out of reach, leaving the area or avoiding the perpetrator and talking to other people – are the most common responses to sexual harassment in nightclubs (Ronen, 2010; Brooks, 2011; Graham et al, 2016). Women are guided by their fear of escalating the aggression through too assertive a rejection and strategise to manage risks in the NTE (Sue, 2010; Nicholls, 2015). One interviewee recalled how a female friend who rejected unwanted advances in a forthright manner was punched by a male stranger. Refusal strategies are not passive responses and need to be conceptualised as agentic behaviours shaped as much by the cultural context of the NTE as they are by broader gendered sexual scripts. While men's persistent unwanted attention is naturalised as 'what men do', women's negotiation of consent can prove to be a delicate balancing act: too forceful a rejection of men's sexual aggressions would risk positioning these women as not only unreasonable and a 'bad sport' (Sue, 2010), but rude and thereby unfeminine, and may expose them to further aggression as in the example given. Intervention from male friends was a well-rehearsed strategy used by many:

> 'Sometimes if this happens, I'd just peek from the queue. They [male friends] pick up on it – and they'll like come over and like pretend like, 'oh, I've been looking for you, where have you been?' And then the other lads will like back off because it's kind of like, so they've got their own males. They're not for us to play with anymore, they're not free girls anymore. So they step back.' (Lucy, white woman)

This interviewee utilises men's proprietary behaviour towards 'their' women to avoid unwanted sexual attention by pretending that she is "not free" for them "to play with anymore". One theatre student, who cited his frustration at the regular groping his female friends were subjected to in nightclubs as his reason for volunteering, recounted how he put his training to use through this strategy. However, he was not the only one to recount his frustration at being called upon to pretend to be a boyfriend, and noted that while lack of consent was not an effective deterrent, men willingly ceded their entitlement to another man:

> 'I might pretend to be her boyfriend. That shouldn't be a reason for them not to touch them just because they have boyfriends. They shouldn't do it anyway. But on a night out in a loud club with these idiots that seems to be the only thing they understand.' (Ethan, white man, theatre student)

Such strategies may indeed create further risk of harassment from familiar men as women's strategic overtures towards them might then become the pretext for unwanted sexual attention from these known men. One woman and her female friend pretended that they were a lesbian couple in clubs to deflect persistent unwanted attention, a strategy that might risk drawing sexual attention from men who bring the hetero male gaze to lesbians or, indeed, risk homophobic abuse.

On the whole, while men's sexual aggressions were minimised and trivialised, women's challenges to aggressive behaviour were often constructed as problematic by bystanders, bar staff and sometimes by students themselves, and were seen as a last resort. One respondent reported how when she challenged a stranger who would not leave her alone in a nightclub, she was told by the bouncers that she was "arguing too much" and told to leave for causing trouble. A programme volunteer recounted how she argued with a bouncer to get him to take responsibility for a young woman who had passed out by his nightclub until she and her friends could summon help. Another programme volunteer mentioned initiatives that she took to "look out for" other female friends – particularly to prevent predatory men "taking advantage" of women who were too drunk to give consent – and how this had led to her being labelled a "cockblocker". Several programme volunteers articulated that making the move from understanding to action was not straightforward, given the strongly embedded norms in the NTE, but also their desire to continue to inhabit this space. Two women reported being so frustrated by these gendered expectations that they had stopped going to nightclubs.

Student accounts point to the impossible contradictions within the postfeminist cultures of consumption in the NTE. Their narratives indicate a reiteration of gendered scripts, as well as some contradictory discourses and actions, as they seek to resist dominant gendered norms within these spaces, while maintaining access to them.

Conclusion

Our findings add to evidence on the prevalence of GBV in student communities, demonstrating the need to engage with spaces within and outside universities where GBV is enacted and resisted. They also shed light on the less-explored issue of what kinds of resistance are possible (see Lewis et al, 2016; and Lewis and Marine, Chapter Six in this volume, for exceptions) and on the challenges/possibilities for prevention education. BI programmes can be effective in changing perceptions and creating confidence to act, albeit within limits determined by the dominant culture, institutions and by broader social structures. The findings suggest there is a research gap in terms of examining the importance of intersectionality in understanding GBV and informing BI programmes. GBV and the gender norms that underpin it may be experienced differently by students depending on (perceived) race and sexuality. Training needs to address the links between these and other axes of inequality such as class, disability and non-binary gender presentations.

The findings also demonstrate the need to engage with postfeminist equalisation discourses within which sexist and heteronormative attitudes and behaviours are re-packaged as individual, freely chosen modes of acting and being; and GBV as essentially a private matter for the victim rather than a community issue. In the postfeminist neoliberal context which de-politicises/de-genders GBV, our findings reiterate criticisms of some US initiatives which overemphasise individualised solutions to GBV and employ problematic, de-gendered concepts of 'power-based violence' (Coker et al, 2011; Katz et al, 2011: 689). Prevention education potentially can raise awareness of these complexities, including shifting de-gendered conceptualisations of GBV:

> 'I was of the opinion [...] that it was sort of 50–50 split of men abusing women, women abusing men [...] But now I realise that's not the case at all. And that made me really think about things differently [...] They're really amazing lessons [...] I would go back and be thinking about it hours later.' (Ethan, theatre student)

Another programme volunteer reported that training enabled her to make connections between the "less serious" and "more extreme" manifestations of GBV, making her less tolerant of the former. Finally, the analysis highlights both the constraints on, and possibilities for, student resistance in the context of responses from other agents (including other students, universities, social media sites and nightclubs), and the nature of 'interventions' in different contexts. What constitutes an intervention needs further interrogation, as does the possibility of defining and measuring 'success'. The Get Savi student union society, established by programme volunteers following the programme, uses social media to challenge GBV. The impact of such engagements is inherently difficult to assess. Simply by making dissent visible, their activities may create space for others including victims/survivors to find support and encounter alternative perspectives. Social media, as a platform, can increase the visibility of resistance, but as this space is deeply embedded in gendered (and other) inequalities, dissenting voices are often marginalised. Online anonymity can both enable students to challenge their peers more easily than in face-to-face settings, and provide indemnity for perpetrators of abuse.

The analysis of students' experiences of the NTE reveals further issues around defining intervention/resistance. In these spaces, acts of GBV are often ephemeral and embedded within dominant cultural norms, meaning collective resistance for women seeking to inhabit these spaces is particularly challenging. Understanding strategies used by students to evade or challenge GBV is therefore instructive in analysing the nature of resistance at this individual, micro-level, as well as in illuminating how available modes of resistance might serve to re-inscribe prevailing gender norms.

Institutional support from the university and engagement with external environments is vital, given that nightclubs, bars and other 'off-campus' social venues are key sites of GBV, but there are limitations. UOL blocked the use of Yik Yak through the University server (O'Dell, 2016) due to concerns about cyberbullying, but students bypassed this through their own internet access.

Prevention education can help facilitate a culture of challenging, rather than a culture of normalisation. Programme volunteers suggested training had made them more likely to intervene. However, the interviews also demonstrated the constraints on resistance. It is therefore vital that BI programmes prepare volunteers for the reality of intervention. In addition, programmes must not become a tool used by institutions to responsibilise students for their 'own' safety. As the incident in the lecture theatre suggests, collaborations between lecturers and students and visible institutional support are crucial to creating violence-free learning environments.

Notes

[1]   While we share concerns about the usefulness of 'lad culture' as a concept (Phipps, 2016), we employ the term as it is dominant in the literature.

[2]   On the 28th April, 2017, Yik Yak announced that it would be shutting down.

[3]   Where interviewees participated in the theatre module (identified as 'theatre student') or in the peer-training programme ('programme-volunteer'), this is indicated the first time they are quoted. This is to differentiate students who took part in the theatrical aspects of the project, but not in the bystander intervention programme itself, from those who directly participated in the BI programme. See the methods section.

4   Although this did not take place on social media, the context was similar in terms of the use of digital technologies and as anonymity allowed the perpetrators to feel empowered to make offensive comments.

References

Ahrens, C.E., Rich, M.D. and Ullman, J. B. (2011) 'Rehearsing for real life: The impact of the InterACT Sexual Assault Prevention program on self-reported likelihood of engaging in bystander interventions', *Violence Against Women*, 17(6): 760–776.

Banyard, V.L., Moynihan, M.M. and Plante, E.G. (2007) 'Sexual violence prevention through bystander education: an experimental evaluation', *Journal of Community Psychology*, 35: 463–81.

Brooks, O. (2011) '"Guys! Stop doing it!" Young women's adoption and rejection of safety advice when socializing in bars, pubs and clubs', *British Journal of Criminology*, 51: 635–51.

Casey, E.A. and Lindhorst, T.P. (2009) 'Toward a multi-level, ecological approach to the primary prevention of sexual assault: prevention in peer and community contexts', *Trauma, Violence & Abuse*, 10 (2): 91–114.

Coker, A.L., Cook-Craig, P.G., Williams, C.M., Fisher, B.S., Clear, E.R., Garcia, L.S. and Hegge, L.M. (2011) 'Evaluation of Green Dot: an active bystander intervention to reduce sexual violence on college campuses', *Violence Against Women*, 17 (6): 777–96.

Connell, R.W. (2005) *Masculinities*, second edition, Berkeley; Los Angeles: University of California Press.

Connell, R. (2011) *Confronting Equality: Gender, Knowledge and Global Change*, Cambridge: Polity Press.

Dempster, S. (2011) 'I drink, therefore I'm man: gender discourses, alcohol and the construction of British undergraduate masculinities', *Gender and Education*, 23(5): 635–53.

García-Favaro, L. and Gill, R. (2016) '"Emasculation nation has arrived': sexism rearticulated in online responses to Lose the Lads' Mags campaign', *Feminist Media Studies*, 16 (3): 379–97.

Gill, R. (2007) *Gender and the Media*, Cambridge: Polity Press.

Gill, R. (2009) 'Beyond the "sexualization of culture" thesis: an intersectional analysis of "sixpacks", "midriffs" and "hot lesbians" in advertising', *Sexualities*, 12 (2): 137–60.

Gill, R. (2011) 'Bend it like Beckham? The challenges of reading gender and visual culture' in P. Reavey (ed) *Visual Methods in Psychology: Using and Interpreting Images in Qualitative Research*, London and New York; Routledge, pp 29–42.

Graham, K., Bernards, S. Abbey, A., Dumas, T.M. and Wells, S. (2016) 'When women do not want it: young female bargoers' experiences with and responses to sexual harassment in social drinking contexts', *Violence Against Women*, 23 (12): 1419–41.

Griffin, C., Szmigin, I., Bengry-Howell, A., Hackley, C. and Mistral, W. (2013) 'Inhabiting the contradictions: hypersexual femininity and the culture of intoxication among young women in the UK', *Feminism & Psychology*, 23: 184–206.

Jackson, C. and Dempster, S. (2009) '"I sat back on my computer... with a bottle of whisky next to me": constructing "cool" masculinity through "effortless" achievement in secondary and higher education', *Journal of Gender Studies*, 18 (4): 341–56.

Jackson, C. and Sundaram, V. (2015) *Is "Lad Culture" a Problem in Higher Education? Exploring the Perspectives of Staff Working in UK Universities*, London: Society for Research into Higher Education.

Jackson, C., Dempster, S. and Pollard, L. (2015) '"They just don't seem to really care, they just think it's cool to sit there and talk": laddism in university teaching-learning contexts', *Educational Review*, 67 (3): 300–14.

Jordan, A. (2016) 'Conceptualising backlash: (UK) men's rights groups, anti-feminism and postfeminism', *Canadian Journal of Women and the Law*, 28 (1): 18–44.

Katz, J., Heisterkamp, H.A. and Fleming, W.M. (2011) 'The social justice roots of the mentors in violence prevention model and its application in a high school setting', *Violence Against Women*, 17 (6): 684–702.

Kavanaugh, P.R. (2013) 'The continuum of sexual violence: women's accounts of victimization in urban nightlife', *Feminist Criminology*, 8: 20–39.

Kelly, L. and Radford, J. (1990) '"Nothing really happened": the invalidation of women's experiences of sexual violence', *Critical Social Policy*, 10: 39–53.

Levy, A. (2005) *Female Chauvinist Pigs: Women and the Rise of Raunch Culture*, 1st. Australian edn., London: Pocket Books.

Lewis, R., Marine, S. and Kenney, K. (2016) '"I get together with my friends and try to change it": young feminist students resist "laddism", "rape culture" and "everyday sexism"', *Journal of Gender Studies*, 27 (1): 56–72.

MacKinnon, C. (1979) *Sexual Harassment of Working Women*, New Haven, CT: Yale University Press.McRobbie, A. (2009) *The Aftermath of Feminism: Gender, Culture and Social Change*, London: Sage.

Mitchell, K.S. and Freitag, J.L. (2011) 'Forum theatre for bystanders: a new model for gender violence prevention', *Violence Against Women*, 17 (8): 990–1013.

Moynihan, M.M. and Banyard, V.L. (2008) 'Community responsibility for preventing sexual violence: a pilot study with campus Greeks and intercollegiate athletes', *Journal of Prevention & Intervention in the Community*, 36: 23–38.

Nicholls, E.M.L. (2015) 'Running the tightrope: negotiating femininities in the night time economy in Newcastle', PhD Thesis, Newcastle University, UK.

O'Dell, L. (2016) 'Freedom of speech concerns as university blocks Yik Yak', *The Linc*, 24 February, http://thelinc.co.uk/2016/02/freedom-of-speech-concerns-as-university-blocks-yik-yak/

Phipps, A. (2016) '(Re)theorising laddish masculinities in higher education', *Gender and Education*, 29 (7): 815–30.

Phipps, A. and Young, I. (2015a) 'Neoliberalisation and lad cultures in higher education', *Sociology*, 49 (2): 305–22.

Phipps, A. and Young, I. (2015b) '"Lad culture" in higher education: agency in the sexualisation debates', *Sexualities*, 18 (4): 459–79.

Potter, S.J., Moynihan, M.M., Stapleton, J.G. and Banyard, V.L. (2009) 'Empowering bystanders to prevent campus violence against women: a preliminary evaluation of a poster campaign', *Violence Against Women*, 15(1): 106–21.

Renold, E. and Ringrose, J. (2011) 'Schizoid subjectivities? re-theorizing teen girls' sexual cultures in an era of "sexualisation"', *Journal of Sociology*, 47 (4): 389–409.

Ronen, S. (2010) 'Grinding on the dance floor: gendered scripts and sexualized dancing at college parties', *Gender & Society*, 24: 355–77.

Scharff, C. (2012) *Repudiating Feminism: Young Women in a Neoliberal World*, Farnham: Ashgate.

Sue, D.W. (2010) *Microaggressions in Everyday Life: Race, Gender, and Sexual Orientation*, Hoboken, NJ: John Wiley & Sons.

Tan, Q.H. (2014) 'Postfeminist possibilities: unpacking the paradoxical performances of heterosexualized femininity in club spaces', *Social & Cultural Geography*, 15 (1): 23–48.

Tinkler, J.E, Becker, S. and Clayton, K.A. (2016) '"Kind of natural, kind of wrong": young people's beliefs about the morality, legality, and normalcy of sexual aggression in public drinking settings', *Law & Social Inquiry*, doi: 10.1111/lsi.12235

Waitt, G., Jessop, L. and Gorman-Murray, A. (2011) "The guys in there just expect to be laid": embodied and gendered socio-spatial practices of a "night out" in Wollongong, Australia', *Gender, Place & Culture*, 18 (2): 255–75.

10

Tackling gender based violence in university communities: a practitioner perspective

Ellie Hutchinson

In recent years, universities across the UK have begun exploring, developing and testing bystander approaches to tackling violence against women and girls (VAWG). Differing in their approaches, the programmes are underpinned by a belief that sexist social norms are at the root of violence and that by utilising social marketing techniques and prevention education programmes, aimed at non-perpetrating men, social norm change can occur. By engaging with men as allies, bystander programmes aim to create positive social environments, upskilling men and women and supporting them to challenge peers engaged in sexist behaviour. At the heart of this approach is a belief that sexist social norms, as they are learnt, can be unlearnt, challenged, and ultimately changed.

This chapter provides a brief outline of how one such approach – Get Savi (Students Against Violence Initiative) – was developed and delivered in Scotland between 2012 and 2015. Focusing first on the broader policy and political context in which this programme was developed, this chapter explores the importance of a political consensus around the causes of VAWG. Crucial to the development of Get Savi was both a political and practitioner consensus around adopting the socio-ecological approach to violence prevention, most vividly represented in national policy approaches developed by the Scottish Government. The financial environment at this time also enabled violence against women organisations to begin utilising partnerships and expertise to develop prevention education work. Alongside the broader context, this chapter also explores the role of partnerships in the development and in the re-imagining of the prevention education programme for a Scottish audience, based on the success of US approaches. Finally, it highlights some of the ongoing challenges such as the difficulties in generating long-term evaluations and in producing robust research around the relationship between programme attendance and campus-wide behaviour change, due in part to the reluctance of institutions to engage at the senior and administrative level. By drawing together learnings from the project this chapter seeks to make recommendations for future policies and programmes on prevention education for student communities in the UK and beyond.

The policy and political context in Scotland

It was no coincidence that Scotland was the first country within the UK to test bystander programmes. Much has been written about the role of female MSPs (Members of the Scottish Parliament) and feminist organisations in promoting a positive policy environment in which to challenge violence against women in all its forms (MacKay and Breitenbach, 2001). The Scottish Parliament was established in 1999 and by 2000 a national strategy to address domestic abuse was published. This strategy noted that, domestic abuse 'is part of a range of behaviours constituting male abuse of power, and is linked to other forms of male violence' (The Scottish Executive, 2000: 5), setting the scene for a sophisticated, and importantly, gendered, understanding of domestic abuse, not seen within Westminster policies at the time of writing. This gendered understanding was no doubt brought about by the successful lobbying of feminist and women's organisations across the country.

This top-level consensus about the very causes of violence and abuse – that is gender inequality – was based on an analysis that made explicit the links between gender inequality and violence, allowing organisations to develop programmes and policies tackling issues across the continuum of abuse (Kelly, 1988). This approach contrasts with a so-called 'gender-neutral' approach which obscures or makes invisible the significance of gender and is unable to address the root causes of the violence. The Scottish policy context used the socio-ecological model to understand VAWG. A public health and a rights-based model, the socio-ecological model enables an understanding of VAWG as a complex, multi-layered issue that can be understood through a focus on the individual and their particular histories and contexts such as education, income, ethnicity; the various relationships they are part of and which influence them; the broader community and its values, norms and practices; and the broader socioeconomic factors and policies related to, for example, health and education, which create a structural context that inhibits or encourages violence and social inequalities between groups. The causal explanation for VAWG is complex and results from a combination of multiple influences on behaviour. It is about how individuals relate to those around them and to their broader environment. The socio-ecological model allows us to address the factors that put people at risk for or protect them from experiencing or perpetrating violence (risk and protective factors) and the prevention strategies that can be used at each level to address these factors (CDC, undated).

The socio-ecological model outlines how, at each level of an individual's life, there are opportunities to challenge, resist and change social norms. For anti-VAWG practitioners this means challenging at the individual level sexist and rigid understandings of how men and women 'should' behave and the acceptability of violence and abuse towards women. A crucial aspect of the Scottish policy on VAWG was the recognition of all three dimensions of responses to this problem – prosecution, protection and prevention, the last of which was much neglected in the UK. With a gendered analysis in place and a top-level strategy to address VAWG, the Scottish Government has developed training strategies, ring fenced and protected funding for children's workers, ring fenced funding for service providers and developed prevention strategies to address all forms of VAWG.

In the early to mid-2000s, VAWG prevention work in Scotland was mainly focused on children and young people, understanding children and young people as both resisters and conduits for emerging social norms. In 2008, the National Domestic Abuse Delivery Plan for Children and Young People Experiencing Domestic Abuse (hereafter, the Delivery Plan) was developed, calling for action across the four Ps – protection, provision, prevention and protection. In 2009, the NSPCC published ground-breaking research into abuse in teenagers' intimate relationships (Barter et al, 2009). This research refocused VAWG organisations on the experiences of young people and reinvigorated policy work to prevent violence in a period when children and young people were beginning to come to the attention of researchers, practitioners and policymakers seeking to understand and challenge VAWG.

It was in this context that the Delivery Plan was rolled out over the subsequent years. While the Plan highlighted specific actions needed to tackle social norms and explore the role of education within prevention, it omitted to place VAWG in a broader economic and structural context. For example, the Plan's work on prevention focused heavily on education, seeing young people as conduits for change. While this approach enabled deeper conversations with educators and young people around sex, relationships and domestic abuse, it failed to address the impact of broader economic signifiers of inequality –

for example, poverty and equal pay, and how they directly influence perceptions of entitlement and ability.[1] Consequently, much work developed from this high-level policy focused on the ability of children and young people to resist social norms, rather than on the adults and institutions responsible for them, or on the broader structural context within which these norms are fostered.

Although the Equality Unit was instrumental in leading this work, it was difficult to work across departments and bring in other work areas – such as Education or Children and Young People. Critically, education in the Scottish context is de-centralised, meaning that in practice each local authority area delivers education priorities inconsistently – with some children and young people accessing prevention education in particularly committed (and resourced) areas, such as Dundee City (Dundee Violence Against Women Partnership, 2010) and other children denied access to this work.

However, with a clear focus on prevention, the Delivery Plan undoubtedly created a positive environment for organisations to develop work based around social norm change. It is argued here that the shift to prevention also occurred during times of relative economic stability whereby battles to secure funding for the very existence of frontline services had been (somewhat) tempered. During this time, Women's Aid groups offered at least one children's worker per group through government funding, enhancing the work they were able to do with children and young people in schools. This established strong networks between groups and schools, and broadened their role within the community to include education and awareness raising. Previously, much of this work had been unfunded; the Delivery Plan made the work and roles explicit and created a mandate for prevention education to occur within education establishments.

Relative financial stability created a context conducive to partnership working unlike in England, where cuts to the funding of domestic violence services, short funding cycles and the tendering process increasingly pitted services against each other for a diminishing pool of resources. The very different context in Scotland enabled national and local VAWG organisations to collaborate effectively, both in the policy arena and in service delivery. Organisations such as Rape Crisis Scotland, Scottish Women's Aid (SWA) and Zero Tolerance,[2] which had historically close working relationships, were able to develop partnerships with newly established White Ribbon Campaign (WRC)[3] as well as Amnesty International. LGBT Youth's domestic abuse project, and worker, were increasingly lobbying the violence against women field for better support and understanding of the issues faced by LGBT young people in accessing domestic abuse services, and thus close working relationships were established (LGBT Youth Scotland, 2011). On an informal level, the size of the sector meant that staff regularly worked in several organisations, had some ties with partner organisations or even shared office spaces, creating a strong informal network of organisations and individuals working to prevent VAWG. The VAWG partnerships at the local level further entrenched these networks, and the Prevention Network, co-ordinated by Zero Tolerance, embedded these relationships. Further, a collaborative, consensus-driven ethos underpinned many of the organisations, explicitly feminist in their praxis, creating an environment of positive and productive partnership working. In sum, then, the stage was set for the development of a collaborative prevention education initiative aimed at children and/or young people.

In the context of this policy-driven working consensus on the meaning of prevention and the causes of VAWG across Scotland, by 2007 many organisations were working on the understanding of prevention as being community-focused with an emphasis on healthy relationships, consent and positive masculinities. The following section outlines how this context enabled the development of the Get Savi programme.

Building consensus, laying the ground work: developing the Get Savi programme

As the largest and oldest domestic abuse charity in the country, SWA was well-placed to promote prevention education with children and young people within a broader focus on domestic abuse. As the national umbrella group of 39 affiliated Women's Aid groups in Scotland, the organisation could draw on the knowledge and experience of workers on the ground to explore and identify gaps in service provision and policy development. During this development phase, each group had at least one children's worker in post, and some were staffed with training or education workers. SWA was also able to appoint a Prevention Worker (and author of this chapter) with a specific focus on prevention policy. This post was situated within the Children and Young People's policy team, which located prevention work within an educational approach, focusing on building positive relationships from an early age. For SWA, this meant a continuation of the work already undertaken directly with children and young people experiencing domestic abuse, and the ethos of co-production and involvement in policy development and campaign messaging.[4] The Prevention Worker at SWA was responsible for developing policy responses to abuse in young people's relationships and promoting healthy relationships as well as supporting the work of local member organisations (Women's Aid groups), local authorities and national policymakers in promoting a prevention education approach to preventing domestic abuse.

Critics of this shift towards prevention education rightly noted that funding for prevention workers and projects was often temporary and that, during times of economic restraint, funding for education and prevention services is often withdrawn, that service provision was still patchy and that crisis support was still underfunded. However, in Scotland, funding was provided through the Scottish Government who accorded higher priority to prevention work than was the case in the rest of the UK, where Women's Aid groups and other VAWG service providers existed in a consistently precarious funding environment with a focus on operational survival and crisis provision, stretching their resources and challenging their very ability to operate (Ellis, 2008). In addition, services in England were operating within a political environment that ideologically favoured a gender invisible approach which (see Donaldson et al, Chapter Five in this volume), as argued earlier, fails to acknowledge or address root causes of VAWG.

The initial work of the Prevention Worker at SWA involved mapping current prevention education methods across the country, bringing together resources within the growing prevention field in Scotland and identifying gaps in practice (Ellis, 2008). This research identified gaps in existing prevention education programmes, which included: institutional reluctance to recognise the existence of and to address the issue of gender based violence (GBV); the limited focus of sex and relationships education where little attention was given to issues of active consent (compared to a focus on sexual health and contraception); and lack of consistent, coherent and accessible policy and practice responses to abuse in young people's relationships, findings which resonate with other literature (Ellis and Thiara, 2014). Inconsistencies across local authorities were also noted, with some dedicating teams and resources to aligning education, health and violence against women organisations, and with others focusing solely on crisis support.[5] In a context where violence, including sexual violence, against young women is not consistently identified as a social problem and recognised as violence, there is an inherent limitation of crisis-led responses as these approaches incorrectly assume that victims recognise and name their experiences as abuse and seek help. Additionally such a response does little in terms of early intervention and prevention, which require an ongoing and active engagement with the underlying causes of violence and abuse.

This mapping research identified the need for and the potential of bystander programmes, and a working group to develop a Scottish response was then established with representatives from Zero Tolerance, Rape Crisis Scotland, LGBT Youth, White Ribbon Scotland, National Union of Students (NUS) Scotland and SWA. The Prevention Worker based within SWA researched existing evidence about the effectiveness of bystander programmes, and assessed their potential value within the Scottish context. This review of existing bystander interventions and the debates surrounding them informed the framing and the content of the bystander programme, Get Savi, developed in collaboration with the above mentioned working group.

The first issue identified was the underlying ideological approach that can inform particular interventions; some interventions focus on individual change and responsibility to intervene in situations, whereas others emphasise broader cultural change. Programmes that focused solely on individual behaviour, particularly those that focused on the potential victims through responsibilisation strategies such as self-defence training and altering their own conduct, were immediately rejected. Approaches that did not identify or sufficiently critique broader social structures that underpin particular acts of GBV – for example, those that individualised problematic behaviour rather than locating it within power relations and structural inequalities based on hierarchies of gender and sexuality – were also deemed inappropriate. Additionally, approaches such as those in the military that took a top-down approach to behaviour change (for example through rote-learning such as 'repeat after me' training scenarios) were discounted as inappropriate for both the Scottish context and long-term impact. The working group also considered approaches that have been utilised in the US which draw upon traditional modes of masculinity as a tool in reducing VAWG – for example 'real men don't rape' or 'my strength is not for hurting' campaigns and terminology. Following discussions, these approaches were rejected as it was judged that their understandings of manhood could reaffirm traditional models of masculinity and femininity which construct women as inherently vulnerable and in need of protection, and known men as potential protectors of women from stranger men (Stanko, 1990), and thereby undermine a structural approach to ending violence that is based on a critique of binary constructions of masculinity and femininity. (For feminist critiques of anti-violence campaigns which draw on problematic ideas of masculinity and femininity, see Escobar (2013) and Ferguson (2015).) Additionally messages that derive from dominant constructions of masculinity also risk a narrow focus on GBV in heterosexual relations, and invisibilise GBV against sexual minorities that is based on hierarchical constructions of gender and sexuality (Namaste, 1996; Cramer, 2011).

Within the bystander movement, one key point of conflict is around the 'gendering' of violence, with some programmes taking a strategic or a politically driven gender invisible approach to enhance attendance.[6] It is argued that this approach may encourage more institutional buy-in in the initial stages in a broader political context which degenders GBV. According to this argument, in terms of engaging students, an approach that – at least initially – invisibilises gender may encourage more attendees, as well as minimise resistance from men and from those women who might feel uncomfortable at the focus on gender. Such an approach may also be premised on the common sense understanding that everyone – at a basic level – wants to be a pro-social rather than an anti-social person, and hence an active bystander in the context of an intervention programme. Given the resistance to recognising the gender-specificity of GBV, the notion of gender is introduced gradually and cautiously to minimise resistance from men. However, one criticism of bystander programmes which take this approach is that men are not 'silent bystanders' of sexism but beneficiaries. To deny men's culpability within an economic and cultural system designed to disempower women and privilege men is to underplay the structural elements at play.

Our approach to the problem of GBV was quite different; our starting point prioritised gender in understanding GBV, and recognised how structural inequalities underpin GBV and how GBV reinforces structural inequalities. We anticipated resistance because prevention education involves calling out and challenging privilege derived from gender and sexuality. A lack of resistance would imply either that the programme was not addressing and challenging the structural inequalities that underpin acts and expressions of GBV or that the participants were already questioning these hierarchies and engaged with these debates (which was often the case for members of feminist societies). Implicit in our feminist understanding of prevention education was that such education programmes would inevitably – and ideally – be delivered to participants who are victimised by GBV in its various manifestations, those who are observers and perhaps condone such behaviour or remain silent, as well as to participants who benefit from gender privilege and actively strive to maintain their privilege. We came to the conclusion that programmes that invisibilise gender fail to address structural and cultural change, and therefore it is posited that they will be unable to achieve long lasting and meaningful impacts.[7]

At the heart of our approach was the acknowledgement that while men's voices are crucial in ending violence against women, they are not central. Rather the experiences of survivors and women must be prioritised in work to end VAWG. By seeking to challenge sexist power dynamics in our own working relationships, we hoped to challenge sexist power dynamics in the classroom and beyond. While the role of men as allies was embraced within our approach, it was not centralised. In practical terms, this meant that in many instances, we sought to deliver the programme as mixed gender pairs, embedding a feminist praxis of *doing* as well as *believing*, and we sought to create a space for and facilitate conversations about GBV that were grounded in participants' real-life experiences of GBV – which meant privileging the voices of women and sexual minorities who experience such violences. To some extent, the delivery of the training in mixed gender pairs was also one way of overcoming resistance to programme content by men and some women.

Central to the development of what would become the Get Savi programme was a recognition that the North American context was somewhat different to the Scottish context. The working group was committed to ensuring the programme would reflect not only the Scottish context, but also the local institutional context in which the training would be delivered. Unlike the institutional context in US universities, Scottish university and college students have comparatively few pastoral care structures and fewer opportunities to develop cross-campus communities. Similarly there is currently no central funding for university-based GBV prevention programmes, supported and housed by the university and funded across state and federal bodies.[8] There are no fraternities or sororities or similar communities of accommodation and, unlike many American campuses, no mandatory training for all incoming students on issues relating to violence against women. There are no university-based violence against women crisis centres and no prevention officer based on campus.[9] In terms of institutional support for addressing (and acknowledging) VAWG, it could be argued the Scottish context provides minimal university-based dedicated support for victims of violence. Indeed, it can be argued that colleges and universities have been loath to engage with the existence of VAWG on campus, particularly when perpetrated by students themselves and even less so when perpetrated by university staff (Weale and Batty, 2016). University responses have been somewhat more responsive when their student is victimised by a non-student or a student of another university (NUS, 2010).

In the Scottish context, university responses to VAWG are therefore somewhat invisible. However, students themselves have been increasingly active and visible in responding to VAWG in universities. The NUS undertook a number of projects to explore GBV on campus, including work on lad culture, stalking and sexual harassment (NUS, 2010, 2012). Feminist activism has been reinvigorated, with offline and online activism becoming more and more vocal (Lewis et al, 2016; Lewis and Marine, Chapter Six in this volume). While this was a welcome development in terms of engaging with feminist activists on campus, it also created challenges as we worked to persuade student unions and university administrators that feminist groups were not solely responsible for challenging VAWG, but that the institution as a whole should also be held responsible.

Given the gender-specific understanding of the problem in the Scottish context and the ideological approach of the partner agencies, the working group came to a decision to utilise a discursive approach of curious non-judgement which is grounded in a feminist praxis of change, whereby the role of the trainer is not to direct but instead to create supportive spaces for individuals to develop their own knowledge and empower themselves. This approach was centred on a feminist understanding of GBV that could be adapted to the Scottish context. Following the review of literature on prevention education and evaluations of bystander programmes, the Green Dot and the University of New Hampshire's programmes were deemed most appropriate as models for development – combining institutional support, social marketing techniques, accessible training models, a non-judgemental discursive approach and importantly, robust and meaningful monitoring outcomes.[10]

The context in which Get Savi was developed was one with a highly energised, active student community, a healthy, well-funded, supportive VAWG sector, and a national, policy consensus supporting VAWG prevention work in local areas with a focus on healthy relationships and active consent. The combination of these three vital factors meant that we could experiment, innovate, try something new, to fail, to experiment, and ultimately to fully engage with young people on the kind of programme they needed to tackle VAWG within their own communities to make real, long lasting change.

Programme development: getting it wrong, getting it right

The Get Savi programme[11] focused on four key themes: i) GBV exists; ii) it is both the cause and the consequence of sexism; iii) we can (and should) challenge it; and iv) there are certain skills and techniques we can use to do this. The original model aimed to develop a peer network, with young people trained as peer educators to deliver the programme in their own communities within the first 18 months. It was intended that this programme would create a sustainable network supported by SWA and/or the WRC.

A peer to peer training method was developed, to ensure that messages were given (and absorbed) by members of the same community, leading to a better understanding of the issues, and a willingness to act and therefore change behaviours.[12] The initial training of the potential peer trainers was delivered by practised trainers working in SWA and WRC. The initial programmes were delivered to student volunteers, and it was immediately apparent that more women than men would sign up to support it and that, common across all VAWG work, many attendees were drawn to the programme through already identifying as feminists or as activists. These factors meant that our initial ability to engage with non-perpetrating (and non-engaging men) was reduced, and that different ways to engage with men would be required. To engage with men, we identified supportive NUS representatives and student societies to act as conduits for engagement, and sessions were held with chairs from a variety of societies including sports, feminist, LGBT, BME and social groups. The most supportive and vocal students for dispersing the programme throughout their institutions were often linked to a number of societies. The programme was also delivered to university staff, student societies and groups in response to requests following media-publicised acts of misogyny and discrimination by young men in leadership positions within the university.

The programme developed as the attendees brought their own experiences of hearing, and collectively devised effective mechanisms for challenging, sexist and homophobic comments made by family and friends such as "that's so gay" and derisive use of the phrase "like a girl". Rather than prescribe scenarios to discuss in workshops, we supported participants to anonymously submit scenarios which were then used in workshop discussions. Other learnings from initial roll-outs of Get Savi were that both the length of the workshop and our expectations of students were unrealistic. With many of them talking about violence for the first time, the leap from educated to educator was too far. Similarly it became clear that weekend workshops would not be attractive for most students.

To support the delivery of the programme and address some of the practical barriers, we created an online wiki on terms and practice tools for students, redeveloped the programme to be undertaken either in one day or in two afternoon settings, and tailored the programme to audiences' needs. As we delivered more and more sessions to more and more students across the country – over 100 in total – it became clear that feminist groups required different conversation starters and introductions to the gendered analysis than other groups, that LGBT societies wanted to dedicate time to talk about homophobia, that staff and students from sports and entertainment societies required more support in developing their understanding of the issues, and that the role of the trainer should shift from trainer/instructor to facilitator/mediator in mixed gender groups. This facilitation/mediator role was particularly important when women disclosed instances of sexual harassment, violence, microaggressions and sexism to their male peers. These conversations provided much more powerful learning moments than theoretical examples ever could. This learning – about how to create an open, non-judgemental space while dealing positively with disclosures – was vital in how we trained peer educators. It was apparent from the early stages that many attendees had an expectation that the course would provide 'answers' to how to challenge VAWG. Creating a space for people to explore their own experiences safely – through anonymously submitting scenarios and discussing them in small groups – enabled attendees to fully explore what worked for them, rather than simply responding with what they thought they 'should' say. Embedding an ethos of person-centred change, of non-judgemental facilitating, and feminist praxis required facilitators to actively listen and respond to issues arising and provide a skilled response to unexpected questions – something that many peer educators felt unable to do initially.

One of the shortcomings of this early phase of Get Savi was that the programme did not fully explore the intersections of race and privilege, a gap that was picked up by some participants themselves. This was likely due to the lack of lived experience of the project board, resulting in a gap in the delivery of the programme. However, due to the openness of the approach, and the levelling of power dynamics within the classroom, we were able to redevelop parts of the programme having learnt from the students directly.

Through listening, reflecting and learning from the positive response to Get Savi, we extended the project to run over four years. At the end of this period, we were able to recruit a number of young people as peer educators from NUS Scotland, Queen Margaret University in Edinburgh, Robert Gordon University in Aberdeen and the University of Lincoln. Students who attended the course were able to develop standalone campaigns and programmes for other students with support from academics. However, with staff changes and shifts in organisational priorities, it was difficult to sustain a conversation with peer educators or trained students to document how the programme evolved over the course of its delivery through the peer students' networks and over the years as it cascaded down.

Monitoring and evaluation: learning through doing

While the delivery of the course was organic, the four themes remained central: that GBV exists; that it is both a cause and a consequence of sexism; that speaking out can help to create anti-violent cultures; that there are ways to speak out safely. Resistance to the first two themes was often encountered by groups who had been mandated to attend (particularly male staff) and some young men; however, as most groups were self-selecting we encountered little active resistance from young men, but we did factor in extra time and facilitation skills to give more space to explore sexism and incidences of violence where resistance was particularly evident. Taking a person-centred and group-ed approach to programme delivery did result in better and more meaningful engagement with groups – this was reflected in positive post-programme evaluations around enjoyment and skill development – but in terms of evaluating the programme long term it became harder to identify change as each session was delivered according to the needs of each group.

Initial plans to undertake long-term evaluation of the programme were thwarted by the lack of institutional support and lack of obligatory responsibilities.[13] The evaluations undertaken at the end of each session were not robust enough to draw any conclusions. The limitations of the type of data we could collect were three-fold. The evaluations did not measure long-term individual change; there was no means of capturing institutional and cultural change; and there was no baseline survey against which to measure attitudinal change. Therefore, although we knew that attendees had intentions to change, we knew little of how they did change, and what impact this intention may have had. Further, without institutional support, behaviour change was limited to individual acts, rather than shifts in whole campus cultures. Meaningful and in-depth change requires not only individual confidence to challenge, but also institutional support for anti-violence cultures. It was this institutional support that was predominantly lacking.

Without collecting baseline attitudes and behaviours from communities we were unable to fully explore the impact Get Savi has had on campus communities and what the needs for further engagement were.[14] While it was possible, then, to gain insight into the process of behaviour change, and we could identify some elements of short-term change, it was harder to gain any insight into long-term behaviour and cultural change.

Conclusion: learning and recommendations

Throughout the period of the project, we gained several insights into the theory and praxis of running a bystander programme for over 16-year-olds in further and higher education. First, the favourable context in which we developed the programme must be acknowledged.

The gendered understanding of violence at the government level enabled us to pitch our explicitly feminist programme to further and higher education establishments. Without this high level of support our ability to engage with students or develop the programme as we did would have been greatly reduced. In the financial and political context, prevention education was deemed not only a legitimate funding arena, but also a necessary one. This not only created an environment where we could experiment with emerging practice, but also enabled us to apply a feminist praxis of collective working, without fear of competing for ever decreasing funding pots.

Second, by applying a feminist praxis, we could take a person–centred approach to facilitating change, creating safe spaces for empowerment. We then enabled groups to develop their own tools to challenge sexism and supported them in a group setting to hear each other's experiences of living within patriarchy. However, this approach created challenges in terms of creating robust evaluation tools. By shifting programme delivery according to the needs of each group, we were unable to fully evaluate the long-term impact of the programme as a whole.

Lastly, the reach of our programme and our inability to evaluate the programme was further compounded by the reluctance of university management to engage with the programme at all. For example, we were unable to engage on an in-depth level with men as allies, and our ability to target traditionally masculine societies (such as sports) was greatly undermined by lack of institutional support. In the main, we ended up working with student societies and individual students, and ran only three sessions involving staff. We were unable to undertake whole-community social marketing campaigns or to support the development of anti-VAWG policy and practice on campus. We were unable to undertake baseline surveys without which we were unable to evaluate what long-term or widespread change may have occurred.

For bystander programmes in the UK to have the success of their North American counterparts, several factors must be in place. There must be institutional support from the outset, involving all societies, staff and students. Support services for students must be visible and accessible, and have a specialist knowledge of VAWG. Baseline surveys must be conducted on attitudes to violence and prevalence. All staff and students should undertake bystander training, and administrations should develop policies around reporting, as recommended by Universities UK (2016). Bystander programmes should also be supported by a social marketing campaign that utilises various media accessed by students and staff. Finally, to ensure robust monitoring and evaluations, there must be post-programme surveys exploring attitudinal and behaviour change in the short and long term.

Without these changes, it is likely that bystander programmes will remain the preserve of feminist, LGBT and particular student societies that have explicit lived experience of the issues and a developed understanding of GBV. For bystander programmes to be successful within and across campus communities, institutions must acknowledge the incidence and prevalence of GBV. They must acknowledge that GBV is a human rights as well as a public health issue, and that as communities and public bodies, they have a duty to protect students from preventable violence and abuse. Innovation requires risk, and risk requires support. Without that support – financial, cultural and political support – innovative programmes to address norm changes at the individual, community and institutional level will simply not succeed. It is our plea that campus administrators invest in this approach and provide students with the opportunity to learn, live and thrive in safe and supportive communities.

Notes

[1] See the Scottish Government's 'National Domestic Abuse Delivery Plan for Children and Young People', www.gov.scot/Publications/2008/06/17115558/0

[2] Zero Tolerance is a Scotland-based prevention education charity working to end men's violence against women by promoting gender equality and by challenging attitudes which normalise violence and abuse. Its work began in 1992 with a series of iconic awareness raising poster campaigns.

[3] The White Ribbon Scotland campaign provides training and information workshops to engage men and give them the skills to stand up to violence against women.

[4] Previous campaigns and research involving children and young people include the Listen Louder campaign around safe contact in the context of abusive fathers and support needs (https://vimeo.com/128989352) and the Support Needs of Children and Young People who have to move house because of domestic abuse (Stafford et al, 2007).

[5] This inconsistency is replicated across the UK, with some children and young people able to access prevention education initiatives, and some barely able to access crisis support. With no ring fenced funding at either the local or the national level dedicated towards prevention, it is often the first service to go.

[6] These ideas on gender and prevention education have been developed through conversations with Sundari Anitha.

[7] For more in-depth analysis, see https://aifs.gov.au/publications/bystander-approaches/challenges-implementing-bystander-approaches-responding-and-preventing-sexual-violence

[8] Within the American context, however, there is federally distributed and centrally ring fenced funding for such programmes: https://fas.org/sgp/crs/misc/R42499.pdf

[9] Durham University created a new post of Student Support and Training Officer (Sexual Violence & Misconduct) in the Academic Support Office in 2016. It is believed this is the first such post in the UK.

[10] See http://cola.unh.edu/prevention-innovations-research-center/evidence-based-initiatives#BEM for the University of New Hampshire programme and https://alteristic.org/progress/for evaluations of the Green Dot.

[11] http://www.preventionplatform.co.uk/?p=3015

[12] See www.eab.com/research-and-insights/student-affairs-forum/custom/2014/09/peer-led-sexual-violence-prevention-program-operationscontent%20page

[13] In many US and some UK institutions, bystander programmes are undertaken as part of a course requirement (such as within the University of New Hampshire) and pre- and post-programme surveys must be undertaken by participants to fulfil course requirements.

[14] A further approach to support social norm change is that of community readiness. A community readiness approach analyses the community's readiness to make change around a public health issue, and provides a framework for campaigning and lobbying. See http://triethniccenter.colostate.edu/docs/CR_Handbook_8-3-15.pdf

References

Barter, C., McCarry, M., Berridge, D. and Evans, K. (2009) *Partner Exploitation and Violence in Teenage Intimate Relationship*, London: NSPCC.

CDC (undated) *The Socio-Ecological Model: A Framework for Violence Prevention*, Atlanta: Center for Disease Control, https://www.cdc.gov/violenceprevention/overview/social-ecologicalmodel.html

Cramer, E. (ed) (2011) *Addressing Homophobia and Heterosexism on College Campuses*, New York: Routledge.Dundee Violence Against Women Partnership (2010) *Our Rights: Children and Young People's Consultation Event Report*, 1 March, www.dvawp.co.uk/sites/all/files/imceuploads/Our%20Rights%20Report%20without%20pics.pdf

Ellis, J. (2008) 'Primary Prevention of Domestic Abuse through Education' in C. Humphreys, C. Houghton and J. Ellis (2008) *Literature Review: Better Outcomes for Children and Young People affected by Domestic Abuse – Directions for Good Practice*, Edinburgh: Scottish Government.

Ellis, J. and Thiara, R. (eds) (2014) *Preventing Violence against Women and Girls: Educational Work with Children and Young People*, Bristol: Policy Press.

Escobar, S (2013) 'Why a mile in her shoes falls short and what people can do to prevent violence', The Gloss, 8 May, www.thegloss.com/culture/why-a-mile-in-her-shoes-falls-short-and-what-people-can-do-to-end-sexual-violence/

Ferguson, S. (2015) '3 Reasons Why Saying "Real Men Don't Rape" Reinforces Rape Culture', Everydayfeminism, 28 February, http://everydayfeminism.com/2015/02/real-men-do-rape/

Kelly, L. (1988) *Surviving Sexual Violence*, Cambridge: Polity Press

Lewis, R., Marine, S. and Kenney, K. (2016) '"I get together with my friends and I change it": Young feminist students resist 'laddism', 'rape culture' and 'everyday sexism", *Journal of Gender Studies*, 27 (1): 56–72.

LGBT Youth Scotland (2011) *Voices Unheard: Domestic Abuse – Lesbian, Gay, Bisexual and Transgender Young People's Perspectives*, www.lgbtyouth.org.uk/files/documents/02_Voices_Unheard/Reports/VoicesUnheardWeb2011.pdf

MacKay, F. and Breitenbach, E. (2001) *Women and Contemporary Scottish Politics: An Anthology*, Edinburgh: Edinburgh University Press.

Namaste, K. (1996) 'Genderbashing: Sexuality, Gender, and the Regulation of Public Space', *Environment and Planning D: Society and Space*, 14 (2): 221–40.

National Union of Students (NUS) (2010) *Hidden Marks: A Study of Women Students' Experiences of Harassment, Stalking, Violence and Sexual Assault*, London: NUS.

NUS (2012) *That's What She Said: Women Students' Experiences of "Lad Culture" at Universities*, London: NUS.

Scottish Executive (2000) *National Strategy to Address Domestic Abuse in Scotland. Scottish Partnership on Domestic Abuse*, www.gov.scot/Resource/Doc/158940/0043185.pdf

Stafford, A., Stead, J. and Grimes, M. (2007) *The Support Needs of Children and Young People who have to Move Home because of Domestic Abuse*, Edinburgh: Scottish Women's Aid.

Stanko, E. (1990) *Everyday Violence: How Women and Men Experience Sexual and Physical Danger*, London: Pandora.Universities UK (2016) *Changing the Culture, Report of the Universities UK Taskforce Examining Violence Against Women, Harassment and Hate Crime Affecting University Students*, London: UUK.

Weale, S. and Batty, D. (2016) 'Sexual harassment of students by university staff hidden by non-disclosure agreements', *Guardian*, 26 August, www.theguardian.com/education/2016/aug/26/sexual-harassment-of-students-by-university-staff-hidden-by-non-disclosure-agreements

Conclusion: setting the agenda for challenging gender based violence in universities

Ruth Lewis and Sundari Anitha

In the UK, we are at a pivotal moment regarding gender based violence (GBV) in universities. The preceding chapters reflect on lessons learned and directions for future approaches to tackling GBV. In this final chapter, we highlight the emerging key themes from the contributions to this volume and identify gaps and possibilities in current research and practice.

Exploring GBV as part of the continuum of violence

The chapters in this volume approach GBV as part of the continuum of violence (Kelly, 1988) that includes sexual violence and harassment, intimate partner violence, and homophobic and transphobic abuse. Rather than taking the narrower focus on sexual violence that some others adopt, especially in the US, our approach has been more broadly on the variety of forms of GBV. While focused examination of the particularities of specific forms of GBV has tremendous value for developing our understanding of the phenomenon and effective responses, it is vital we see these specific forms as part of the greater whole of the continuum of abuse that Kelly (1988) identified. Broader understanding of the various types of GBV as part of a continuum helps to highlight the connections between these different types of GBV, for example, advertising Freshers' Weeks events in ways that sexually objectify and demean women helps create a culture whereby sexual assault is normalised and victim-blaming is commonplace. This broader perspective highlights the role of not only behaviours but also attitudes and cultural norms in scaffolding sexism and misogyny, as identified by Sundaram (Chapter One in this volume) in her analysis of young people's conceptualisations of violence which lead to its toleration, normalisation and trivialisation. Understanding the attitudes and norms that underpin GBV helps recognise that interventions need to target a range of behaviours, attitudes and cultural norms; interventions such as *The Intervention Initiative* (Fenton and Mott's chapter), Stand Together

(Jordan et al's chapter) and Get Savi (Hutchinson's chapter) recognise the continuum and the connections between different manifestations of GBV.

However, some of the contributions to this book have tended to focus on sexual violence, sexual harassment and the 'wallpaper of sexism' (Lewis et al, 2015) in the context of the renewed interest in 'lad culture', rather than, for example, intimate partner violence or homophobic and transphobic abuse, both of which warrant further scholarly and policy attention. We recommend that future scholarly activity and interventions around GBV in universities continue to see the individual manifestations as part of the myriad of behaviours that constitute the continuum of GBV.

The UK's late attention to this problem means there are significant gaps in research evidence from which to develop effective practice. The NUS (2010) survey provided a valuable starting point of information about women students' experiences of harassment, stalking, violence and sexual assault and, perhaps most importantly, a vital platform from which to agitate for change. A new national study of the prevalence of GBV across UK universities is required to address its shortcomings and provide a reliable evidence base to guide future policies and interventions. Such a study would ideally build on the NUS (2010) survey and would also include: a continuum of sexual violence and domestic abuse including 'coercive control' (Stark, 2009), homophobia and transphobia; experiences of GBV among men and trans people; GBV in online as well as offline environments, and staff-on-student experiences of GBV. Individual institutions need local data about the 'climate' (including incidence and impact of GBV; patterns of reporting to the institution and other formal and informal contacts; and institutional responses), and the sector as a whole needs reliable, robust national quantitative and qualitative data, using consistent definitions of the different types of GBV. This will allow, inter alia, the mapping of continuities and differences throughout the country and will make available baseline data for measuring the effectiveness of future interventions. Cantor et al (2015) report wide variations in prevalence of sexual assault and misconduct between the 27 US institutions they surveyed. The reasons for these variations are unclear but suggest that sexual assault is by no means an inevitable feature of university life and that institutional factors may prevent or facilitate sexual assault and, by extension, other forms of GBV. A new national study of GBV in the UK would help us to identify and account for any such variations in the UK, in order to understand how to transform universities into GBV-resistant environments.

A significant gap in recent scholarship and practice is around staff-on-student and staff-on-staff violations. While this has been the subject of recent media attention (see Weale and Batty, 2016a, b; Batty et al, 2017; Willgress, 2016; Pells, 2016), it has received very little academic research attention since 'workplace harassment' was first exposed by feminist campaigners and scholars in the 1970s and 1980s (see MacKinnon, 1979; Hearn and Parkin, 1987). Anecdotally, many contemporary women scholars recall their days as young students and staff when sexual advances and coercion by some male staff were part of the academic terrain and they reflect with pleasure on the changed academic environment. However, the *Guardian* investigation (Batty et al, 2017) and the publicity around Sara Ahmed's resignation from Goldsmith's reveals that this kind of sexual violation is not a thing of the past. Scholarship and campaigning in the 1970s and 1980s about sexual harassment in the workplace were part of a wider challenge to gender inequalities, and women's exclusion, marginalisation and subjugation at work; it was informed by an awareness of the power dynamics at play in environments where large numbers of women were relative newcomers. Those power dynamics are particularly stark in the relationship between a supervisor/lecturer (typically a man) and student (typically a woman) which can be exploited, especially if the institution does not take steps to set and maintain standards of behaviour. However, as women have achieved greater representation in the workplace, notwithstanding remaining inequalities, and have changed those workplaces and cultures, have we, as scholars, taken our eye off the enduring forms of gendered hierarchies which have perhaps become more hidden in response to progress achieved in the gendered academic landscape? A fresh examination of the extent of these kinds of gendered intrusions in the lives of staff and students in the academic workplace, and of the institutional responses, is warranted as part of an effort to transform universities into GBV-resistant environments.

Recognising gender, resisting gender based violence

The chapters in this volume draw strongly on a feminist analysis of GBV and share a recognition of the significance of gender and the value of a feminist, intersectional approach to tackling this phenomenon. For example, Klein highlights the limitations of research about university violence which fails to recognise gender and the 'sexist male culture of sexual aggression and exploitation'. Chapters by Hutchinson and by Donaldson et al identify that a gendered understanding of GBV at the national policy level in Scotland and Wales has generated a policy environment conducive to initiatives that adopt a gendered approach. Fenton and Mott describe strategic efforts to de-centre gender in order to minimise (political and inter-personal) resistance to interventions. In different ways, all the contributions prioritise a gendered understanding of and approach to GBV in universities.

However, several of the chapters (for example, Jordan et al, Lewis and Marine) have highlighted the difficulties in conducting intersectional analysis of GBV in UK universities. There is then, a gap in knowledge and understanding of the intersections of different forms of oppression as part of GBV at universities. We call on future scholarship, policies and interventions about GBV in universities to explore and address the significance of gender as it intersects with, for example, racism, classism, disablism, homophobia and transphobia. As Phipps (in Chapter Two) highlights, 'lad culture' takes different forms among working class and privileged men. This begs the questions whether it also takes different forms among, for example, different ethnic groups; how are contemporary conceptualisations of young Asian men as dangerous – to national security and to women – enacted in the context of masculinities, heterosexuality, and GBV? How do homophobia and heteronormativity intersect to maintain the gender binary at a time when many young people are exploring a myriad of forms of gender and sexual identities?

A feminist intersectional framework for researching, theorising, and responding to GBV enables recognition that people are positioned differently along the various axes of power; for example, black and white men, heterosexual and queer men enjoy different kinds of 'masculine capital' (de Visser et al, 2009) which may influence their orientation to GBV. Such intersectional approaches reveal how these systems of power support each other to maintain the status quo. They also reveal how masculinity is played out differently by men according to where they are positioned in this matrix of power, revealing opportunities for disrupting problematic enactments of masculinity and promoting 'inclusive masculinities' (Anderson, 2005). By highlighting how widespread, normalised and 'everyday' sexism is experienced in different ways in different demographic and cultural groups, feminist intersectional approaches also help explain why some women support misogynistic attitudes and cultures – whether by adopting 'victim-blaming' attitudes, condoning aggressive masculinity as 'just a laugh', or by participating in ratings of sexual attractiveness and performance.

As argued in the Introduction and in chapters by Sundaram, Phipps, and Lewis and Marine, a structural intersectional feminist approach understands this violence as a form of gendered power which maintains the patriarchal, heteronormative status quo. This understanding of GBV helps us recognise the similarities among victims'/survivors' experiences and the similarities in behaviours of perpetrators which can inform tactics for intervention. Recognition of the shared experiences reveals GBV as a *social* problem, resulting from systematic, structural, gendered inequalities in power, rather than an individual problem of 'bullying' resulting from randomly distributed power differentials.

Approaches that centre gender are likely to meet with high levels of resistance, and that poses an additional set of challenges which future research and practice need to consider. Resistance to the progressive agenda of tackling GBV in universities comes from various directions: from those eager to protect their male privilege (men's rights activists and libertarians); from individual and groups of male students who feel criticised for what they see as reasonable masculine behaviour or because they feel they are being targeted as problematic because of their gender; from some men in academia who wish to protect the privilege of their status including unchallenged sexual access to students; from senior management who may be reluctant to reveal that GBV affects their institution, especially in times of increased competition for students; from those who have some sympathy for feminist politics but who fear that the focus on GBV highlights women's 'dreaded victim status' (Baker, 2008: 59). Activists, student leaders, university management and administrators, and scholars who wish to address GBV in universities tread carefully in this minefield of resistance to their efforts.

We encourage critical engagement with resistance. Resistance is an inevitable part of this work to dismantle powerful hierarchies and, indeed, an indication of success. After all, hierarchies do not willingly relinquish power; they resist attempts to challenge their 'rightful' retention of power. They challenge, deny and silence efforts to expose their power. They depict as problematic those who bring attention to the problem (as Ahmed details in her 'feministkilljoys' blog).[1] Work to expose GBV at universities is resisted in these ways (see Hutchinson, this volume) and such resistance is an indication that our work is taking hold and having an impact, although there may be a disproportionate amount of resistance in comparison with the successful challenge to power; as Phipps argues in her chapter, 'a *sense* of victimisation on the part of the privileged does not mean victimisation has occurred'. Part of the resistance to our work is the claim that it depicts universities as sites of 'sexual paranoia' (Kipnis, 2017) where all sexual encounters are conflictual and abusive, and women and queer students are at constant risk of harassment and oppression. Such discourses are part of wider debates about the nature of universities (should they be sites of 'free speech'? Is 'no platforming' a reasonable tactic?) and the characteristics of generations of young people (are they 'precious snowflakes' or activists imagining alternative societies?). Other attempts to theorise resistance – such as Jordan's (2016) insightful analysis of 'backlash' and postfeminism as 'active resistance to what is perceived to be the current gender order' (p 29) which has 'the potential to shape, challenge, and/or reinforce dominant constructions of ... norms around gender and gender politics' (p 42) – may prove helpful in understanding and responding to the resistance our work generates.

Resistance and the discourses generated by resistance are an inevitable part of work against GBV in universities and can be a productive force, helping the development of more nuanced, effective strategies in scholarship and practice. After all, most bodies of political thought, feminism included, have developed in response to critique and challenge from both within and outside its ranks. Resistance in GBV work warrants further attention in terms of theorising the nature of resistance and in terms of developing strategic, tactical responses which are effective at dismantling gendered power.

Moreover, our work to end GBV may also be conceived of as resistance; resistance to the status quo, to patriarchal power. We can conceive of our resistance as a sign of life, energy and hope in civic society. This resistance is part of ambitious efforts to destabilise the current gender order, to imagine and enact a world free of gender oppression. As Foucault (1997: 167 cited by Ahmed, 2017) wrote, 'if there was no resistance ... it would be just a matter of obedience'.

A key element of this resistance is student activism to challenge GBV. As detailed in some of the chapters in this volume (Jordan et al, Lewis and Marine) some UK campuses are alive with feminist resistance to GBV and the contemporary gender order. However, to date, there has been relatively little research about this resurgence in university-based feminist politics. There is a pressing need, given the relatively short life and rapid regeneration of student bodies, to capture and record this activism, particularly in terms of which students participate, how they conceptualise and approach GBV (and other issues they tackle), how they strategise their activism, the relationships they build with university staff (academic, support and management) and with outside organisations, and the impacts and consequences of their activism.

Developing a jigsaw of strategies

A beneficial consequence of the slow awakening of policymakers and scholars to GBV in universities is that we can draw on the lessons learned elsewhere over the previous four decades to inform the direction and focus of our future efforts. A wealth of scholarship discusses the attempts, particularly in North America, to reform university environments through policy development and use of the law. Durbach and Grey's chapter examines the shifting institutional responses in Australia. In the UK there are several legal opportunities, outlined in Louise Whitfield's chapter, for challenging GBV in universities which could be adopted by individuals seeking redress or by activists seeking to change university practices. What is telling, perhaps, is how infrequently they have been used. In the US, despite seeming advances in policy and legal approaches, such as Title IX, scholarship in this volume (see Klein's chapter) and elsewhere highlights the pitfalls of this approach. There are lessons to be learned here about the dangers of striving for institutional accountability and change through the use of such measures, which can produce a mechanistic approach which fails to bring to the fore the wellbeing of victims/survivors. Recent work about GBV in wider contexts also raises concern about feminists' reliance on formal justice systems, with their investment in racism, patriarchy, classism and heteronormativity; Rentschler (2017) for example, proposes a 'feminist politics of transformative, anti-carceral justice' which 'requires a re-orientation of practice towards models of survivor-centred transformative justice' (p 579). However, given it is only recently that UK universities have started to consider GBV as within their responsibility, we are cautious about rejecting strategies to hold them to account and to provide some measure of protection and justice for survivors. Rather than disavow formal systems of justice and accountability, but mindful that approaches which rely on formal legal mechanisms can never be the panacea to GBV (due in part to the obstacles Whitfield highlights in her chapter), we instead propose that they are best considered as one piece in the jigsaw of strategies for tackling GBV at universities.

We call on scholars, activists and university leaders to explore, develop, pilot and evaluate a jigsaw of responses to tackle GBV. This jigsaw of strategies might include legal responses (see Whitfield's chapter), national policy frameworks (see the chapters by Donaldson et al and Durbach and Grey), institutional policies and procedures for recording, investigating and dealing with complaints (see Klein's chapter), curriculum-based initiatives such as bystander intervention programmes and other educational initiatives (see the chapters by Fenton and Mott, Hutchinson, and Jordan et al) and consent workshops, victim/survivor-centred support services provided by universities and in collaboration with external agencies, and activist (student and community) mobilisation, which might include awareness-raising campaigns (such as those described by Lewis and Marine, and Hutchinson). With their different, sometimes opposing strategies, audiences, aims and methods, these contrasting but potentially complementary approaches can contribute to the transformation of university environments into spaces where GBV is genuinely not tolerated.

Essential to this jigsaw of responses are the actors who piece together the complementary pieces. Who are the key actors in tackling GBV in universities? University leaders – senior management in academic and support services – need to embrace the possibility of developing GBV-intolerant campuses. The absence of institutional leadership to tackle this problem is reflected in the Universities UK (2016: 58) report's recommendation 'that all university leaders should afford tackling violence against women, harassment and hate crime priority status and dedicate appropriate resources to tackling it'. As the chapters in this volume illustrate, there is some very promising, innovative, coordinated practice to tackle GBV in UK universities, which is grounded in robust empirical and theoretical evidence about the problem and effective interventions. However, this is not found consistently throughout the country; not all universities have risen to the challenge. Therefore, at the institutional level, universities need to move beyond the patchwork of un-coordinated activities among academic and non-academic staff and students to develop, as Universities UK (2016) highlights, an institution-wide approach (see Towl, 2016, for an account of how one university has embraced its civic and educational responsibility and developed leadership around sexual violence).

Universities do not face this challenge alone. Higher education institutions (HEIs) can support each other to develop leadership and good practice; inter-institutional collaboration can highlight and share lessons from the range of current good practice in those institutions that have not been frightened to lead the way in tackling GBV. In addition, key agencies in the sector can support HEIs to embrace their responsibilities. For example, following the Universities UK (UUK) Taskforce to examine violence against women, harassment and hate crime, a Catalyst funding programme provided by Higher Education Funding Council of England is a valuable start for developing a programme of evidence and knowledge about effective interventions.

The development of a coordinated gendered approach to violence against women and girls in Scotland (as described in chapters by Donaldson et al and Hutchinson) provides an example of the leadership required. Moreover, university leaders can draw on the expertise within their institutions; many HEIs have academics working on issues related to GBV who can contribute to the strategic planning and cultural transformation required.

Academics have roles to play in tackling GBV both as scholars and as members of university communities who contribute to their cultures. Much of the impetus to bring attention to GBV in universities has come from scholarship that has highlighted the existence and nature of this problem (see, for example, Jackson and Dempster, 2009; Phipps and Smith, 2012; Phipps and Young, 2015; Jackson and Sundaram, 2015). Conferences, symposia and networks[2] are key to developing knowledge, but also provide support to scholars whose attempts to change their own institutions have met with resistance. These experiences can feed into our efforts to theorise and respond to resistance, as discussed earlier. Staff trade unions also have a role to play in transforming the working environment and preventing GBV among staff. UCU's work on domestic abuse, sexual harassment, bullying, gender identity and sexual orientation equality in the workplace[3] provides valuable resources for staff challenging GBV in their workplace.

Students and their local and national unions play a crucial role in addressing GBV. NUS leaders have been at the forefront of agitating for change, contributing to national debates and policy development (for example, through membership of the UUK Taskforce) and providing evidence about GBV (for example, NUS, 2010). Student activism, through students unions, feminist societies and other groupings, seems to be developing throughout the country but, as described earlier, reliable research evidence about the spread of such activism is lacking; without coordination and documentation of such efforts, an important part of the jigsaw may be lost to history.

These various actors, in collaboration and as collectives, are crucial parts of the jigsaw of strategies required to tackle GBV. They enact their roles against a backdrop of significant changes to the academic landscape, which present a unique set of challenges. Not only have neoliberal values (such as faith in the market, an audit approach to nearly every aspect of university activity, and an instrumental approach to education) taken hold as never before, but universities' nature, purpose and role in society is in flux. As we write, there remains tremendous uncertainty about the impact of Brexit, the implications of which will unfold in the coming years. And with the changed funding base of universities which results in the highest level of student fees in the world (Kentish, 2017), the struggle to afford GBV high priority will not be easily won but we owe it to our students, current and future, to work to eradicate GBV from their experience of university.

Summary

This collection contributes to the conversation about how to avoid the missteps that have hindered efforts to address GBV and how to develop productive, effective approaches to hold universities to account, improve institutional prevention and responses to GBV, and transform university cultures so that students need not fear victimisation nor have to deal with its consequences. This is a huge task; universities do not operate in a vacuum, immune to the wider social and economic forces. GBV is a normalised, everyday aspect of the wider society of which universities are a part and, as Sundaram argues in her chapter, efforts to transform attitudes about GBV need to start before university, with young people in school. The UK's late attention to this topic means generations of students have been left unprotected from GBV and unsupported when they experience it. However, this late start does mean that we can learn from countries where institutions, activists and scholars have generated a wealth of knowledge about how the problem manifests and how it is best tackled, and we can use that as a springboard for future developments in research and practice.

Notes

1   https://feministkilljoys.com/
2   Such as Universities Against Gender Based Violence: https://uagbv.wordpress. com/
3   See www.ucu.org.uk/publications

References

Ahmed, S. (2017) 'No', Feministkilljoys, 30 June, https://feministkilljoys.com/2017/06/30/no/Anderson, E. (2005) 'Orthodox and inclusive masculinity: Competing masculinities among heterosexual men in a feminized terrain', *Sociological Perspectives*, 48 (3): 337–55.

Baker, J. (2008) 'The Ideology of Choice. Overstating Progress and Hiding Injustice in the Lives of Young Women: Findings from a Study in North Queensland, Australia', *Women's Studies International Forum*, 31 (1): 53–64.

Batty, D., Weale, S. and Bannock, C. (2017) 'Sexual harassment at "epidemic" levels in UK universities', *Guardian*, 5 March

Cantor, D., Fisher, B., Chibnall, S. H., Townsend, R., Lee, H., Thomas, G., and Westat, Inc. (2015) *Report on the AAU Campus Climate Survey on Sexual Assault and Sexual Misconduct*, Rockville: Westat.

De Visser, R.O., Smith, J.A. and McDonnell, E.J. (2009) '"That's not masculine": Masculine Capital and Health-related Behaviour', *Journal of Health Psychology*, 14 (7): 1047–58.

Foucault, M. (1997) *The Politics of Truth*, New York: Semiotext.

Hearn, J. and Parkin, W. (1987) *Sex At work: The Power and Paradox of Organisation Sexuality*, Brighton: Wheatsheaf Books.

Jackson, C. and Dempster, S. (2009) '"I sat back on my computer … with a bottle of whisky next to me': Constructing 'cool' masculinity through 'effortless' achievement in secondary and higher education', *Journal of Gender Studies*, 18 (4): 341–56.

Jackson, C. and Sundaram, V. (2015) *Is 'Lad Culture' a Problem in Higher Education? Exploring the Perspectives of Staff Working in UK Universities*, Society for Research into Higher Education, Lancaster University and University of York, www.srhe.ac.uk/downloads/JacksonSundaramLadCulture.pdf

Jordan, A. (2016) 'Conceptualizing Backlash:(UK) Men's Rights Groups, Anti-Feminism, and Postfeminism', *Canadian Journal of Women and the Law*, 28 (1): 18–44.

Kelly, L. (1988) *Surviving Sexual Violence*, Cambridge: Polity Press.

Kentish, B. (2017) 'University tuition fees in England now the highest in the world, new analysis suggests', *Independent*, 28 March, www.independent.co.uk/news/education/university-tuition-fees-england-highest-world-compare-students-student-loan-calculator-a7654276.html

Kipnis, L. (2017) *Unwanted Advances: Sexual Paranoia Comes to Campus*, London: Harper Collins.

Lewis, R., Sharp, E.A., Remnant, J. and Redpath, R. (2015) '"Safe spaces': experiences of feminist women-only space', *Sociology Research Online*, 20 (4), www.socresonline.org.uk/20/4/9.html

MacKinnon, C.A. (1979) *Sexual Harassment of Working Women: A Case of Sex Discrimination* (No. 19), Yale University Press.

NUS (2010) *Hidden Marks*, London: NUS.

Pells, R. (2016) 'Sussex University let senior lecturer continue teaching after he beat up student girlfriend', *Independent*, 16 August.

Phipps, A. and Smith, G. (2012) 'Violence against women students in the UK: Time to take action', *Gender and Education*, 24 (4): 357–73.

Phipps, A. and Young, I. (2015) 'Neoliberalisation and 'lad cultures' in higher education', *Sociology*, 49 (2): 305–22.

Rentschler, C.A. (2017) 'Bystander intervention, feminist hashtag activism, and the anti-carceral politics of care', *Feminist Media Studies*, 17 (4): 565–84.

Stark, E. (2009) *Coercive Control: The Entrapment of Women in Personal Life*, Oxford: Oxford University Press.

Towl, G. (2016) 'Tackling sexual violence at UK universities: a case study', *Contemporary Social Science*, 11 (4): 432–7.

Universities UK (2016) *Changing the Culture: Report of the Universities UK Taskforce Examining Violence Against Women, Harassment and Hate Crime Affecting University Students*, London: Universities UK, www.universitiesuk.ac.uk/policy-and-analysis/reports/Pages/changing-the-culture-final-report.aspx

Weale, S. and Batty, D. (2016a) 'Sexual harassment of students by university staff hidden by non-disclosure agreements', *Guardian*, 26 August.

Weale, S. and Batty, D. (2016b) 'Scale of sexual abuse in UK universities likened to Savile and Catholic scandals', *Guardian*, 5 October.

Willgress, L. (2016) 'Feminist studies professor resigns from London's Goldsmiths university over alleged sexual harassment of students by staff', *Telegraph*, 9 June.

Index

Note: Page numbers followed by an 'n' indicate end-of-chapter notes.